FULL COUNT

FULL COUNT

The Education of a Pitcher

DAVID CONE *and* **JACK CURRY**

GRAND CENTRAL
PUBLISHING

NEW YORK   BOSTON

Grand Central Publishing
Hachette Book Group
1290 Avenue of the Americas, New York, NY 10104
grandcentralpublishing.com
twitter.com/grandcentralpub

First Edition: May 2019

Grand Central Publishing is a division of Hachette Book Group, Inc. The Grand Central Publishing name and logo is a trademark of Hachette Book Group, Inc.

The publisher is not responsible for websites (or their content) that are not owned by the publisher.

The Hachette Speakers Bureau provides a wide range of authors for speaking events. To find out more, go to www.hachettespeakersbureau.com or call (866) 376-6591.

Library of Congress Control Number: 2019930191

ISBNs: 978-1-5387-4884-8 (hardcover), 978-1-5387-4882-4 (ebook), 978-1-5387-1641-0 (B&N signed hardcover), 978-1-5387-1640-3 (signed hardcover)

Printed in the United States of America

LSC-C

10 9 8 7 6 5 4 3 2 1

For Mom, who understood about regression to the mean before it was popular.
For Dad, who was my first and best coach.
David Cone

For Mom, who will forever be my guiding light.
For Pamela, who is always my brightest light.
Jack Curry

CONTENTS

Contents

Extra Innings

FULL COUNT

Introduction

A REFLECTION

Staring into the bathroom mirror, I saw a sweaty-faced and steely-eyed man who was wondering how the next few minutes of his life would unfold. He looked serious and he looked concerned. I kept staring at the man, studying every inch of that weary face and those focused eyes, and I wondered if the man was powerful enough to pitch one more spotless inning. *Please*, I thought, *just get three more outs*.

Obviously, I was that man, the man who placed both hands on the sink, leaned forward, and pushed his nose within six inches of the mirror. I wanted some answers, and I needed some reassurance inside the Yankee Stadium clubhouse bathroom. After tossing eight perfect innings against the Montreal Expos on July 18, 1999, I changed into a fresh undershirt by my locker and retreated to the bathroom. I was alone, all alone, before the ninth inning and I gave myself a specific command: "Don't blow this."

Of all the inspiring words that I could have used, my first words were *Don't blow this*. I challenged myself because I knew what motivated me, and I knew I responded well to being challenged. As an aspiring nine-year-old pitcher, I received tough love from my father, who was my first coach, so I used the same technique on

1

myself. I let my forceful words sink in, the staring contest continued, and I added, "Don't you dare blow this."

I wanted the reflection to talk back. I really wanted the man in the mirror to tell me he could do this and tell me everything would be all right. Taking inventory of how I had retired the first twenty-four batters, I knew my slider had been floating like a Frisbee, I knew my fastball was nicking the corners, and I knew the Expos seemed helpless as they swung early and often. Based on that mounting evidence, I finally told myself, "You can do this. You have to do this."

Did I believe I could get the final three outs? Well, part of me believed it. Every pitcher has that mental tug-of-war with himself in almost every game. It doesn't have to be a potential perfect game for pitchers to wonder if they're about to get a strikeout with a nasty slider or if they're about to allow a homer on a hanging slider. For pitchers, the questions are never ending.

Throughout my career, I asked myself questions about the way I gripped my pitches, about the spin and velocity on my pitches, about the arm angles I used to deliver pitches, and about the smartest strategies for attacking hitters. Those questions and hundreds of others hover over pitchers, steady reminders about what we should or shouldn't do. I have lots of answers to these pitching questions and I have lots of pitching stories. All of these theories and opinions and tales will be unveiled in this book, an array of ideas from me and from others, a detailed assessment on the art of pitching and my life as a pitcher. I always believed pitchers need to be searchers, mound investigators who determine the best pitch to throw and the best way to throw it. Then do that again and again.

On that day in the stadium bathroom, I took deep breaths as the conversation between the dueling sides of my personality continued. The confident Cone was poised for perfection and envisioned it happening, while doubting David questioned whether it would ever happen. Even if a pitcher has the biggest ego in the world, he's going to experience doubts in pressure-filled situations. Back in 1999, I was trying to do something only fifteen other pitchers in major league history had ever done. I would have been delusional if I didn't have a doubt or two.

I was in my fourteenth major league season and, through all my creativity and quirkiness, I had never stopped and studied myself in the mirror during a game. And I never did it again. But this game was a special situation, a time where I was mature enough to pause, slow my brain and my pulse down, and absorb what was happening. As a thirty-six-year-old, I might never get another chance to pitch a perfect game, and I wanted to prepare myself in the best way possible.

Part of preparing myself meant preparing myself for failure, too. Pitching is a job that involves a lot of failure; even the greatest of pitchers throw balls about 40 percent of the time. So my frenetic mind told me that something could go wrong. There could be a bloop single or a ball that rolled sixty feet for a hit or one of my fielders could make an error or I could walk a batter. If any of those things happened, I needed to be OK with that result. Would I be OK if I ended up being less than perfect?

"Forget that," I said. "No, I won't be OK with that." Thankfully, the aggressive and confident me fought the equally aggressive and doubting me and told me to stay calm and keep pitching the same way. *Don't even think about those bleak scenarios*, I told myself in a conversation that felt like a devil-versus-angel chat. I guess I was the angel and the devil.

My internal struggle continued inside the bathroom, a bathroom so quiet that I heard water draining through the pipes. The adjacent clubhouse was empty because my superstitious teammates didn't want to talk to a pitcher who was working on a perfect game. No problem there. I just spoke to myself. Knowing the ninth was fast approaching, I had one final question: "What are you going to do now?"

For two or three minutes, I stood by myself and evaluated the man who was pursuing perfection. The last time I glanced in the mirror, I saw someone who looked energized. Maybe I had been revived by my strange pep talk. I knew how I would attack the Expos, so the physical side of my game was ready, but the detour to the mirror was a way to enhance my mental approach.

While I had never stared at myself in the mirror, I perpetually analyzed myself and tried to determine if I was capable of throwing one more strike, notching one more out, and pitching one more inning. Pitching is a constant test; you're always trying to prove you're better than the batter who is standing in the box. I hustled to the mound in the ninth and believed, truly believed, I would get those three outs.

Pitching is never simple, not even for those who succeed at the highest levels. It is complex and confounding, daunting and demanding. It is an art that I still study, still adore, still analyze, and, quite honestly, still miss. The lessons about pitching are constant.

It's time for us to get started on this journey. I'll be your tour guide. I will stare in the mirror again, study myself again, and tell you everything I see.

Chapter 1

MANIACAL ON THE MOUND

I<small>T WAS EVERYTHING</small> I <small>WANTED</small> and, really, everything I didn't want. I always longed to be on the mound so I could perform and be the center of attention, with thousands of fans screaming and waiting for me to throw a pitch. But I wanted to experience that type of atmosphere when I was dominating a game, not when I was sputtering. In this memorable moment, I wasn't dazzling. I was barely breathing.

Huffing and puffing my way through Game 5 of the 1995 American League Division Series between my Yankees and the Seattle Mariners, I was a weary pitcher with an aching arm and a deteriorating plan. The Yankees had acquired me from the Toronto Blue Jays in July, and I was supposed to help lead them to the postseason and maybe even to the World Series. This sort of high-leverage game was exactly why the Yankees pursued me as a hired gun. But, pitch after suspect pitch, my situation grew more and more distressing.

We started the eighth inning with a 4–2 lead, but that shrunk by a run when Ken Griffey Jr. blasted a one-out homer. After I retired Edgar Martinez on a groundout, I exhaled because he had been so lethal against us and because I was one elusive out from pushing the game into the ninth. But I couldn't get it. I became too careful, too defensive, and too nervous. I walked a batter, allowed a single, and walked another Mariner to fill the bases. After not throwing four balls to anyone in the entire game, I had walked two of the last three Mariners, a glaring sign that I was squeezing the ball too tight or aiming it or just being passive. My pitches were eroding, and I wasn't close to being the same effective pitcher I had been in the earlier innings.

Still, I had blind faith as Doug Strange, a left-handed batter, was announced as a pinch-hitter. I stood behind the mound while Strange took some swings in the on-deck circle, idle time in which I tried to convince myself I could still get this last out. Buck Showalter, my manager, later said he didn't want to remove me from the game because he trusted me and because I deserved "the chance there to finish it." I appreciate Showalter's trust in me, but I wasn't glancing into the dugout for any reassurance. And I didn't want Showalter analyzing me, either, and I didn't want him to see how lifeless I was and, honestly, how scared I was. I was so spent that it felt like I was lifting a hundred-pound dumbbell every time I raised my right arm to throw a pitch.

In that defining duel against Strange, I felt like a bystander in my own final scene. Throwing strikes was supposed to be my focus, but I couldn't do it. It was a circle-of-life moment, and I was mor-phing into a tense nine-year-old kid again. I threw a decent slider that Strange swung over for the first strike, but then I unleashed three straight balls, my location worsening with each pitch and my body clearly sagging. After securing a second strike on a fastball that was right down the middle, Mike Stanley signaled for a split-ter, which I had missed badly with earlier in the at bat, and I never hesitated. I thought that was the right pitch to throw on 3-2. I still think it was, but I threw it way inside and also bounced it. It was my 147th pitch. No man has thrown more pitches in a postgame game since then.

"And they gambled with the split-finger," said Jim Kaat, the former major league pitcher who was calling the game. "Three-two. Two out. Wow."

Once I walked Strange to force in pinch-runner Alex Rodriguez with the tying run, I almost collapsed, immediately slumping over, putting my hands on my knees and remaining in that bent position for several seconds. I trudged off the mound, my head bowed and my senses in disarray as I was replaced by Mariano Rivera, a converted starter in his rookie season who was not yet viewed as a dominant reliever. We lost to the Mariners in eleven innings and our season ended. I always believed I could have done something different, something ingenious, to get one more out, and the splitter was designed to be that get-me-out-of-trouble pitch.

But, on that fateful night, everything was a blur. I didn't want to come out of the game, but I didn't have the strength, physically or mentally, to get through that last batter. Everything I understood about executing pitches, the vast knowledge and endless experience, was in tatters because, at that moment, the five-ounce ball felt like a bowling ball. There was nothing I could do to revive myself because, for those pitches, I wasn't the same confident pitcher. I was a frightened nine-year-old.

From the time I was nine, being on a mound was where I needed to be and where I had to be. I wanted to be the most important player on the field, I wanted every pair of eyes staring at me, and I wanted to be in control. Maybe it's an ego issue, but it takes a certain type of controlling personality to climb atop a mound, a place that can be as lonely as it is exciting, and decide that's where you belong. It's the responsibility, the intensity, and the desire for the spotlight that appeals to pitchers. It's what you do. It's who you are.

All of these years later, I can still hear my mother yelling, "Throw strikes! Throw strikes!" at Little League games, and I can still feel the stress that would smother me when I couldn't do it. No matter how talented a pitcher is, there is incredible stress involved in harnessing all the power in your body to try and throw a pitch to a specific location, a location as tiny as a cocktail napkin. And failing. And then trying to do it again and failing again.

Every pitcher knows those feelings of being uncomfortable and flustered, feelings that can be exposed after one shabby sequence of pitches. I would chastise myself in a blitz of expletives and ask myself what was wrong. Should I use more finger pressure on the ball? Is my front shoulder flying away from my body and causing my pitches to sail? Is my front leg landing directly in line with the catcher's target? Stress follows pitchers and clings to them like a sweaty Dri-FIT shirt—and still I loved every aspect of that demanding position, even the unnerving moments.

Anytime I ascended the mound and stared in for a sign, I was a little jumpy and a little hyperactive because I wanted to succeed so desperately. The mound was a heavenly spot for me, a hill of hope that I first discovered as a boy: a get-out-of-my-way kind of kid. There has never been a place where I've felt more powerful—and, of course, on some days there has never been a place where I've felt more depressed.

Even when I wasn't close to the mound, I still imagined myself there. When I was lumbering through my living room, I would stop, close my eyes, and envision myself pitching. I was always ready, always aggressive. I'd do the same thing as I stood on a subway platform or as I waited in line for a cup of coffee. Stop. Close my eyes. Transport myself to the mound. No matter where I was or how awkward I might look, that feeling always rejuvenated me, always made me feel as if I was back in the right place.

It's been more than fifteen years since I've thrown a baseball in a major league game, but I can still see myself pitching. My eyes are darting from the catcher to the batter to the umpire, my face is bathed in perspiration, and my mind, my ever-frenetic mind, is hunting for solutions. I hope I always see myself like that. I need that adrenaline rush, as counterfeit as it might be, and I need to know that it could still be me out there, even if it isn't. In my mind, I trick myself into believing that it is. I am still pitching.

There is no experience like it, really. Not for me or for thousands like me. The pitcher has a weighty responsibility that is like no other in sports. In baseball, there's no running back or wide receiver who can take the ball from you. It's our ball and our game, a game that is like no other because the defense actually has control of the ball, and that control starts with the pitcher. Like other pitchers, I chose this difficult position, knowing the requirements, the expectations, and the emotional swings. When you watch a game, you watch the pitcher. You watched me and the pitcher after me and the pitcher after him. I loved that attention, craved that attention. I still do.

Being a pitcher means being a creator, an orchestrator, an improviser, and a magician, a person willing to devise some way to throw the ball so that the hitter is deceived and defeated. Curve it, sink it, cut it, bend it, explode it, and then do it again. But just make sure that the next pitch is even better. Make the ball dance. Make it do whatever you need it to do. Pitchers are required to test themselves and trust themselves, notions that don't always mesh on the mound. As a pitcher tries to throw the perfect slider, a pitch that is designed to break late and confuse a hitter, does he believe he will succeed? He had better believe it.

Through all of the long, lazy days or the quick, hectic nights at the ballpark, I was intent on being a smart student and a clever thief, roles that every pitcher should emulate. As a maturing pitcher who was learning how to be a professional, and even as a veteran pitcher who had won a Cy Young Award, I studied and I stole. I analyzed other pitchers and tried to determine the reasons they were successful and if there was anything they did that

I should be doing. If a pitcher isn't trying to swipe something valuable from other pitchers, whether it's a grip on a pitch, a positioning on the rubber, or a strategy against a particular hitter, he's being careless.

During the Wiffle ball games in my backyard in Kansas City, I typically mimicked Luis Tiant, my pied piper, and called our field Coneway Park after Boston's Fenway Park. If I was imitating Juan Marichal and his high leg kick, the venue was dubbed Conedlestick Park after San Francisco's Candlestick Park. My father even installed floodlights so we could play night games.

Tiant had immense talent while winning 229 games for teams like the Indians, the Red Sox, and the Yankees, but he had style and deception, too. When Tiant threw a pitch, he didn't simply step back with his left leg, raise it in front of him, swing his arms over his head, rotate his hips, and power his body forward to throw the ball, as coaches teach. There were no lessons for what Tiant did. He was a pitching contortionist. Tiant turned away from the plate, twisted his body so that he was looking toward center field, tilted his head toward the sky, pirouetted back to home, and then threw a pitch. He made the unnatural look so natural. I wanted to do that or something like that, too.

Sitting on the floor so I could closely analyze Tiant's movements on television, I was convinced that Tiant's unusual delivery confused batters. The batters saw more of the number on Tiant's back than they saw of Tiant's eyes or the ball. Hitters never knew when Tiant would release the ball or from what angle. That's deceiving the hitter. That's pitching. Tiant's funky motion was telling batters that he was so sneaky and so confident that he didn't even need to look at the plate as he prepared to throw the pitch.

Trying to fully replicate Tiant's distinctive style would be disastrous because pitching styles need to develop naturally. But Tiant's unorthodox approach was a reminder to study every pitcher, from your teammates to your opponents to the pitchers you see on TV. Pitchers need to be students, forever students, because there's always a chance to learn something or poach something that will make you better.

With a baseball in their hands and control of what happens next in the game, pitchers feel invigorated and energized. I loved to slide my fingers over the cowhide surface, my index and middle fingers combing the red seams until I had touched all 108 of them. I wanted to locate the thickest seams, the place on the ball where the seams felt larger, even if they weren't. If I felt seams that seemed the slightest bit thicker to me, I'd be more content because that gave me a better grip and a better way to create spin and velocity on my pitches. Pitchers chase edges, whether they are real or imagined.

In this world, this fascinating and complicated world of pitching, I challenged myself to be better, be nastier, and be the last man standing, gladiator style. Give me the ball and I would devise something, no matter how sore my arm felt. I had a relentless attitude as a pitcher, a feeling of responsibility that caused me, honestly, to behave maniacally on the mound. I wanted to sweat, stew, and scream until we had notched the twenty-seventh out. Even if it meant throwing 160 pitches. Even if I was putting my arm in danger. Even if I wasn't the best choice to pitch anymore because I was fatigued or just ineffective. The hell with those fears and concerns. I would worry about them tomorrow. In my scouting reports on pitchers, a little craziness is a positive trait.

That dose of craziness can be helpful because it can cause a pitcher to be daring and take some chances, choices that might be unexpected and might unnerve the batters. A first-pitch curveball or a 3-1 changeup aren't pitches a batter is likely to anticipate. By shrewdly and selectively taking chances and throwing them, a pitcher can get strikes and give the batter something extra to ponder. Or a pitcher can take a chance with a 3-2 splitter and the bases loaded in the postseason, as I did on my 147th pitch of the game to Strange, and it backfires.

As much as I wanted to stay in games and as much as I knew pitchers who were just as stubborn as me, I eventually learned, a little too late, that pitchers need protectors. I never thought about the repercussions of throwing 160 pitches in a game because I had been taught, lectured, and counseled to believe that every start was my responsibility and I needed to exert myself to pitch for as long as I could. Actually, I still believe in that philosophy, with the caveat being that pitchers need to be durable and smart, not durable and foolish. My mentality was "go until you blow," and that was detrimental, at times, in my career. As Exhibit A, I required surgery to remove an aneurysm from under my right armpit in 1996. The aneurysm, which is the swelling of an artery that results when the lining of the blood vessel is compromised, came from the stress I put on my arm while throwing thousands and thousands of pitches in my life.

What are you doing in the trainer's room again, rookie? That question reverberated off the walls of the clubhouse when I began my career with the Royals and the Mets. I watched, warily, as young pitchers who frequented the trainer's room were belittled and called soft and unreliable. Some of the veterans would scoldingly tell the pitchers they were too young to be hurt, a hazing of sorts that doesn't exist today. That bullying I witnessed stayed with me and molded me, motivating me to want to pitch deep into games to earn the respect of my peers.

In those days, the finish line wasn't a starter's pitch count. It was the number of innings he could complete. But, nowadays, it's rare for a starter to even throw 120 pitches. Managers become antsy if a pitcher nears 100 pitches or if he has to face a batting order for the third time. I didn't worry much about pitch counts as a pitcher, but I understand why teams are obsessed with protecting arms that are worth millions to an organization. It's a sensible way to treat such a valuable commodity, especially with teams trying to comprehend why an inordinate number of pitchers have ended up tearing a ligament in their elbow and needing Tommy John surgery.

Still, there needs to be a better balance between haphazardly throwing 160 pitches and worrying as someone nears 100 pitches. Pitchers need to push themselves to discover what their limitations are and learn if they can still be as effective on their 115th pitch as they are on their 75th pitch. If a pitcher's splitter isn't diving, he needs to use his fastball or his slider and survive until the splitter returns. Or maybe it won't return at all. Those experiences, which multiply as a pitcher goes deeper into a game, are the building blocks to becoming a more confident performer.

Unless pitchers are given the opportunities to rumble through some of those pitch count limits, they probably won't ever know how strong or successful they can be later in games. A minor league prospect who is accustomed to being removed from starts after five innings isn't going to be prepared to pitch in the seventh or the eighth and is going to encounter new obstacles when he finally gets that opportunity. In many ways, today's pitchers are too coddled and aren't allowed to test themselves to determine how much they can endure. Except for a handful of durable pitchers, that's never going to change, because teams are very protective of their pitchers and managers are conditioned to bring in fresh relievers who throw fastballs in the upper 90s and accumulate lots of strikeouts.

If my shoulder felt as if someone had jabbed a plastic knife in my labrum, I pushed through the pain. If my fingers were throbbing and influencing the way I held the ball, I'd flex them and try a different grip. If I was sapped for energy, I'd take a deep breath, curse at myself, and create something different to try. A different arm angle, a new grip, a change in velocity. Anything.

Lift your front leg a little higher and you can stride closer to the plate, giving your fastball more velocity because you are releasing the ball later. As a right-hander, target off-speed pitches inside to righty hitters because they won't expect them and they might be off balance. With two strikes, throw your curveball as low as a batter's cleats because he could be jumpy and he might swing. These are just a few tweaks that pitchers can make, changes that could help them maneuver through a precarious situation.

I know a few pitchers who were crazier than me, and I know a lot more pitchers who were saner than me, but we all shared the same vision and the same goal: Deceive the hitter any way possible. One of my reliable approaches against left-handed batters was to get a first-pitch strike with a four-seam fastball or a curveball, then throw a cut fastball inside to get them to foul it off for a second strike, then throw my splitter in the dirt or a backdoor slider as the strikeout pitch.

But that was different from what Greg Maddux, Jack McDowell, or Andy Pettitte did, and I wanted to understand why. I wanted to know how Maddux could throw two-seam fastballs that looked like they were about to hit a left-handed batter's hip and then dived right and clipped the inside corner. I wanted to know how Mc-Dowell's slider maintained its sharpness deep into the game and made batters buckle. I wanted to know how Pettitte's cutters had such late and sharp left-to-right action. Even if I didn't imitate these pitchers, I wanted to analyze them, quiz them, and have that knowledge in my database. Maybe it would help me get an important out someday.

Some pitchers have a Plan A and, if that doesn't work, a Plan B or C. I wanted to have a Plan A through Z. If what I was doing wasn't working, I'd throw sidearm or I'd twist my body completely around or I'd invent a pitch. I wasn't afraid to try different things, which helped make me difficult to dissect and made some batters uncomfortable against me. But that experimental side of me also infuriated some coaches. They would insist that I couldn't throw certain pitches from different arm angles or to certain locations, and I would tell them, "It's my career. I'm going to do it the way I want to do it."

That refusal to acquiesce to the standard operating procedure was my way of following what had been working or what I thought would flourish. I believed throwing a specific pitch to a specific location was going to be effective because that's what I felt at that moment. It might change thirty seconds later, but when I threw a pitch, any pitch, I believed it was the proper pitch to throw. Every pitcher should feel that way, or the pitch isn't worth throwing. That faith, which was faulty at times, helps explain a part of my philosophy and how desperate I was to get outs. There was a maniacal quality to being on the mound, an urgency to excel and to avoid repeating my mistakes. If my slider was flat or my fastball lacked its usual life, changes were always possible and even probable.

As a pitching student, I was always thinking about what I might want to do deeper into the at bat. Before every pitch, I envisioned the outcome. If a pitch didn't generate the outcome I expected, I wanted to know why. Quite often, the batters told me. I would study the batter's swing, the batter's body language, and the batter's eyes to get instant feedback. Anything the batter did, any half swing or futile swing or positioning in the box or twitch, gave me some extra information. If a batter was late swinging at a pedestrian fastball and barely fouled it off the opposite way, that could be an indication that he was waiting on an off-speed pitch. I would digest that information and decide how to counter.

Once I had unearthed any evidence from the batter, it could help me strategize about what to do next. My mind was always rotating through a series of questions: Was my slider spinning the way I wanted it to spin? Did my fastball have extra life? How was my command of the strike zone? How patient should I be with some of my pitches? Was my body staying balanced and in sync with my delivery?

It became instinctive to ask and answer these questions, which is what pitching is. Posing those questions and seeking those answers was how I made myself feel more comfortable, even if it was an edgy kind of comfort. Unlike those pitchers who wanted to throw just one pitch at a time and not think a few pitches ahead, I was a better pitcher when I was scrambling for information and feedback. Both approaches, the passive and the aggressive, can be successful, but I would rather be the pitcher who had more insight and had it quickly.

If I was pitching in 2019, I would still focus on my strengths and I would still be a "feel" pitcher, but I would definitely embrace the abundance of data that is now available for pitchers. For instance, I would be obsessed with knowing the spin rates on my pitches, the vertical and horizontal breaks on my pitches, and my release points. During bullpen sessions between starts, those are specific elements that pitchers can dissect. I would have fiddled with the grips on my slider and my curveball to determine if I could increase my spin rate, which would give those pitches more life and make them even more difficult to hit. Sometimes, a pitcher's eyes can lie and he might think his pitches are moving more than they actually are. With the high-speed cameras that are now used to evaluate pitches, there's no lying. A pitcher will know precisely how many inches his splitter dropped and how much side-to-side movement his slider had. That's priceless information.

Because of that inseparable relationship between a pitcher and the main tool of his craft, a pitcher often grips a baseball even when he's not pitching. Or is it the opposite of that? As former major league pitcher Jim Bouton eloquently said, "You spend a good piece of your life gripping a baseball and, in the end, it turns out that it was the other way around all the time."

Anyway, those countless hours of caressing and holding the ball can lead to one aspect of pitching that every pitcher adores: the ability to develop a new pitch and add it to your repertoire. There's a combination of anticipation and tension as a pitcher cultivates a new pitch because he's waiting for it to finally spin, break, or move the way he wants it to, the way it needs to, so that it can be used in a game.

In a dicey situation with runners on base, it's very difficult to debut a new pitch and feel confident in it. Establishing a new grip during a bullpen session doesn't compare to throwing the pitch with runners on base and Mike Trout batting. Pitchers might panic in those spots because they have been told, over and over, that it's criminal to allow a game-altering hit with their third- or fourth-best pitch.

Eventually, a pitcher has to take the baseball, use that new grip, exhale, and try to throw it against a dangerous hitter like Trout. Desperation can be the fuel that causes a pitcher to use a new pitch. Maybe a pitcher's fastball isn't reacting the way he wants it to react, so he needs to try a cut fastball that he's only worked on in the bullpen and see if that's a solution.

Pitchers are fascinated with weapons, meaning the pitches that they have in each game. An artist like Masahiro Tanaka throws six different pitches, including a splitter, a slider, a sinker, and a curve, so with the variation of speeds he uses, he has a myriad of choices for attacking hitters. The more trustworthy weapons a pitcher has and the more ways he's able to use them, the more successful he's likely to be.

I always wanted to be an expert at developing my craft, not just somebody who strolled to the mound with a fastball in the mid-90s and a solid breaking pitch and thought that was all I needed to thrive. Earlier in my career, I could do that. Some pitchers have the talent to do that and to be intimidating forces, but I was always more intrigued by outwitting hitters and wanted to know why something was or wasn't producing positive results.

That curiosity was beneficial because I tinkered with grips and changed arm angles as I tried to make the ball juke and move and fool batters. One of a pitcher's most gratifying outcomes is when he throws a nasty pitch that absolutely freezes the batter, shocks him so severely that he never even tries to swing. When a batter stared at one of my sliders and then shook his head or cursed, he helped me. His reaction told me how superior that pitch had been, and his helplessness also gave me a mental boost because I knew I had flustered him and therefore believed I could do it again.

Deceiving hitters required being thorough with my preparation and occasionally being ready to throw some pitches they would never expect. I practiced bouncing curveballs in front of the plate, knowing there would be situations where I would want to entice some hitters to chase those difficult-to-hit curves. I even practiced pumping fastballs that were above a batter's eyes to tempt free swingers to chase them. Without having practiced those types of pitches, it isn't simple to throw them in those out-of-the-strike-zone locations. Bouncing a curve takes as much precision as throwing a curve that pierces the bottom of the strike zone. It's one more lesson I learned in a life that's been filled with pitching lessons.

Regardless of how much experience and insight pitchers have, there will be situations where they feel helpless on the mound. They know what to do, but, because of fatigue, nervousness, or ineffectiveness, they can't complete the most basic of actions by throwing the ball for a strike. It happens to all pitchers. It happened to me, most notably in Strange's at bat against me in the 1995 postseason loss to the Mariners.

If I could, I would go back and pitch today, tomorrow, and the next day. I would sprint to that mound, get in the same comfortable position I always cherished, and get ready to throw a baseball. There is nothing in my life, maybe nothing in any pitcher's life, that equates with the feeling of being on a mound, being in control, or, actually, trying to be in control. I will make the pitch this time. I know I will. I still think like a pitcher. Most of us do.

Chapter 2

WHEN THE GOING GETS TOUGH

I CAN STILL SEE MY FATHER in his work clothes, his long-sleeve shirt wrinkled and soiled after he had toiled through a twelve-hour shift as a mechanic in the Swift meat processing plant. I can still see a man who looked like he needed to sit down or, on many days, needed to lie down and take a nap. My father was a hard worker, a provider, but Ed Cone was also my first and best pitching coach.

Thankfully, I can also still see a man who changed into a T-shirt or a sweatshirt and told me to get prepared for pitching practice. Without hesitation, I dashed to my room in our modest three-story house in Kansas City, grabbed my glove, and rushed to meet my father. I didn't want him to remember how weary he was or get distracted by a household project. I wanted my father all to myself so he could teach me how to pitch, something I had pleaded with him to do for months. And now the day was finally here. I was the happiest nine-year-old on St. John Avenue.

Across the street from our house sat Budd Park, a place that might as well have been Royals Stadium or Yankee Stadium to me. Since I had two older brothers (Danny and Chris) and an older sister (Christal), I was always trying to compete with them, the little brother who wanted to be a lot bigger and a lot stronger than he was. When they traipsed over to Budd Park, I followed them and tried to be just as athletic and just as cool. Man, I just wanted to play sports, any and all sports.

Interestingly, both my father and Joan, my mother, were reluctant to let me become a pitcher and assume the stress of the most important position on the field. They were protective of their youngest child, their very competitive and scrappy youngest child, and they repeatedly asked me if I was serious about becoming a pitcher. Of course, I gave them the same emphatic answer every time because I was drawn to being in the center of the field and being the center of attention. All pitchers, even kid pitchers, have egos. My father wanted to train me as a hitter and even tried to name me Theodore as an homage to Ted Williams. But I wanted to be the player holding the baseball. I always wanted to pitch.

I can still remember standing on the mound, which seemed like a mountain, and being so eager to clutch the baseball, a baseball that I needed four fingers to grip because my hands were so small. But, before I threw the ball, my father counseled me about pitching. He was a serious man and a disciplinarian and, if I wanted to pitch, I was going to do it properly.

Anyone who met my dad once I began my professional career would describe him as gentlemanly and mild-mannered, a short man with a soft voice and sagging eyes. But when I was a kid learning to play sports, my father was a tough dude and a tough coach. He ran demanding practices and insisted we keep performing drills until we perfected them. He would scream at umpires like an Earl Weaver wannabe. He would toss his son out of practices for misbehaving. Yes, that feisty son was me.

While I wouldn't say he was a clone of Bobby Knight, the no-nonsense basketball coach from Indiana University, I would say that my father admired Knight's style. I remember watching the replay of an enraged Knight tossing a chair across the court because he was upset with the officials, and I could swear I saw a gleam in my father's eyes. He didn't object to that behavior, theorizing that Knight was trying to intimidate the officials to make a point to try and help his team.

As a serious student of sports, my father devoured books and articles about pitching and baseball and, since he also coached me in basketball, about basketball, too. On many nights, I would watch my father almost slip into a trance as he read a book about John Wooden, the legendary UCLA basketball coach, siphoning those strategies off the pages and delivering them to me and my teammates on the fields and courts. My father was smart, strict, and intense, so we didn't share many jokes on the short walk from our home to Budd Park.

Lesson number one began with my father slowly telling me every pitch should be thrown with a purpose, words that were empty to a nine-year-old. Nine-year-olds want to pick up a baseball and throw it as hard as they can, just like their idols do. But my father wouldn't let me throw a ball off a mound until I understood what he meant. I nodded and repeated his words, but I'm not sure I fully understood them. Not at that point, anyway.

Then my father pointed to my right arm and told me "Less is more" to emphasize the importance of taking my time and not always throwing a ball at maximum velocity. My father built a small mound and a home plate in the backyard so that I could pitch to him every night, and we spent hundreds of nights as the pitcher and the catcher in that sliver of our yard. He taught me a drill in which he would instruct me to throw at 100 percent of my strength and then quickly lower that to 75 percent and then to 50 percent—which, at that age, meant I was essentially lobbing the ball. Despite having a powerful arm, I had difficulty throwing strikes, so my father was teaching me to navigate around my wildness by focusing on control, not velocity.

It was excruciating to be forbidden from throwing my hardest. But as pitchers graduate to higher levels, lessening the velocity on pitches and trying to trick batters can be just as effective and less taxing as trying to throw the ball by them. While I grasped those words and thought about them during my career, they really resonated after my fastball had lost velocity and had become less of a weapon and I needed to adapt. That occurred in the final few years of my career as I tried to survive in the majors with an 85-mile-per-hour fastball. And it was 85 on a good day.

Still, as dedicated as my father was and as desperately as I wanted to pitch, we still clashed because, as always, I sometimes wanted to do certain things my own way. I could be a punk and I could throw temper tantrums, and my father had no time for that immaturity, disciplining me in front of the entire team when it was needed. I hated being singled out like that, especially by my own dad, but I typically accepted the punishment.

Whenever I evaluate why I thrived as a major leaguer, I highlight my stubbornness but also the stringent way in which I was raised as being significant in guiding me to that success. I was an Irish Catholic kid who grew up in the corporal punishment era so, if I needed to be reprimanded, absorbing a stick to the butt from my father was always a possibility. I think that rigid atmosphere led to my approach on the mound, an almost manic and desperate fight to make this work, to become an effective pitcher and, I guess, to not have to worry about being hit with a stick, figuratively, later in life.

Obviously, I'm not a psychologist, but I know that rebellious and aggressive attitude was a staple of my personality as a kid, as an adult, and on the mound. In one Little League game, I allowed the game-winning hit in the final inning and I was furious. I bolted off the mound, tore off my jersey, and shunned the opposing coach as he tried to shake hands. The other coach was a family friend, so my petulance infuriated my father. Hey, what can I say? I could be a little pain in the ass. Learning how to control my emotions was hard. To this day, if something pushes my hot button, I might react in a cranky manner. It could be a cabdriver making the wrong turn because he's talking on his phone. It could be someone barreling into me on the subway. But, believe me, I can still snap. Just like the boy who ripped off his jersey and pouted.

By urging me to be purposeful with throwing a baseball, my father also helped to create the delivery that I used throughout my career. When I delivered a pitch, I always had a point where I lifted my front leg and had a bit of a hesitation before I completed my motion and tossed the ball. That slight hesitation came from my father reminding me to gather myself, and it stayed with me, one final checkpoint of sorts before I powered the rest of my body forward.

When I was thirteen, my father—surely sensing that I wasn't going to grow up to be six foot four and 225 pounds—proposed that I use a drop-and-drive style of pitching, a la Tom Seaver, because it focused on a pitcher's legs. Seaver would drop down so low during his delivery that he would routinely scuff his back knee across the dirt of the mound, but that drive forward was where he generated his velocity. When a pitcher uses this style, he's generating power from his legs and his core and isn't relying as much on gaining all his strength from his shoulder or his upper body.

My father was friends with Rocco Stasi, a respected amateur coach and a former minor league player, so he asked Rocco to tutor me. That's how I perfected the drop-and-drive style. As I said, my father was progressive in his thinking about sports and was consumed by offering the proper advice and making sure I was pitching the right way. Rocco taught me to drive forward off my back leg, but he stressed that I still needed to land seamlessly on my front leg and be able to bend that leg and finish my delivery with a flourish.

I didn't know it then, but my father's lessons were setting me up to have options as a pitcher. As overpowering as my fastball was as a teenager, as a minor leaguer, and even as a major leaguer, there will be many games for every pitcher when the fastball isn't enough. If a pitcher is solely reliant on his fastball, he's going to be mired in situations where the fastball is fickle and he's a lost soul. By reminding me that less was more and instructing me to focus on hitting different spots with my pitches, my father was making me tougher to hit and, in essence, was making me a tougher pitcher.

Postseason baseball is intense, pressure filled, and it can also be magical. At least that was the way I viewed it as a baseball-obsessed teenager. I had studied these monumental games on television and always wondered what it would be like to pitch in the most meaningful games of the season. I would lie in my bed, eyes closed, and imagine pitching for a pennant or a World Series. Now I was in that exact position, that rarefied position with the Mets in 1988, and I was sweating before I had even thrown a pitch to the Dodgers.

Once upon a time, I wanted to be a sportswriter, believing I could have been like Oscar Madison, the funny and sloppy writer from *The Odd Couple*. He loved his job, he loved sports, he never seemed to make his bed, and he stored stale sandwiches in his bedroom, which were all commonalities for me. So when the New York *Daily News* asked me to ghostwrite a column with Bob Klapisch, their beat writer, for the National League Championship Series, I agreed, even though it was a distraction I didn't need before the most important start of my career.

After we scored three runs in the ninth inning to beat the

Dodgers, 3–2, in Game 1, I made some unfavorable remarks about them to Klapisch. I said Orel Hershiser, who was the best pitcher on the planet at the time, was lucky to pitch eight scoreless innings; and I said Jay Howell, the Dodgers' closer, reminded us of a high school pitcher because he threw so many curveballs. In the giddiness of our clubhouse, I lost focus on what mattered—my subsequent start—and in trying to be sarcastic and facetious, I put myself in an unenviable position.

When I arrived in the visitors' clubhouse at Dodger Stadium to pitch Game 2, I hadn't even read what Klapisch had written, since these were the pre-Internet days. But, really, it was what I had written. The story had my byline on it, and those words, littered across the page of a tabloid, had infuriated the Dodgers and made my teammates uneasy, too. Tommy Lasorda, the Dodgers' manager, taped it to a bulletin board and made sure all of his players knew every word that appeared in the column. It was immediate motivation for a team we had defeated in eleven of twelve games that season.

Nothing my father had told me or nothing any coach told me could save me on October 5, 1988, the day of that start. The veneer of toughness I thought I possessed began to chip as I learned just how massive a story I had foolishly created. Before I pulled on my uniform pants, Jay Horwitz, our loyal media relations director, told me how the Dodgers had seized upon my reckless column and were using it as a rallying cry.

As I warmed up before the game, I felt like a pariah, hoping someone would assure me that it wasn't that problematic. Incredibly, I wasn't thinking about pitching in this critical game. I was thinking about who I had irritated, why I had been careless, and how I could hide from this fiasco. It was the modern equivalent of sending a dozen hasty tweets to your boss and awaiting the repercussions.

There were almost fifty-six thousand people howling at Dodger Stadium, and it seemed as if each fan had read the column, had despised it, and had sat down in front of me on the field. I noticed everything, including how the Dodgers shouted at me from their dugout and diverted my attention from actually pitching.

I felt like I was drowning on the mound, the dirt sinking around me and swallowing my feet, then my legs, then my torso, then my neck. As I was figuratively plunging underwater, I was trying to throw anything that resembled a strike and I couldn't come close. I lifted my arms to begin my motion, but my legs provided no stability, causing me to teeter and bounce pitches.

I walked Mickey Hatcher, the second batter of the game, on a close 3-2 pitch, instantly agonizing over it and letting the potential for trouble linger in my brain. With two outs, I balked, another sign that I was uncomfortable, because the slow-footed Hatcher wasn't a threat to steal a base. I threw a slider to Mike Marshall, a pitch that would have been a ball on the outside corner, and he reached out and blooped it into left field for a run-scoring single. I've never heard a more raucous reaction to a soft two-hundred-foot single. *Everyone really hates me*, I thought.

To me, that single had the impact of a four-hundred-foot homer because I was tense and mortified. I threw pitches that bounced because I was so out of sync and so focused on the wrong things. I gazed in for signs from Gary Carter, but my eyes strayed toward the opposing dugout to see what the Dodgers were doing. There was nothing in that dugout that could help me, so that was a ridiculous choice, but I did it because I was still a novice, a tough guy no longer. My pregame meeting with Carter was a blur. I couldn't remember what he said or what pitches I was supposed to throw. I didn't have the emotional strength or the mental toughness to understand that the reaction to my column was irrelevant and that I needed to perform.

In the second inning, I plunked Jeff Hamilton, who was a .236 hitter that season, with a 1-2 pitch, another wayward pitch and another indication of how wayward a pitcher I had become. Still, I was one out away from escaping the inning, but I allowed a first-pitch single to the opposing pitcher. Yes, Tim Belcher, who had four hits in fifty-six at bats that year, looked as confident as if he were Tony Gwynn in smacking a single to center. That unnerved me, but, again, I was distraught and didn't have the ability to rebound. At times, I remember feeling as if I was watching someone else experiencing this sluggish inning, watching another guy in a Mets uniform who was melting faster than a crayon in a toaster.

When Steve Sax slapped one of my fastballs into center field, it bounced five times before it actually touched the outfield grass. Five bounces? Ten bounces? It didn't matter because Sax's single gave the Dodgers a 2–0 lead. The fans responded as if Sax had ripped a baseball through the outfield fence. In moments like this, I eventually learned to slow down and calm myself down by thinking about making one good pitch, but at this tender point in my career, I didn't have those skills.

"David Cone has nobody to blame but himself," said Tim McCarver, one of the television analysts for the game. He added, "Don't be a sportswriter," because it can only incite the opposition.

Naturally, he was right. Still, if I had made it through the second inning with a 2-0 deficit, that would have been a major accomplishment, but I didn't. I couldn't stop the avalanche from coming, couldn't direct my pitches to the precise locations. I hung a 1-2 slider to Hatcher, which was one of my worst pitches of a dreadful outing, and he hammered it down the left field line for a two-run double. Marshall lined a first-pitch fastball for a single that gave the Dodgers a 5–0 cushion that felt like 15–0. As I watched the excitable Hatcher rumble into the dugout, he looked as if he had won $10 million in the lottery. And the rest of the players acted as if he was sharing the money with them.

Athletes marvel about having out-of-body experiences, those exhilarating feelings when they have performed so exceptionally that their actions seem almost otherworldly. I had an out-of-body experience, too, but it wasn't exhilarating. It really sucked. I was overwhelmed in that game, a distracted pitcher who lasted two dismal innings.

I always thought I was extremely tough, a middleweight pitcher who was rebellious and mouthy and who, most of the time, acted the way I wanted to act. When I had the baseball, I wanted to be the most intimidating player on the field, the guardian who would make sure no runs scored. In my first complete season with the Mets, I learned, harshly, that I wasn't as tough as I thought. No pitchers can throw strikes when their arms are trembling and their legs are limp. If I had accumulated more mental toughness, I would have blocked out those disturbances, dismissed the Dodgers for being so sensitive, and simply focused on reviewing scouting reports and pitching effectively.

The questions I should have asked myself were: Who cared what I had said about the Dodgers? Why don't the Dodgers worry about trying to hit my fastball? But I wasn't mentally tough enough to behave like that. I was in La-La Land, literally, as I gave up five runs in a 6–3 loss. My father sat in the stands for that game, watching in despair as his son and prized pupil was eviscerated and embarrassed.

Stunned and discombobulated by what happened, I spoke to waves of reporters after the game and admitted I had made those comments, although I really didn't mean to offend anyone. Too late. I did offend the Dodgers and they retaliated on the field. Before the reporters peppered me with questions, I offered some gallows humor by saying, "Do I get a last request?"

Using my cleats to dig a landing spot on the Dodger Stadium mound six days later, I wasn't making any jokes because my leg was twitching. I was nervous, again, even after having pitched one inning of relief in Game 3. Carter kept flashing one finger, almost pleading with me to throw one fastball for a strike. My nervous system was overloaded and I threw balls on eight of the first nine pitches, bouncing pitches and walking the first two batters. I was drowning again.

But Kirk Gibson, an intelligent hitter who won the NL MVP that season, popped up a bunt to me, which was one of the greatest gifts a batter has ever given me. I hustled forward and put my right hand in the air to let Carter know I would snatch it. Although I wasn't clever enough to let the bunt drop to the grass and try to collect a double play, I was still relieved.

After that one out, I relaxed and got angrier, smarter, and tougher. "Get another out," I said, challenging myself. I stopped torturing myself for making a mistake with the column and concentrated on making specific pitches to specific locations. It's one thing to act like a tough guy, which I sometimes did, but it's much more important to pitch like a tough guy, which I also did. I relied heavily on my fastball and pitched a complete game as we won, 5–1, in Game 6.

Late in the game, Al Michaels, the play-by-play announcer, said, "And the decibel level doesn't bother David Cone one iota," an obvious reference to how I wilted in Game 2.

My humiliating experience in Game 2 was the worst of my career, a collision of my valuable pitching career and my unimportant and brief journalism career. I wish it hadn't happened, because even though I stabilized myself and won my next start in Game 6, we lost the series in seven games. My meltdown and my lack of toughness might have, in part, prevented us from winning a World Series title.

But, as wretched as that experience was and as much as I still think about what might have happened if I hadn't floundered in that game, I know the ordeal helped me. It made me tougher and strengthened me to never feel that unnerved again. Players need to be challenged and tested until they become comfortable with the most unsettling situations, and if it's something as extreme as what I experienced, they will feel idiotic and they will learn quickly.

With every experience I collected, both positive and negative, I created a mental file and used those notes to help me in future outings. As forlorn as I was after Game 2, I suddenly had tremendous confidence after Game 6. Less than a week after flopping against the Dodgers, I had become mentally tougher. I knew it.

Every professional pitcher will endure something chaotic and humiliating in his career, although probably not as extreme as what I experienced before a postseason game. How they handle those frustrating situations and what they learn from them will dictate how tough they are and how much tougher they can become. Sometimes, a slap in the face is good because it's a reminder of what a pitcher doesn't want to feel again.

The vocabulary in baseball conversations rarely produces words that appear on the SATs, which is why words like *tough* and *toughness* are often sprinkled throughout these discussions. With two strikes, his slider is a tough pitch to hit. He's a tough hitter with runners in scoring position. They're a tough team against left-handed pitchers. On and on, toughness is a topic that permeates baseball.

The players who are talented and fortunate enough to make it to the major leagues are the best in the world, players who were usually the premier players on their teams since they first started playing. They are incredibly talented, but in the majors so is everyone else. Beyond the talent, these players need to have mental toughness, too, which is significant in a sport where there can be emotional swings from one pitch to the next, never mind one inning to the next. Baseball is a sport that's filled with failure, emotions churning and changing with every hanging slider or misplaced fastball.

What is mental toughness for a player? It's a mind-set, an approach, and a way of acting and reacting to the good, the bad, the unexpected, and the uncertain. As the intensity of a game increases, players preach about slowing the game down, which is a euphemism for not getting panicky.

Toughness is not letting one game or anything that happened in that game rattle you, which can be challenging because adversity is disconcerting. The annoying pain in your shoulder? Get a massage, stretch it out, and work through it. The umpire with the floating strike zone? Be consistent with locating your pitches and persuade him to call strikes. The soggy mound created by the rain shower? Remove the dirt from your cleats, establish some steadier footing, and pitch consistently. Whenever a player experiences these kinds of irritations, teammates notice how they react and gauge how resilient they seem to be.

The pitcher has been efficient for three innings, throwing a 95-mile-per-hour fastball that is cutting inside on batters and a slider that is bending beautifully, causing him to strut back to the dugout. But his fastball loses velocity in the fourth and his slider becomes flat, making him less confident. After allowing a few runs, he's not standing as tall anymore, moving slower and searching for help.

The pitcher can find some help, help from himself, because there are always other options to explore. He can throw the curveball that he abandoned in the second inning, or try to locate his diminished fastball more precisely. Work. Think. Create. Keep trying different pitches to every quadrant of the strike zone to challenge hitters, but don't dare look in the dugout. Is he staring in the dugout? The pitchers who do that, the doubters who routinely display that subtle sign of surrendering, aren't considered mentally tough.

Like judges at a talent competition, my teammates and I would sometimes evaluate a player's toughness and, based on what we had witnessed, rate him as someone who was very tough, someone who should be tougher, or someone who wasn't tough. We might as well have held up cards with numbers on them as they strolled past us. Some teammates believed a player either had or didn't have toughness as part of his DNA, and there was no amount of coaching or experiences that would transform a passive player into a tough player. Push him, prod him, test him, and haze him, but it wouldn't matter.

I believe that some amount of toughness is inherent and is obviously related to how a person was raised and the different situations he encountered in life. We are all influenced by whether we grew up poor, middle class, or privileged; whether we came from a one- or a two-parent family; whether we had siblings who helped mold us; how much adversity we endured in our lives; and just how committed we were in an extremely competitive business. As I've said, I know I was heavily influenced by having two older brothers and a father who was both a dutiful and a demanding coach.

But with all the responsibility and pressure that exists in the major leagues, I think toughness is a trait that has to be drained out of a player and developed when he finally reaches that elite level and he is challenged. To develop and learn to be tougher, a player usually needs to get humbled and feel what it's like to fail.

Toughness involves being realistic, and that includes being prepared for the worst and knowing something could eventually go awry. In every game I pitched, there was a pitch or a sequence where I either failed or could have failed and that did change or could have changed the outcome of the game. Pitchers need to be as confident as possible in what they are doing, but they need to be honest and understand that there will be games where they don't have their best pitches and they will sputter. If they understand that inevitably will happen, they won't be as skittish when it does.

The more comfortable I became as a pitcher, the more daring and aggressive I became, traits that are all part of being confident and tough. After the Blue Jays acquired me from the Mets for their postseason push in August 1992, I was a fatigued pitcher, having had pitch counts of 166, 142, and 140 in some of my final starts with New York. But once I made some mechanical adjustments with where my left leg landed on the mound, I felt rejuvenated with Toronto, especially since I had a chance to pitch in my first World Series.

The gambling side of me was evident during a tense Game 2 of the American League Championship Series between the Jays and the Athletics. With runners on second and third and one out in a scoreless game, I tossed a 2-2 fastball to Walt Weiss that narrowly missed being a strike. Now I was one ball away from allowing the A's to load the bases in the fifth inning, so the situation begged for me to throw another fastball.

Weiss and everyone else with a pulse in Toronto probably figured that I had to throw another fastball. Pat Borders, my catcher, felt that way, since he called for a fastball three times. I refused to pick the safer choice. I wanted to be more creative and throw a backdoor slider, a pitch that would start several inches off the outside corner before breaking from right to left and surprising the left-handed-hitting Weiss. I believed in that pitch, believed in it because I was tough enough to believe in it and because I thought it would surprise Weiss. It worked. Weiss's eyes tracked the pitch, thinking it would stay outside, but those eyes followed it right into Borders's glove for a called strike on the corner.

After the strikeout, Weiss lugged his bat back to the dugout with a confused look that seemed to be asking, *What the heck was that?* If I was willing to throw a gorgeous 3-2 slider in a fastball count in that perilous spot, the A's couldn't even fathom what I'd throw for the rest of the game. That one pitch, that one slider, built confidence and toughness because it showed the A's that I was going to be unpredictable, and it gave me an advantage. I followed that by striking out Rickey Henderson. I lasted eight innings, and we won, 3–1.

As much as I trusted Borders, I had to throw the 3-2 slider because that was the pitch I believed in. A pitcher knows how the ball feels leaving his hand and how much spin and velocity he should be able to generate. A pitcher feels the stiffness in his knee or the tightness in his lower back, nagging pains that may impact how he follows through in his delivery. A pitcher has the most knowledge about himself and his pitches, so I always wanted to make the final decision about what to throw. Some pitchers disagree with me and don't mind having a game called for them, but once I became an established pitcher, that wasn't even a debatable issue for me.

I have seen many younger pitchers encounter problems when they don't have 100 percent conviction about throwing a specific pitch. If a pitcher wants to throw a slider, he might ignore his instincts and throw a fastball because that's what the catcher requested. Sometimes that's understandable. But if the pitcher feels strongly about using the slider, I would rather see him throw it because it's probably going to be a better pitch.

No pitcher ever wants to be called a Mister P or Mister Perfect, a degrading nickname for pitchers who can flourish only when everything about the outing is perfect, from his pitches to the strike zone to the mound to the weather to any of the dozens of elements that pitchers can use as excuses. The pitchers who were Mister Ps were the type who would pitch until they experienced some adversity and then hoped to disappear from the game. There are a lot of Mister Ps, even if they don't realize that's what teammates are calling them.

Pitchers need to adapt to evolving situations, which can mean developing a new plan because some pitches are lagging. One quality pitch and a considerable amount of toughness can be life preservers for pitchers, especially when they are hunting for an approach that works. Andy Pettitte was tough and determined because he focused on making one effective pitch as a way to get through a delicate spot. As unsettling as a game situation might be, Pettitte believed he needed only one pitch to get the necessary strikeout, pop out, or double-play groundout.

So, even if he fell behind 2-0 or 3-1 in the count, Pettitte was obsessed with getting the count to two strikes and then utilizing his cutter as a finishing pitch. When he knew he didn't have his best control or his sharpest stuff, he always felt he had one more cutter that could rescue him.

It takes a certain toughness to think like that and pitch like that because a pitcher is taking risks when he's pecking away with decoy pitches to set up one potentially clinching pitch. The tough, smart pitchers, pitchers like Pettitte, tell themselves that they have enough pitches left to succeed. The pitchers who worry "What do I do now?" aren't tough, but the pitchers who say "I know exactly what I'm going to do now" are.

My father had it right all along. He wanted me to understand everything I was doing on the mound, so he taught me specific lessons about pitching, even when I was just beginning to pitch as a nine-year-old. He had been a pitcher and he recognized how enamored I was with the prospect of being a pitcher, so he studied the craft, shared his knowledge with me, and watched me succeed a lot and fail sometimes, too. Just like every pitcher. I can still hear his advice. I always will.

Chapter 3

START ME UP

IF A CAMERA HAD BEEN following me on the days that I pitched, it would have shown me dressed in full uniform, from the cleats on my feet to the cap on my head, at least a half hour before I needed to be in the bullpen. My scouting meeting with my catcher was long completed, and my arm had been stretched out and massaged because I was obsessed with being ready with time to spare. I wanted to be as comfortable as possible.

But there was no such thing as being comfortable when I was the visiting pitcher in the crowded Fenway Park bullpen. The home and visiting bullpens were constructed in 1940 because Red Sox owner Tom Yawkey wanted the right center-field fences to be closer so the sweet-swinging Ted Williams could hit more homers. They don't seem as if they've been updated much since Ted's days. It's an intimidating place to warm up because the fans are almost crammed in the bullpen with the pitcher, hovering over the five-and-a-half-foot fences and creating a hostile setting for anyone wearing a gray Yankees uniform. The drunker the fans were, the more intense the verbal abuse got in the place that we called the chicken coop.

"Hey, Cone, you're a garbage pitcher," a fan would howl. "The Sox are going to tear you apart tonight."

Of course, that type of comment was benign compared to some of the other things fans yelled, like "Your mother is a this-and-that," and "Your wife is hanging out in the clubhouse with our team." Warming up there felt like a death cage match because I often wondered if someone might lean over the fence and grab my shoulder as I was about to release the ball or chuck a beer can at me. Or worse. I appreciate passionate fans and I was treated very well when I pitched in Boston for one season, but, man, that bullpen was as difficult a pregame environment as I've ever experienced. Eventually, I tried to turn it into a positive and forced myself to focus sooner, almost willing myself to have a game face before my first warm-up pitch.

The Red Sox fans were intense and smart, so they would have something to say about every pitch. If I threw a slider that hung because I was still getting a feel for the pitch, they would scream, "Nomar is going to crush that." My first few fastballs were always pedestrian because I needed to loosen up my arm, but they seized upon the lack of velocity and said, "That's all you got? That's going to get destroyed." I remember bouncing one of my splitters because, again, I was just trying to get into a rhythm with the pitch, and a fan drolly said, "Oh, I feel bad for you. That's not going to work." The fan said it with such resignation in his voice (for me) and such confidence in his voice (for the Red Sox) that it lodged inside my head for a few minutes. *Was he right?*

When I was pitching games at Fenway, I could block out the fans. But when there was one loudmouth whooping it up near the bullpen, it did get on my nerves. I finally developed a defense mechanism for those fans. After they seemed to exhaust some of their best material, I would react to one specific fan's barbs and smile and say, "That was a good one." They weren't expecting me to react at all, so it usually surprised them and even quieted them for a while. As soon as a pitcher showed those fans that he was unnerved by what they were doing, he was sunk because they would simply increase the abuse. Obviously, long before I faced Boston's leadoff batter, the first enemies were the fans hounding me around the bullpen.

Moving methodically to establish some control, I dug at the dirt around the bullpen rubber to create a comfortable spot for pushing off the white slab. The feel of the first baseball I threw had to be comfortable, too, as if the ball was an extension of my hand. I would toss a baseball or two back in the bucket if it didn't feel perfect. That action invariably caused a fan to scream, "It's not the ball. It's you," a humorous line that I couldn't ignore. During the 2018 World Series, the Los Angeles Dodgers had complained about how close the fans were to their pitchers and I thought, *Been there and lived that*.

That contentious environment was much different than the calm environment I enjoyed before I journeyed to the bullpen. As much as I relished talking about baseball with teammates, coaches, and reporters on the days I started, I still crawled into my own bunker about an hour before the first pitch. I would find the quietest spot in the clubhouse, even if it meant hiding in one of the bathroom stalls, to avoid any interactions and any distractions. My personality changed dramatically in those minutes leading up to the game because I didn't want to be burdened by last-minute discussions about the hitters, the weather, the music blaring in the clubhouse, or the cold coffee in the food room.

My alone time was important and meditative because it helped me control my anxiety. Most pitchers get that bunker mentality several hours earlier than I ever did and are much more unapproachable than I ever was. To relax myself and block out the world, I closed my eyes and envisioned a peaceful scene, like a comfortable lounge chair on an empty beach.

Since I loved experimenting, I approached pregame bullpen

sessions as if I were in a laboratory, even if it was a chicken coop laboratory in Boston. There were always possible refinements to be made. I would assess how my pitches were reacting as they left my hand, the best barometer of how they would respond during the game. I needed to know if my fastball had extra life and if my slider and splitter had the requisite depth and movement.

Every pitcher wants to hear his fastball pop into the catcher's mitt, no matter how hard he throws, because that familiar and re-freshing sound is a psychological boost. From the time I was a fifteen-year-old Royals fan and watched the Yankees' Goose Gos-sage in the bullpen in Kansas City, saliva flying, his motion a tangle of arms and legs and the sound of his explosive fastballs reverberat-ing off the walls, I wanted to unleash my fastballs in a major league bullpen.

On that fateful visit, I bought a general admission ticket and leaned over the bullpen wall and watched Gossage pitch, and I was in shock. He was so strong, so powerful, and so intimidat-ing. That *bam, bam, bam* into the catcher's mitt was intoxicating to me and almost made my head snap back. After Gossage whipped a dozen or so pitches, Yankees manager Billy Martin approached the mound and lifted his right arm, like a warden signaling for an executioner, and made a pitching change. So Gos-sage fired a few more pitches and rumbled into the game.

All pitchers are human and all pitchers want to believe, really believe, they have superb fastballs. Because the mental aspect of pitching is so crucial and confidence can be so fleeting, a pitcher who thinks he has more power on his fastball will be more confi-dent. How psychologically important is it for a pitcher to hear that explosive sound in the bullpen? Rick Sutcliffe once asked Joe Gi-rardi to use a new catcher's mitt because Girardi's broken-in mitt no longer popped noisily enough when Sutcliffe's fastball hit it. One of the Yankees' bullpen catchers had a mitt we called the "ego glove," because the sound that erupted when the ball clashed with the mitt made every pitcher feel like Nolan Ryan.

Visualization is important for pitchers. They can help themselves and relax themselves by forecasting which pitches they will throw to batters and the results they want to achieve. If a pitcher has a slider that's breaking sharply on a given day, he should envision batters swinging over that pitch for a strikeout or tapping it weakly to an infielder. That's what I did.

As vicious as the fans frequently were to me in the Fenway bullpen, I know they were much nastier on a memorable night in May 2003. Roger Clemens, a former Red Sox deity and the winningest pitcher in franchise history, was now a Yankee. The fans blistered him and let the Rocket know he was no longer welcome in a city where he had won three Cy Young Awards. There were three police officers and two security guards positioned near the bullpen, so the fans were forced to voice their insults from farther away, which, of course, they still did. They called Clemens a traitor, they told him he should be pitching in a high school JV game, and they called him a litany of profane names that would not be permitted on an episode of *Sesame Street*.

"I got a better arm than you," one hefty man incorrectly squawked. "You're nothing."

As energized as Clemens was before games, the sight of that extra protection by the bullpen and the heightened verbal abuse surely fueled him through an eleven-minute throwing session. One usher theorized that the fans would be "hanging over the fence" if the police and security weren't in place. Clemens was a machine, throwing fastballs to different sides of the plate, working on his splitter and grunting on every pitch. He never looked up at the fans and never acknowledged them. When Clemens felt he was game ready, he trudged to the dugout, counting the minutes until he could finally throw a pitch that mattered.

Clemens was in his own world, but it was a world impeccably designed to get his body best prepared to pitch a game. I've never seen another pitcher endure as physically demanding a workout even before he made it to the bullpen to warm up his valuable arm. Clemens would run at a brisk pace for several minutes, something starting pitchers rarely do on the days they are pitching, and return to the clubhouse in a sweat.

On the days he started, it was riveting to watch Clemens huddle with the athletic trainers and test his body the way a mechanic tests every aspect of a luxury car. He wanted to know that his right shoulder, his right elbow, his back, his hips, his hamstrings, his calves, and every other part of his body was tuned up and ready to go. If his shoulder felt sore, he would get a massage. If one of his hamstrings was stiff, he would stretch it out. Nothing went unchecked. And, as I witnessed during a Royals–Red Sox game in June 1994, Clemens really didn't ignore anything, even if it was only marginally related to his body.

About fifteen minutes before the scheduled first pitch, both Rocket and I were warming up in our respective bullpens at Fenway. I would guess we were both about three-quarters of the way finished with our sessions, but I began watching Clemens closely because I didn't want to finish before him. Since he was pitching the top of the first inning, I wanted to time my session so I lingered a little longer than him in the bullpen. If I completed my warm-ups at the same time as Rocket, it could have been as much as a half hour before I threw another pitch in the bottom of the first. So I was waiting on Rocket.

Suddenly, I heard a shrill voice screaming, "Rocket! Rocket!" and I saw a blond woman dashing through the lower level of the Fenway stands. Like I said, that area could be boisterous, so I was surprised that one person's voice was cutting through all of the noise, but it was. As the woman made it closer to the bullpen area, she raised her hand and waved something in the air.

"Rocket," she said, "I've got your lucky socks."

Lucky socks? Seriously? The woman was Debbie Clemens, Roger's wife, and she had rushed to the bullpen to make sure that her husband would have his footwear. I had never seen anything like this, but Rocket grabbed the socks from Debbie and disappeared into the bullpen bathroom. An astonished Bruce Kison, my pitching coach, said, "You've got to be kidding me."

At that point, I wasn't sure what to do because I didn't know how long it would take him to remove his cleats, his stirrups, his other socks, and maybe his pants, and pull on those socks. I tossed a few pitches and then I stopped throwing and sat down. It seemed like it took Rocket several minutes to change, which was an unfortunate delay, as I was trying to get ready for my start. Finally, Rocket emerged wearing his lucky socks, order having been restored to his baseball world.

It's kind of weird, but I remember that sock exchange as much as I remember what happened on the field. We both pitched seven strong innings and both allowed two runs, but neither of us received a decision as the Red Sox won, 4–2. I guess Rocket's socks were a little luckier than mine. When I became teammates with Clemens on the Yankees, I never worked up the nerve to ask him about that day. I could have had some fun and rushed a pair of socks to him before a spring start for a déjà vu moment, but I missed that opportunity to tease him.

I don't think too many players ever teased Mariano Rivera in the bullpen, which was his kingdom. And, like Clemens, me, and every other pitcher, Rivera had a specific routine he used to get ready in the late innings. After John Flaherty made the Yankees as a backup catcher in 2003, he heard the bullpen phone ring, he saw Rivera stand up, and he rushed behind the plate to begin catching Rivera's warm-up tosses. It was Flaherty's first official day as a Yankee, so he didn't wait for Rivera to say anything and quickly crouched behind the plate to catch the mighty Mariano. Rivera threw three or four pitches and then he stared icily at Mike Borzello, the bullpen catcher, who looked uncomfortable while standing a few feet away. Borzello approached Flaherty and said, "I'm really the only one who ever catches him." With that one sentence, Flaherty learned Rivera's preferences and went back to his seat. Interestingly, the polite Rivera put the onus on the bullpen catcher to tell Flaherty about his desire, surely not wanting to disrespect a new teammate.

While it might not have been as exhaustive as Clemens's pregame checklist, I had my own checklist during my bullpen sessions. After finding a baseball that felt perfect in my hand, I placed my index and middle fingers on the cross seams of the ball, which are called the horseshoe seams, and put my thumb underneath those two fingers on the leather side of the ball to establish my grip on a four-seam fastball. The four-seamer is a pitcher's fastest pitch—there are four seams rotating as the ball slices through the air—and it's also usually his most dependable pitch because it doesn't have excessive side-to-side movement. I wanted to be absolutely certain I could pinpoint my four-seamer at a right-handed batter's knees and on the outside corner, the appealing down-and-away location that is about the size of a grapefruit and is a pitcher's definition of the perfect strike. I needed to command that pitch as a weapon and as a security blanket.

Helpless and powerless are terrible ways to feel on the mound, but when I had a four-seamer that I could control, I felt strong because it was my get-me-out-of-trouble pitch. Throwing a down-and-away fastball shouldn't typically get you into as much trouble as a pitch that's over the middle or on the inside corner because batters must reach across the plate and try and hit it the opposite way, something that they don't usually do with as much power. I was a stubborn pitcher, even in my bullpen sessions. Until I could repeatedly unleash fastballs that were down and away for strikes, I wouldn't work on another type of pitch.

If I missed my spot by even a few inches, I would roll the ball around in my hand, get my grip again, and start all over. I never considered myself robotic, but I was robotic in my desire to throw that pitch to that spot at will.

Flash back to the first time you picked up a baseball and threw it. It was a fastball. Well, it was really a slow ball because that's the easiest pitch to throw. After you graduate beyond just tossing a ball and you are trying to subdue hitters, you will likely be throwing both a four-seam fastball and a two-seam fastball.

To be a consistent strike thrower who can repeatedly throw a fastball that is at the knees and on the outside corner, your mechanics have to be perfect. In my case, I knew my results would tell me if the various aspects of my delivery were in unison. There are probably fifty things a pitcher does before throwing every pitch, actions as basic as standing upright on the mound, not tilting his chin toward the ground, and staring solely at the catcher's target, but I was always particularly focused on being balanced.

Pitchers aren't walking across a four-inch balance beam and flipping like gymnasts, but we are tiptoeing through our own balancing exercises because there are so many parts of the body that must coalesce to produce an effective pitch. To stay balanced and avoid any disruptions in my delivery, I knew the lower half of my body, especially my left hip, needed to be my axis. Unlike what some pitching coaches profess about the upper body being most important for keeping a pitcher aligned, I thought my lower body was more critical.

Imagine you are watching a right-handed pitcher like me from the third base coach's box. As I lifted my left leg in my delivery and pivoted toward the plate, I wanted my body to stay "sideways" longer, with my left side parallel to the plate and my left knee pointed toward third.

The longer I kept my lower half and my shoulder in that sideways position, that in-between part of the delivery, the more I could stay on top of the ball, which meant my hand was behind the ball as I drove forward and I wasn't sacrificing velocity or movement. That in-between part of the delivery is called a glide. Pitchers are reminded to gather themselves to begin their delivery, glide through their delivery, and then throw the pitch. Gather, glide, explode. It's an easy shorthand to remember, especially in daunting spots.

Besides staying sideways with my left hip, I needed to make sure I lifted my leg to its highest point as I rotated toward the plate and separated my pitching hand from my glove hand. If the ball is still in a pitcher's glove when his body is moving forward, he will struggle with locating pitches. If I was pelting the edges of the outside corner with my four-seamer, I knew my mechanics were uncluttered, the execution married with the results.

With each fastball in the bullpen, my arm was getting looser, and I was fighting through any aches or soreness. If I was in the middle of a bullpen session and, hypothetically, someone told me that I could use only one pitch for the entire game, I'd curse and panic. Thirty seconds later, I would bypass my slider and my splitter, two of my best pitches, to use the four-seamer. If my location was precise, meaning I was putting pitches exactly where I wanted to, I could win a game with a solid four-seamer.

Rare is the starting pitcher who is comfortable relying on one pitch, but sometimes he has no choice. I watched Clemens, Dwight Gooden, and others thrive with mostly four-seamers in some games. There were dozens of starts where my fastball was enabling me to get quick outs, so I kept throwing it in the early innings, saving my secondary pitches for the second or the third time through the batting order and therefore remaining more of a mystery to hitters. I loved being creative, as I said, but if my fastball was effective, I didn't have to veer from what was working. In those games, I wanted batters to keep wondering and waiting on the appearance of my slider or splitter.

Whether it was Gooden or Clemens in my era, or Max Scherzer or Justin Verlander nowadays, there are games where a pitcher feels invincible. The baseball feels lighter in his hand, the seams feel higher and easier to grip, the ball shoots out of his hand like a missile, and the movement of his pitches is nasty and precise.

I was fortunate enough to stand on the mound for 471 regular season and postseason games, and in almost all of them, I threw a fastball that was down and away to the first righty hitter. Depending on how much finger pressure I used, it's a pitch that could tail away from the batter and could catch the outside corner for a strike, totally flustering the batter. I used that same pitch and that same location to come inside on lefty batters and freeze them. It's exhilarating to get a batter to start swinging and then catch him looking at the pitch, leaving him as motionless as a statue.

In the final weeks of a forgettable 1991 season, during which the Mets underachieved and won a mere seventy-seven games, I pitched a game where I felt machinelike while throwing perfect fastballs and almost recording a no-hitter. Every fastball that I threw before the game made me feel a little bolder because I was pounding those pitches into Charlie O'Brien's glove, loudly and accurately.

In the early innings, we simply continued my routine from the bullpen with a succession of fastballs. It was a hazy night with the temperature dipping into the fifties, and I sensed that the Cardinals weren't reacting to the pitch, so I continued throwing it, moving it in and out and high and low to force the batter's eyes to look up and down and side to side. O'Brien was smart about studying hitters, and he told me the Cardinals couldn't get the barrel of the bat through the strike zone quickly enough to connect with my fastball, so there was no reason to throw anything else. If I had thrown a slider, a breaking pitch with less velocity, I would have been helping the sluggish batters. I relied on my fastball all night; I didn't allow a hit until Felix Jose doubled in the eighth inning, and I ended up with a one-hitter and eleven strikeouts. That experience merely reinforced my views on the importance of having a trustworthy fastball for every start.

When I was on those bullpen mounds, the sweat collecting on my forehead and on the back of my neck, my two-seam fastball was almost an afterthought. Unlike the four-seamer that a pitcher can pinpoint to the outside lane and the inside lane, another name for the extreme corners of the plate, pitchers can't control two-seamers as readily because those fastballs are designed to sink and move from side to side. Because of the way it's thrown, the two-seamer has two fewer seams hitting the air than the four-seamer, which causes it to move more.

I never had great control of my two-seamer and would only occasionally throw it to left-handed hitters to try and produce grounders, or as a decoy pitch to give batters another option to ponder.

The fastball is an ever-present weapon, even if it's a straight fastball. One of the falsehoods I have tried to dispel is when I hear fans and even broadcasters say a straight four-seam fastball is problematic. That's a convenient theory to express, but it's not true if the pitcher has the ability to locate the pitch. Trust me, if Dellin Betances throws a 99-mile-per-hour pellet on the black of the plate, it doesn't matter if the pitch is straight. It will still be an above-average pitch and a very difficult pitch for a batter to drive. I've seen many pitchers succeed with straight four-seamers that they throw extremely hard to specific lanes. The best and tightest four-seamers are the pitches that look smaller to batters, causing them to grudgingly say, "He's throwing aspirin tonight."

In the bullpen, on the game mound, and in so many batters' nightmares, no one threw more aspirin tablets than Gooden. When Gooden was dominating batters, he would throw his four-seamers to the inside and outside lanes, and they were relatively straight fastballs. Since batters could barely see Doc's fastball as he targeted locations on the edges, it didn't matter how much the pitches moved or didn't move. There was a difference when he elevated his four-seamers above the zone, as those fastballs had some hop to them and weren't as straight. Still, Gooden was electrifying while often throwing a straight fastball, which is significant evidence to prove that pitch isn't a bad thing.

With everything that a pitcher must ponder, the brilliant Greg Maddux once said, "You want to be able to only have to worry about pitching, not how to throw pitches." I love that quotation because Maddux was stressing the importance of preparation, and that resonated with me. Maddux was fanatical about honing his fastball command during bullpen sessions. If he could throw his fastball to an index-card-sized spot and change speeds with it, he felt he was in a perfect position to subdue batters and didn't worry about doing too much else in the bullpen. Of course, Maddux's command wasn't just great. It was legendary.

A pitcher longs to know that each of his pitches is ready and that they can be used in any count and in any situation in the game. When and if a pitcher has that confidence, he can devote himself totally to attacking hitters in a variety of ways. But that isn't always the case, and there will be many days where a pitcher lacks that confidence and cohesiveness and must scramble and adjust.

In the bullpen, I never counted how many pitches I threw or fretted about the number. My guess is I threw a few dozen, but it was contingent on what type of lineup I was facing and how strong my arm felt. If a team started six or seven left-handed hitters, I'd spend more time perfecting my curve because that was a breaking pitch I would employ more often against lefties.

Creativity is imperative, and that included bouncing some curves on the plate, an area that wasn't even close to being a strike. If teammates peeked in the bullpen before the game and saw me bouncing curves, they might have figured that I had lousy stuff and that I couldn't control what I was doing. But it was actually the opposite. Bouncing curves is a challenge, and it takes skill to get batters to chase a pitch that ends up below their ankles.

When I had 0-2 and 1-2 counts, I was always eager to bounce a curve in one of those low-risk positions because it's a savvy way to secure a strikeout. Believe me, there are plenty of strikes to be mined on pitches that are thrown on top of the plate or right behind it, and I think more pitchers should try and bounce pitches there to swipe some strikes.

Soon after I turned twelve, I was tinkering and throwing curves, which defied every rule about how to handle a kid pitcher. But my father taught me the proper way to throw a curve, and he limited how many I was allowed to throw in practice or a game. Sometimes, I wasn't allowed to use my curve at all in a game. To throw a curve, you put your middle finger along the bottom seam of the ball, place your index finger beside it for control, and position your thumb on the back seam. You snap your wrist when releasing the curve so it's a finesse pitch, a pitch you're trying to get to bend into the strike zone and trick a hitter. As a way to refine my curve, I was taught to imagine that I had a keg of beer strapped to my chest. When I threw a curve, I wanted to reach over the top of the keg as I got ready to deliver the ball, then pull back underneath the keg to throw the pitch.

To throw a curve that lands near the top of the plate, you use the same grip and you throw it with the same arm speed, but you snap your wrist more aggressively when you release it because you're not trying to throw it to a particular spot. Your goal is to keep the ball down and out of the strike zone, so you don't need to finesse it. If pitchers can produce that type of curve, they will end up throwing a poor-looking pitch that can deliver positive results.

On a quiet November day in 2011, there was an unfamiliar number buzzing on my phone. When I answered it, I was surprised to hear from Bobby Valentine, who had recently been hired as the manager of the Red Sox. Valentine, who is smart and excitable, engaged me in small talk before asking if I would be interested in becoming the Red Sox pitching coach. I was flattered by the overture, but I was also startled because I'd never worked as a coach at any level, and I simply wasn't expecting that kind of opportunity. I wasn't ready to pursue that job at that stage in my life, but it made me ponder what kind of coach I would be.

While I've never compiled all the plans and strategies I would use as a pitching coach, one of my minor rules would be to instruct pitchers to throw curves in the dirt. If the catcher called for a low curve with runners on base, he would be bracing for that pitch, so that really isn't a risky choice. I never believed in avoiding curves in the dirt because I might allow a runner to advance from second to third. I believed in having catchers who were ready to block those potential swing-and-miss pitches.

A flushed face, wide, suspicious eyes, and no smile was a perfect description of how I looked before most games. I was tense because of my competitiveness and my anxiety, a combination that led me to get hyperactive before starts. That combustibility was even worse for the 1992 season opener because I had endured an unsatisfying spring in which my fastball was a few miles slower than the year before. Do you want to make a pitcher feel naked? Strip a few miles off his fastball and shove him onto the mound.

After a series of listless fastballs disarmed me that day, I made an unusual and impromptu decision to deviate from everything I normally did and switched to throwing curveballs, nothing but curves, during my warm-ups. I tossed looping curves that dropped into the strike zone, I tossed sharper curves that I wanted to land under the batter's knees, and I tossed biting curves that bounced off the plate or right behind it. This curveball bonanza was spawned by my fear that my fastball just wasn't robust enough to guide me much that day. When pitching coach Mel Stottlemyre noticed the abundance of curves, he asked if I was OK. I just told him I thought I would need the curve on this day, partially concealing the drastic plan I was hatching.

The Cardinals were speedy, pesky, and notorious for having players with level swings who would peck away at fastballs. If I threw pedestrian fastballs to the likes of Ozzie Smith, Milt Thompson, and Ray Lankford, I envisioned them flicking away the pitches they didn't like before zoning in on something they could hit squarely. In a prescient moment born from panic, I decided to do my best imitation of Bert Blyleven, who had the best curve I've ever seen, to try and keep the Cardinals off balance.

The curve was my fourth-best pitch, but I liked the spin and movement I was getting, so I kept taking the ball, putting my index and middle fingers in the same spot, and kept spinning that pitch for strikes. For eight innings, I succeeded in confusing the Cardinals, limiting them to two runs while striking out nine and walking one. I threw 110 pitches, and it felt as if half of them were curves, a reminder that I needed to trust my own instincts and my own pitches. The pitcher knows his repertoire better than anyone, so if there's an urge to move in an unusual direction, it makes sense to do it. I didn't have Blyleven's curve that day or any other day, but I had a curve that was sharp enough to help me stifle a good team.

I rarely smiled on the mound, but once my plan began working, I grinned when I glanced in the front seats at Busch Stadium that day. Bob Gibson, the Hall of Fame pitcher and the owner of an imposing fastball, had a premium seat for an unscheduled curveball show. Gibson was as intimidating as any pitcher of the last half century and I imagined him muttering, "Does this guy even have a fastball?" On that day, I didn't need one—a decision I made because of the way I felt in the bullpen.

For pitchers, the bullpen is a second home, a home that has a much different vibe for the pregame throwing session than it does for the one or two sessions that a pitcher has between starts. Those sessions are used to keep a pitcher's arm loose, to experiment with new pitches or new grips, and to begin to outline a game plan for the next start. There's scant pressure during one of those in-between sessions, but there's a lot of pressure in the sessions that occur less than one hour before the game.

As the minutes expired before game time, I grew more impatient, a trait that followed me throughout my career and a trait that follows virtually every starting pitcher. It's rare for a starter to be completely calm before the first pitch. There's always some edginess.

I was always relieved when I advanced to the point in my bullpen session where I pretended to face some hitters from the opposing lineup because that meant the game was inching closer. It was imperative to treat those imaginary at bats realistically, including having a coach stand in as the batter, and using the same approach for each imaginary hitter that had been established for that game.

Standing in the bullpen and continuing to remain focused on my pitches, I played mind games and convinced myself I was already pitching in the game. To test my splitter, I wouldn't just throw five straight splitters. I would navigate through a sequence against an imaginary batter, say Kenny Lofton, and try to set him up for the splitter, just as I would in the game. I might start with a fastball to see if I could catch the outside corner for a strike, and follow that with an inside fastball that could startle the batter and that he might foul off. If I felt I succeeded in executing those first two pitches, I would throw my splitter as if I were trying to strike him out. Those hypothetical at bats were beneficial because they forced me into game mode, the place that I was rushing to get to for the last hour.

"Strike three," I'd say under my breath, just as a way to get even more motivated.

When pitchers leave the bullpen, as I've said, they want to feel confident about their pitches, but they also want to feel comfortable. In some rare instances, pitchers can have great bullpen sessions but the quality of their pitches doesn't translate into the game. On those days, they probably tried to do too much with their already useful pitches. If a pitcher's fastball was humming, he might try to throw it harder in the game and overthrow it, losing command and spraying pitches out of the strike zone. If a pitcher's slider had great tumbling action, he might try to get extra spin on it and get it to break even more. Sometimes by doing that, he might grip the ball too tightly and lose the feel for it. Naturally, a pitcher should always try to improve his pitches, but he has to recognize when he's comfortable with what is working and try to preserve that feeling.

Again, in the very few times where a pitcher is erratic in the bullpen and becomes more consistent during the game, it's because he made adjustments, and those adjustments require patience. If his slider was hanging or his splitter wasn't diving, he still needs to use these pitches in the game to try and gain a feel for them and gain some confidence in them. I would use those pitches in less pressurized situations, like with the bases empty or against hitters in the bottom of the order, until I knew I could trust them in more important spots.

Despite the occasional quirk, how a pitcher performs before the game usually carries over to the game. Then again, there are times when a pitch that had been ineffective suddenly turns into a weapon, which is one of the reasons why pitching can be infuriating for even the most accomplished pitchers.

There are new factors to consider once a pitcher leaves the bullpen mound and reaches the game mound. Pitchers are usually throwing in a different direction in the bullpen, likely west-to-east or east-to-west, than they are during the game, which is north-to-south. While that might sound insignificant, it's not. In addition, a pitcher's depth perception is different in the bullpen than it is on the field. Once he's in the more open area on the field, that can be an adjustment, like going from swimming in a one-lane lap pool to swimming in the ocean.

The footing on the bullpen mound is different from the game mound, which is typically comprised of firmer clay and is better maintained by the grounds crew. But a pitcher has to share that mound with the opposition, meaning he must be adaptable. If the other pitcher has a size 14 cleat and you have a size 11 cleat, and he has dug out a larger hole in front of the rubber for his landing leg, you have two choices: repeatedly fill in the hole with more earth or adjust and create a different landing spot. It can be irritating, but the pitcher must make adjustments.

Strange, unexpected events can also occur in the bullpen, developments that can make a manic pitcher like me even more maniacal toward my catcher. I will discuss the relationship between pitchers and catchers at length in a later chapter, but I do want to highlight the importance of catchers in getting a pitcher prepared in the bullpen. As indispensable as Joe Girardi was to me as a savvy, encouraging, and trustworthy catcher, the sensitive side of my pitching personality made him catcher non grata, briefly, on a chaotic day at Yankee Stadium.

When Girardi caught my starts, he'd arrive in the bullpen toward the end of my session so we could go through the process of facing an imaginary hitter and review which pitches were working. For a game in 1999, Girardi appeared early, and I was in a horrendous mood because I didn't have any reliable pitches: no fastball, no splitter, no slider, and no feel for what I wanted to do. Borzello, the bullpen catcher, was at least trying to make me think I had decent stuff by catching erratic pitches and sliding them closer to the strike zone. There's an art to the way catchers receive a ball, even in the bullpen, and Borzello was trying to frame some impossibly bad pitches. Even though I knew they were atrocious pitches, Borzello pacified me by catching them and pulling them into the strike zone. I knew what he was doing, but it eased my concerns and made me think I was slogging closer to finding some consistency with my pitches.

Whatever false protection Borzello provided vanished when Girardi crouched behind the plate. He caught the first pitch and jabbed at it, like a toddler waving at a balloon. Then he snared the second pitch and was just as lazy. When he caught the third pitch and didn't move his glove and at least act as if it was an acceptable pitch, I was livid. As innocent as Girardi's behavior was, it destroyed my fragile confidence and I yelled, "Get out!" He was miffed, but I wanted Borzello back because I needed him, in a sense, to continue lying to me.

Half embarrassed and half incensed, I turned away from a confused Girardi as he left. I spewed profanities and felt like throwing my glove against the bullpen wall. From one inning to the next, pitchers can morph into irate and insecure human beings, which was what I was that day and on so many other days. I think I pitched six or seven decent innings and we won, which was much more than I expected at the beginning of my bullpen fiasco.

A few hours after I verbally squashed Girardi, he located me in the clubhouse and asked why I had done it. I shook my head, stuttered, and told him I didn't want him to see my miserable pitches because I didn't want that to influence how he called the game. Once I completed my warm-ups in the bullpen, I wanted Girardi to have complete confidence to call for any of my pitches because my hope was they would eventually become more useful. That's the lunacy pitchers experience when we can't make the baseball do what we want it to do in the bullpen.

Chapter 4

$47 PAYCHECKS AND SLEEPING ON THE FLOOR

WILLIE MAYS IS A SACRED name in baseball and, like most baseball icons, was also a sacred name in my house. While I was too young to have witnessed Mays's greatest feats, my father told me vivid tales about him. From the way Mays hustled as if his cleats were on fire, to the way his cap fell off as he pursued fly balls, to the way he powered baseballs over the fence as if he was playing stickball on the New York streets, to the way he threw, slid, and smiled, Mays played with style. He simply did things other players couldn't do or wouldn't even try to do.

As a teenager growing up in Kansas City, I saw Mays as a superhero, a man who was so renowned that he should have been wearing a red cape on the field. I put Mays on such a pedestal that I grew giddy when I met someone with a loose connection to him. Joe Presko was a rookie pitcher for the St. Louis Cardinals in 1951, the same year Mays debuted with the New York Giants. Joe eventually became a baseball coach in Kansas City and my brother, Chris, was buddies with Joe's son, Tim, so we knew their family very well.

Since I had been told about Presko's link to Mays and how they opposed each other in the early years of Mays's Hall of Fame career, I was riveted before Presko ever said a word to me. I didn't know he had surrendered a homer to Mays in 1951, the season when the twenty-year-old Mays won the Rookie of the Year Award. But, even if I knew that Mays was 6 for 20 off Presko in his career, those statistics would have simply embellished the questions that were swimming in my mind.

When I saw Presko, a lean, athletic man standing in front of me, I focused on this: He had pitched in the major leagues for six seasons. Six seasons! He had pitched to legends like Mays, Jackie Robinson, and Duke Snider, and played on the same team as Stan Musial, and he was talented enough to do something I desperately wanted to do. But pitching at the highest level of the sport was something I wasn't sure I'd ever be good enough to do. As a fifteen-year-old, I had no clue if I would ever be as accomplished as Presko, the man who won twenty-five major league games.

On a warm and hopeful day, I auditioned for Presko because he was an influential coach in the Ban Johnson League, a summer league filled with college players who were as old as twenty-one. Compared to these men, I was a baby. I was nervous and excited and excitedly nervous, the same types of swirling emotions I would experience for the rest of my career. I had clammy hands and an unsettled stomach because I was trying to impress a pitcher who had pumped fastballs to Mays, something that seemed not quite believable to me.

In that moment, any fifteen-year-old would do exactly what I did: Throw the baseball as hard as possible. I could spin the ball and throw a decent slider, but I didn't want to feature that pitch. I had been throwing curveballs since I was twelve, so I could snap off some nifty curves, too. But, once again, I surmised that Presko wanted to see velocity. I figured he was wondering, "What does this skinny kid have in that right arm?"

I fired fastball after fastball, the ball feeling powerful as it left my hand and popped loudly into the catcher's mitt. Even at that age, I had a good feel for how hard I threw, and my guess is my fastball was humming across the plate at about 85 miles per hour. Damn good for a kid who looked like he should be delivering newspapers on his bike, not being considered to challenge college hitters.

Presko, who had a slender face and optimistic eyes, stood near me during the workout, and his expression changed from curious to very surprised to very interested. By the time I had finished throwing fastballs, Presko altered my life with one sentence: "You can do this." With those words, I believed that Presko meant that I could pitch in the majors, just like him. Hearing that endorsement from a former major leaguer was utterly motivating and was something I held on to throughout my ascension to the big leagues. *You can do this.* Those four words were as powerful as any I had ever heard and were imprinted on my brain. In subsequent years, Presko told friends I was the most advanced teenage pitcher he'd ever seen.

Every time I mentioned to my major league teammates that I didn't play high school baseball, they were typically stunned. Most of them thought I was joking and wanted to know how that was possible. As recently as 2018, Paul O'Neill squirmed in his seat and his face twisted into a confused look when I mentioned that to him, a tidbit that we'd never discussed when we played together for five and a half seasons. I can't remember one major league teammate who shared that odd distinction with me.

Despite my obsession with baseball, I attended Rockhurst High School, an all-boys Jesuit school in Kansas City with excellent academics, a $1,500 tuition, strong football and basketball teams, and no baseball team. Still, baseball always tugged at me, much more than the other sports. After my sophomore year, playing football and basketball wasn't fulfilling enough, so I tried to convince my father to let me transfer to Hickman Mills. It was a public school with a coach who was a scout for the St. Louis Cardinals. But my father was adamant about the importance of a Jesuit education, and he believed I would get enough baseball experience by playing during the summer. Still unhappy, I created a petition in my junior year to start a baseball team at Rockhurst and collected hundreds of signatures. My attempts were denied.

Instead of playing against other high school kids, my baseball experiences came against accomplished college players from schools like Missouri, Kansas, Iowa, and Iowa State in the Ban Johnson League. Wearing my Boyle's Famous Corned Beef uniform and weighing about 140 pounds, I understood how much of an unknown I was. And I reveled in it. As the youngest of four siblings, I was ferociously competitive, and this type of underdog situation made me even more so. I loved to overpower the college players who wondered why the bat boy was actually pitching.

Even without the benefit of a high school team, I received modest attention from the two major league teams that were within 250 miles of my doorstep by the time I turned seventeen. I participated in a tryout camp for the Cardinals at a baseball facility in Kansas City, and I also auditioned for the Royals, which was much more captivating to me because it was held on the grand stage known as Royals Stadium. In those days, I'm pretty sure the Royals advertised it in the local newspapers, so there were about two hundred kids in attendance. If one or two players ended up being signed, that was a lot. Honestly, it was a free-for-all and it was incredibly difficult to get noticed in such a crowded setting.

I waited for what seemed like two hours before I finally got the chance to pitch, but I was smart enough to toss on the side a lot so I could stay loose. I knew this was my one opportunity to impress the Royals, maybe the only opportunity I'd ever get to audition at a major league stadium, so I kept myself as prepared as possible.

And, when my name was finally called, I had about ten or fifteen pitches to dazzle a few scouts so, just like that day with Presko, I reared back and pumped fastballs as hard as I could. I knew scouts wanted to see arm strength, so I used my right leg to push hard off the rubber as I imagined myself throwing 90 miles per hour. At the end of my session, I mixed in a few breaking pitches to prove that I had more than a fastball. Walking off the mound, I saw a few scouts scribbling notes. Still, I was uncertain if I had passed or failed the most critical test of my life.

Thankfully, a thick-haired and thick-chested gentleman named Carl Blando ambled over, introduced himself as a Royals scout, and told me he was impressed by my workout. Blando spoke the language of a scout, saying he liked the "life" on my fastball and telling me he thought I had a good chance to be drafted out of high school. Yes, the pitcher who didn't even belong to a high school team might catapult straight from Rockhurst to the pros. I was euphoric and hopeful. Blando also told me he would keep a keen eye on my performances in the Ban Johnson League.

Not long before the 1981 amateur draft, I pitched in the Ban Johnson season opener. But it wasn't just a fun summer league game anymore. In my mind, I convinced myself I would have one make-it-or-break-it chance to pitch for scouts from the Royals and the Cardinals, the only teams who showed any interest in me. When I reflect on that day, it's intimidating to think how much pressure there was on me to succeed in that game. If I threw 78 miles per hour and lasted two innings, would I have even been drafted?

The time and money that teams invest in scouting players has increased exponentially since I was trying to get noticed almost four decades ago. These days, most draft-eligible high school and college players have been scouted in dozens of games. Obviously, advancements in technology have made it so much easier to scout players, too. If I wanted to find videos of the best high school pitchers in Missouri today, I'm sure they exist on YouTube or on some other baseball or scouting website. There was no extensive video of me as an eighteen-year-old. While I was a little spooked when I saw the scouts pointing radar guns at me to gauge my velocity, I reminded myself this was the stage I desired, and I thought about throwing hard and throwing strikes.

I think I pitched four solid innings in the Ban Johnson game, but the scouts informed my father that they liked my fastball, which hit 88 miles per hour, and they also felt I had good bite on my curveball. I was so naïve about the draft process that I was also practicing at the same time to play quarterback in a Missouri-Kansas high school football challenge at Arrowhead Stadium. How dangerous was that? I was slammed to the ground during a football game in my senior year and felt disoriented when I wobbled back to the huddle. I had to leave the game, but I did return, still a bit wobbly. Whenever I see a player get destroyed in an NFL game, I think about my high school experience and how I might have had a concussion and never knew it. Everyone knows quarterbacks can get sacked and land on their shoulders or arms and injure themselves. At such a critical time, why would an aspiring pitcher ever think about playing in an exhibition football game? Once Blando learned I was moonlighting as a quarterback, he strongly suggested that I bypass the game and protect my arm. That's when I realized how close I was to becoming a professional pitcher.

And, on draft day on June 8, I received the remarkable news that the Royals had selected me in the third round. I was the seventy-fourth player picked overall, and I guarantee you there were many executives from other teams who said, "David who?" when I was chosen. Again, as extensive as scouting is today and as many video highlights that exist for any elite high school player, I still chuckle to think that I merited being a third-round pick mostly off one try-out camp at Royals Stadium and one summer league game. Blando scouted me enough to recommend that the Royals choose me and

I'm thrilled and thankful that he was so confident in me. Interestingly, I was also told the Cardinals were poised to pick me later in the third round. Sid Fernandez, my future teammate with the Mets, was chosen one spot ahead of me, while Ron Darling, my buddy for life and another future Met, was selected ninth overall.

Moments after my first phone conversation with the Royals, I told my father I wanted to sign a contract as quickly as possible. In some ways, I still thought this was a lucky opportunity and that the Royals could call me back and say they had changed their minds. I received a $17,500 signing bonus to become an official member of the Royals organization, the team I had always cherished as a kid, and I left to play minor league baseball in Sarasota.

I had never seen a check for $17,500, and I didn't even know what $17,500 looked like, but I acted like it was $175,000. Although I gave my parents a chunk of the money, I bought a red Camaro Z/28 and was reckless with the rest of the bonus. Regrettably, it was gone in six months. I had my dream job, but I couldn't afford to buy myself a decent dinner.

My situation worsened when I decided I would wait a year to pay taxes on my signing bonus, theorizing incorrectly that I could combine the $17,500 with my earnings from the next year (about $5,000) and only pay taxes on half of that. Of course, it doesn't work that way, and the Internal Revenue Service notified me about my failure to pay taxes on roughly $11,000. We needed a family friend to cosign for a loan so that I could begin to pay the IRS the several thousand dollars I owed. In addition, the IRS also garnished my earnings, so my earliest minor league checks were for a whopping $47. I should have framed one of the $47 checks because that was an excruciating lesson in accounting at the outset of my minor league career.

On the field, I was living a cheap form of baseball nirvana. Yes, the long bus rides were draining. Yes, I ate a lot of peanut butter and jelly sandwiches and ketchup sandwiches on a paltry minor league salary. Yes, I had backaches from the places I slept. Yes, I drank too much cheap beer, chased too many girls, and stayed up too late (a precursor to my raucous days with the 1980s and 1990s Mets). But those factors didn't distract me because I was eating, sleeping, and drinking baseball, which is all I ever wanted to do. Every day, I felt as if I was one day closer to becoming a major leaguer.

Away from home for the first time, my free-spirited approach helped me as I went 6-4 with a 2.55 earned run average in rookie ball in the Gulf Coast League. In 1982, I blossomed and combined to go 16-3 with a 2.08 ERA and 144 strikeouts and 72 walks in 177 innings for Charleston and Fort Myers, a low Single A team and a high Single A team. I was named the Minor League Pitcher of the Year in the Royals organization, outperforming dozens of other pitchers for that honor and putting myself on the fast track toward Royals Stadium. At twenty, I envisioned myself climbing to the majors by 1984 or, if I continued to excel, maybe even by 1983.

Suddenly, the dream was much more than some fantasy and was creeping closer to becoming a reality. Once upon a time, I thought it would be a tremendous achievement to play a couple of years in the minors and reach Double A. Maybe some teammates would make it to the majors, and I could always say I had played with them in the minors. That would have been a badge of honor, some stories I could share when I became a coach or a teacher. After I had played two years in the minors, my thoughts changed completely, and I believed I could be the guy who made it to the show.

Did those major leaguers get to participate in twenty-five-cent beer night in the show? We did that in Charleston. Every Wednesday night was twenty-five-cent beer night and, as long as we won the game, the players were allowed to guzzle a bunch of quarter beers while hanging out with the ushers and the usherettes. They were usually college students who worked at the ballpark, so this was as close as any players were getting to a college mixer or frat party.

Guess what? We were undefeated on Wednesday nights.

Having spending money was constantly an issue, just as it still is for minor leaguers, so it was a relief when we befriended Red the Bartender in Charleston and he allowed us to purchase meals and drinks on a layaway plan. Red the Bartender trusted us to pay him when the Royals paid us, and we always did. I don't remember the name of the bar, and I don't think I ever referred to our benefactor as Red. It was always "Red the Bartender," as if that was the name his parents had given him.

There were weeks and weeks in the minor leagues where I never slept in a bed and was content to sleep on the floor. I would take my dirty clothes, roll them up into a ball, and use that as a pillow. Sometimes, I would spread out a few shirts and use them as a sheet or a blanket. Sometimes, if I had consumed a few drinks, I would mistakenly use my clean clothes as the pillow, and I would show up at the ballpark in a shirt that looked as if it had survived a tornado. At some point during my stay in Charleston, I scored a used mattress, and I treated that find like it was a king-sized bed at the Ritz-Carlton. My red Z/28 became a memory because I couldn't keep up with the payments, so I traded it in for a...gulp...blue Buick Regal. Another financial lesson for me.

Halfway through my second minor league season, I was promoted from Charleston to Fort Myers because Tony Ferreira, a close friend, had been called up to Double A. Tony told me to go to the house where he had been living. When I knocked on the door, there were six other players in the house. One of them pointed to the end of a couch and said, "That's your bed. That's where Tony slept." So my big minor league promotion included sleeping on a part of a couch.

You know what? As uncomfortable as it sounds, I was fine with the arrangements. I knew I was the low man on the totem pole and, if I pitched well, I hoped I wouldn't be there long.

Though I was sometimes impetuous and sometimes immature, I was also a keen observer, and I noticed the importance of having a routine as a pitcher. Starting pitchers are nomads, maneuvering from throwing sessions to running sessions to workout sessions as they wait for their one chance in five days to make a major contribution. That off-and-then-finally-on-again schedule creates a lot of downtime, time to tinker with grips, revamp mechanics, and even perfect impersonations. Since pitchers are together so much, they mimic each other's deliveries for levity and, as I discovered, to learn some things, too.

Gloves dangling at their sides, sunglasses perched on their noses, and mouths moving, the pitchers who aren't starting that day will patrol the outfield during batting practice. Every pitcher participates in this mundane routine, which involves more standing around than zealously pursuing fly balls. What made these hours of idling worthwhile for me were the conversations I had with my peers and the chance to dissect the intricacies of pitching, everything from what to do in a 3-1 count against an aggressive hitter to how much finger pressure to apply on a slider.

On one of those not-so-busy days with the Royals in the fall of 1982, Bret Saberhagen, Mark Gubicza, and I, none of us older than twenty, transitioned from talking about our motions to parroting each other's motions. We were bored minor leaguers who were in Sarasota for some extra instruction, so we used the grass as an improv stage and did exaggerated imitations of each other, complete with fractured play-by-play accounts of our fake pitches.

It began as a playful exercise, with Saberhagen widening his eyes and raising his hands high to match my mannerisms and my motion, and Gubicza nearly scraping his right knee on the ground to mimic my follow-through. But, as the imitations continued, both pitchers focused extensively on how I bent my wrist before releasing the ball, bending their wrists so severely that their hands resembled swans whose beaks were pointed downward.

Once I was balanced on the rubber, I would lift my hands above my head, have a slight hesitation as I rotated my hip, then push as hard as I could off my back leg, which was the drop (your lower body) and drive (toward the plate) approach. When I separated my right hand from my glove hand and extended my arm behind my pivoting leg to get ready to throw the ball, I cupped the ball by bending my wrist and then threw it. Scouts called pitchers who bent their wrist "hookers" or "wrappers" because of the unnatural way the wrist looked before they released the ball. But what I didn't fully comprehend at the time was that wrapping provided extra momentum that gave my pitches additional power.

As teams assess a pitcher's mechanics, they want deliveries that are the equivalent of someone who is cracking a whip: a controlled motion as the arm (the whip) is brought behind the body, a smoothness that continues as the arm accelerates forward, and all the force of the arm exploding when it rushes toward the plate like the crack of a whip. The simpler and cleaner a pitcher is in delivering the ball, the more appealing he is to scouts because they believe that sort of delivery will result in fewer injuries. Obviously, having a pitcher who bent his wrist at the release point clashes with that philosophy.

Since I have small hands, I was always searching for different ways to manipulate the ball and create more action with it. As a teenager, I presume that I started hooking my wrist to generate some extra power on my pitches. Wrapping my wrist happened so naturally that I can't pinpoint exactly when it began.

While I didn't consciously think about wrapping my wrist until Saberhagen and Gubicza imitated me, their mimicking of it caused me to examine precisely what that hooking action did for me. It only took one bullpen session to confirm what I would have guessed: Bending my wrist before unleashing the baseball gave me additional snap on my pitches. That snap, which is the finishing touch before letting go of the baseball, helped me produce more velocity on my fastball and more movement on my other pitches. Some pitchers compare that wrist action to the final brush stroke that a painter uses, a flourish that completes the work of art.

Pitchers strive to make a ball move, snap, and spin, some of the possible avenues to trick a batter. According to Robert K. Adair in *The Physics of Baseball*, a 90-mile-per-hour fastball will rotate about ten times as it travels sixty feet and six inches to the plate. By bending my wrist, I felt I could add another half rotation and get even more late movement on my pitches, which would make them dart or dive and be more deceptive to the hitters.

In layman's terms, imagine if a man was about to punch someone and wanted to hit that person with as much force as possible. The more he cocked his fist back before throwing the punch, the more powerful the punch would be. That's the same principle with a pitcher bending his wrist before releasing a pitch because that subtle move, that extra snap, can help promote more force behind the baseball. When I wrapped my wrist, it acted as a coil to get the rest of my body to power forward and give my hand extra speed as I was throwing the ball.

But, as much as I have always supported the value of wrist action because it promoted more velocity and more movement, it's a facet of pitching that is mostly ignored or shunned.

Minor league coaches implored pitchers to avoid doing what I did with my wrist because they said it was unnatural and it wasn't sustainable. Some coaches theorized that a pitcher who bends his wrist will engage the muscles from the elbow to the wrist; that extra movement is unnecessary, they say, and has the potential to create undue stress in the arm and lead to injuries.

That theory isn't sensible to me because I've never seen specific evidence that proved a pitcher who bent his wrist was placing himself in more danger than a pitcher who didn't. Why wouldn't a pitcher want to engage all of the muscles in his arm while throwing a baseball? Shouldn't a pitcher want to use every part of his body, even the wrist, to alleviate pressure on other parts of the arm? My supporting evidence is that I pitched more than three thousand career innings, I went about nine straight years without missing a start, and I never had any elbow issues.

Impersonations aside, I enjoyed discussing the art of pitching with Saberhagen, Gubicza, and Danny Jackson, and I loved the developing script that we were all going to be part of a superb Kansas City rotation in the near future. The Royals had a group of talented pitchers, and we were all producing and trying to vault our way to the majors. Gubicza and I were scheduled to start 1983 at Double A as twenty-year-olds. Saberhagen, who was nineteen, started the season at Single A and was promoted to Double A, and Jackson actually reached the majors as a twenty-one-year-old that season. As a new season dawned, *Baseball America* listed me as the sixth-best prospect in the Royals organization, one notch behind Gubicza. I was soon going to be pitching in the majors, my ultimate dream, and doing it with some close friends, too.

But, on a sleepy afternoon in the sleepy town of Bradenton, Florida, everything about that plan changed because of one collision at the plate. I was pitching in a spring training game against the Pirates in Pirate City, a field with a chain-link fence backstop that was within spitting distance of the catcher.

There was absolutely nothing memorable about that day until I threw a wild pitch that reached the backstop. The errant pitch created a race as the runner on third tried to sprint ninety feet before I could rumble sixty feet and also retrieve the throw from my catcher, Mitch Ashmore. I reacted slowly and, as I got closer to the plate, I also got my legs tangled as I tried to straddle it. With my legs blocking home, the base runner was already sliding for a piece of the plate, and his back leg collided with my left leg and tore my anterior cruciate ligament.

I heard a cracking sound and felt an electrical shock of pain in my knee, and I knew I was in trouble. Instantly, my career plans would be altered. The base runner immediately said he was sorry, another indication of how gruesome the injury looked and sounded. My last step caused the problem. Before I caught the ball from Ashmore, my legs were too close together and were in the path of the runner's slide.

The ACL is one of the four ligaments that are essential to stabilizing the knee joint and the front and back movements of the knee. This was a significant injury because my left leg was my landing leg, the leg I put a lot of pressure on after I finished throwing a pitch. I missed all of the 1983 season, but it actually took me a lot longer to fully recover from that surgery because it was almost as if I had to learn to pitch all over again. I had to trust that my knee could handle the weight of every pitch as I landed on it. When a pitcher finishes delivering the baseball and lands on his front knee, the knee absorbs all the force of the body as it moves forward. The ACL is designed to keep the kneecap from moving forward.

In those days, the surgery to repair an ACL was much more invasive than it is today. The surgeon entered my knee from both sides and didn't even touch the ACL because it was snapped in two. They rerouted my iliotibial (IT) band, a thick layer of fibers that run along the outside part of the thigh, and ran it down my leg and used that to take the place of the ACL. I still have white scars on both sides of my knee, which are my ACL battle scars.

The rehabilitation was painful and torturous, with the only

fringe benefit being that I rehabbed at Royals Stadium with the major league training staff and got to mingle with the major league players. I would sit in the camera well with my leg propped up on a chair and videotape the games for the Royals, but I also hobbled around the clubhouse and befriended players like George Brett, Dennis Leonard, Hal McRae, Vida Blue, Gaylord Perry, and others.

Still, that was one of the most exasperating and deflating seasons of my life. I spent so many hours on the exercise bike that the trainers covered the seat in Vaseline to help me avoid getting saddle sores. More than anything, I missed the simple act of being able to throw a pitch and to perform as a pitcher. I talked pitching with anyone who would listen to me and even tried to get Perry to teach me his trademark spitter—stay tuned for that story...

When I finally made it back to the mound with Double A Memphis in 1984, I wasn't the same confident and efficient pitcher. Not even close. I didn't trust my knee yet. If I did my usual drop-and-drive delivery and really extended my front leg to get the maximum power from my body, would my knee hold up? I taught myself to use a shorter stride, and that impacted how aggressively I could extend my leg to get enough finish on my pitches. I went 8-12 with a 4.28 ERA, but most concerning was the fact that I walked more batters than I struck out (114 to 110) in 178⅔ innings. It was my worst minor league season.

My knee was pain free because I had recovered from the surgery, but there was a lack of strength and my leg had atrophied. To this day, my left calf is smaller than my right. I didn't have enough stability when I landed, which disrupted my release point, and that made me a marksman with a wayward shot. But in true minor league fashion, I did have one of my most embarrassing moments on the mound in Memphis.

Living on a minor league salary meant I didn't have much money, so I ate mostly fast food and drank cheap beer. Before one game, I had a gurgling stomach that was caused by a combination of too many burgers and some nerves. I was two levels away from the majors, so every start was an audition of sorts. I had plenty of time to use the restroom and reduce my stomach pains, but I didn't bother to do it. Instead, I walked out to pitch the first inning, and that was a mistake. While I was trying to throw effective pitches, my nervous stomach took over and, well, I lost the battle and actually...let loose...as I stood on the mound.

Holy crap, I thought, without irony. *What do I do now?*

All I could do was ignore the messy situation I had created and keep pitching. It wasn't as if I could call time-out. Not surprisingly, I've never been more motivated to complete an inning. When I secured the third out, I sprinted down the left field line to get to the clubhouse. I took off my uniform, my underwear, and my socks, and I scrubbed and scrubbed in the shower. It was as disgusting as disgusting could get. I didn't have an extra set of uniform pants so, after changing my underwear, I wore the same pants again. I dashed back for the second and barely made it in time. No one knew why I left, but anyone who watched me closely probably could have guessed what happened. I avoid sharing this story at dinner parties.

Still struggling with my command and still trying to figure out how to land properly on my surgically repaired knee, I had another inconsistent season at Triple A Omaha in 1985. My body continued to feel compromised by my uncertain knee, I had a difficult time controlling my pitches, and I went 9-15 with a 4.65 ERA and 115 strikeouts and 93 walks in 158⅔ innings.

At that point in my career, I was a lost soul, and I felt even more dejected when Saberhagen, Gubicza, and Jackson—the three pitchers I had been grouped with as the future of the Royals—combined for forty-eight victories and helped Kansas City win its first World Series title. Saberhagen was the World Series MVP and also snared the Cy Young Award. The future became the present without me. In my moments of depression, I reminded myself that I was supposed to be there with the trio, but I couldn't keep pace with them. I didn't deserve to be in the majors. I was too inconsistent. My damn knee.

Compounding my frustration about my knee was being introduced to Bill Fischer, a no-nonsense, do-it-my-way type of coach in the Royals organization. Fischer was a former major league pitcher and legendary pitching coach who had a long association with John Schuerholz, the general manager of the Royals. With a leathery face and the blunt style of the Marine drill sergeant he once was, Fischer taught a simple style of pitching. He wanted pitchers who stood tall on the mound, picked up their front leg to start their delivery, lowered it quickly, then drove forward and threw the pitch. Fischer hated anything that differed from his standard approach so, of course, he hated many of the things I did.

We had some legendary bullpen sessions in which we spent two hours screaming at each other. Fischer, who would end up being the pitching coach for the Reds, the Red Sox, and the Devil Rays in his decorated career, would tell me that his way was the right way to pitch, and I would counter by telling him that he shouldn't create pitching clones. I never felt comfortable with Fischer, because he nitpicked everything I did.

"Don't bounce your hands," Fischer would say.

"But," I would say, "that's part of my delivery."

Fischer would look at me, maybe spit or shake his head, and say, "Not when you're with me, it's not."

Fischer didn't want me to change arm angles or drop down and throw sliders from the side. He didn't want me to throw breaking pitches on the inside corner to right-handed batters. He didn't want me to hesitate before I dropped down in my delivery. When we disagreed, he would bark at me and make me feel like an idiot.

As a pitcher who went 84⅓ consecutive innings without issuing a walk in 1962, Fischer firmly believed he knew how to pitch and I knew nothing.

"You know that little hesitation in your delivery?" Fischer would say. "You can't do that. You'll hurt your arm. And why are you dropping down from the side? Don't do that, either. Once you start your delivery, just keep pitching."

I kept pitching, but I kept doing things my way, and that's why Fischer and I shouted our way through bullpen sessions. Almost every time Fischer told me my pitching style was ugly and would cause me to get injured, I would debate him. I was never afraid to fight and never afraid to stand up for what I believed in, especially when it came to pitching. I also wasn't afraid to try different things, and I know my creativity helped make me a better pitcher. I had to be different. That caused some Royals coaches and executives to label me as a flake, but I didn't care.

"We would marvel at what Coney was able to do and still keep his balance," Gubicza has said. "He was able to change his delivery during a game. Everyone else, we were always taught to have the same delivery and the same landing spot. That way, we would be in the same throwing position. He was able to hesitate in his delivery, turn in his delivery, turn his back a la Luis Tiant, all of these different things, but still maintain the strike zone, which is pretty amazing."

I appreciated Fischer's passion and his willingness to teach a stubborn kid like me, even if we sparred all the time. I actually learned a lot from him, but I just didn't like how he stuffed those lessons down my throat. Maybe he thought that was what I needed. He would repeatedly tell me he was trying to protect my arm and teach me the proper way to throw a baseball, but I argued there isn't one way. There's lots of ways to throw a baseball, depending on a pitcher's body type. Fischer was the pitching coach for the

Red Sox when Roger Clemens won three of his seven Cy Young Awards, and they had a great relationship. But with me, the relationship never worked.

.I didn't win every battle, because Fischer did convince me to change my delivery to an old-school windup, in which I brought my hands over my head then brought them back down and broke my hands apart at the knees. I used that early in my career, and it worked because I was young and I had powerful stuff. Still, years later, Fischer made an admission to me.

"You fooled me," Fischer said. "I was wrong about you."

Searching for consistency and command, I left the States and pitched winter ball in Puerto Rico for Lobos de Arecibo (Arecibo Wolves) in 1985. I had thrown almost 160 innings at Triple A, but I was restless. I really felt that I needed more innings and more repetition to work on landing on my front leg so that it felt seamless. Pitching in Puerto Rico was a relief for me because there were no Kansas City coaches like Fischer to hound me, so I could relax. I started to think less about my mechanics and landing in the exact spot every time, and just let my motion develop naturally. When I finally started to let things fly a little bit, it paid off. As much as I prided myself on being a thinking man's pitcher, thinking less helped me finally get comfortable with using my knee.

Spending the 1986 spring training with a bunch of players who had just won a World Series title, especially with Saberhagen, Gubicza, and Jackson, made me even more excited about trying to get to the big leagues. I was so close to realizing everything I had wanted, but I needed some more innings. Apparently, I also needed to obey a manager's orders, even when I disagreed with him. In my first spring game with the Royals, Manager Dick Howser told me to throw at Russ Morman of the White Sox in the tenth inning. The teams had already combined for a hit batter and a handful of brushback pitches, and Howser wanted me to retaliate. So I fired my first pitch high over Morman's head and to the backstop, knowing it wouldn't hit him. I was ejected, and the game ended because we didn't have any more pitchers available. Being thrown into the middle of a spring training beanball spat wasn't ideal, but I did what I was told, sort of, because I was trying to make the team.

When the Royals made me a reliever at Triple A Omaha in 1986, I never complained, because I realized how established their rotation was and I figured it would be my quickest path to the majors. And it was. Oddly enough, Gubicza, my buddy, was the reason I was summoned to the majors. He was hit in the head with a fly ball during batting practice in June 1986, so the Royals wanted to rest him until his dizziness subsided. They needed a fresh arm. Gene Lamont, my Triple A manager, called me into his office and said, "Congratulations, you're going to the big leagues. They need you there now." There was nothing dramatic about the way Lamont delivered the message, which, in hindsight, I appreciated because he treated it like the next logical step on my baseball journey. That made me feel as if I was ready and I belonged.

In a daze of happiness, I called my parents and told them, "I'm coming home and I'm staying home." I paused to see if they would understand what I meant, but I didn't pause long before shouting, "The Royals just called me up." They were speechless. All those years of them watching me play baseball, and now I was coming home to play for my Royals. And, oh, by the way, I was going to be living with Mom and Dad, too, which was just surreal. I was going to wake up in my parents' house and drive to the ballpark, something that was indescribable for a kid who always felt he was so close and yet so far from a full-time gig at Royals Stadium. Finally, I had won this part of the competition.

"The one thing I always loved about Coney is that he was so darn competitive," Gubicza has said. "He didn't want to give up a hit or a run in any game, no matter who it was. That's what I always loved about him. He was a quiet guy, he was a funny guy, but, when he was on the mound, he was an assassin."

A few minutes or a maybe a few seconds after Lamont told me the life-altering news, I grabbed my equipment bag and jumped into my brown Ford Granada to drive from Omaha to Kansas City. My father had bought that car for me for $500, and I used to describe its color as "doo-doo brown." But, on that day, that Ford Granada, that old man's car, felt like a Rolls-Royce because I was using it to drive myself to the majors. Maybe, just maybe, I could be even better than Joe Presko.

Chapter 5

KANSAS CITY, HERE I COME

Making the fifteen-minute drive to the ballpark was a blur, putting on my white-and-blue uniform with CONE etched across my shoulders was a blur, and speaking with my teammates was also a blur. I was standing inside the clubhouse at Royals Stadium on June 8, 1986, and I was finally a major leaguer, but, in those moments, I felt like a kid from St. John Avenue who had sneaked into the room and grabbed an empty locker.

In my first hours in the big leagues, I didn't know how to act. No one does. Maybe the coolest-of-the-cool players do, but I wasn't sure if I was supposed to act like I belonged or if I was supposed to kiss the carpet. I was much more likely to kiss the carpet because it was so surreal to be playing for my hometown team. Simultaneously, this felt so weird and so wonderful.

As I sat in the bullpen and surveyed my new home, I continued to feel like a straggler who was left over from a fantasy baseball camp. Did the Royals really think I could help them win games? As confident as I should have been after my recent success in the minor leagues, I was filled with varying emotions, from excitement to anxiety to fear.

When I was finally able to call Royals Stadium my working address, I experienced a bunch of flashbacks. I loved that place.

Loved it when I had the chance to attend games and hugged the railing near the bullpen and studied every pitcher. Loved it when I watched games on the TV or listened on the radio and envisioned myself on the mound. Loved it so much that I devised a secretive plan to bypass classes at Holy Cross School one day during the 1976 season so that I could see the Royals. It was a doomed plan. I was thirteen, I didn't drive, and I didn't know anyone who was willing to give me a ride. Books beat baseball. Oh, how I wish Uber had existed in the 1970s.

As I was sitting in the bullpen and trying to act calm, the phone rang, and a coach told me to start warming up. I felt nauseous. Replacing Bret Saberhagen, the Most Valuable Player in the 1985 World Series, to pitch the ninth inning, I was so unsettled that my upper body felt disconnected from my lower body. It was the first time in my life that I couldn't feel my legs. For that brief jog into the game, my legs moved because my brain told them to work. But honestly, I couldn't tell you what one of those strides felt like. Coincidentally, it was five years to the day since the Royals had drafted me. I guess I had a five-year plan to make it to the majors.

Standing, ever so wobbly, on the mound, a destination that once seemed as probable as me walking on the moon, I tried to ignore the fans, the noise, and everything else, and focus on Jamie Quirk, my catcher. Throw some strikes and take some deep breaths, I told myself. I retired Gary Gaetti on a groundout, but then I allowed three consecutive singles as the Twins extended their lead to 5–1. I was just trying to survive and advance through this outing against a team that would defeat the St. Louis Cardinals in the World Series sixteen months later.

My survival seemed to be in doubt when the next sound was a bat destroying a baseball in an alarmingly loud way. That was because Kirby Puckett, an All-Star center fielder who had the physique of a bowling pin and the power of Paul Bunyan, belted a ball so viciously that I thought it might knock over Buddy Biancalana, our 160-pound shortstop. But Biancalana corralled the smash, and, fortunately, he was still standing and threw a runner out at the plate. I notched a groundout for the final out and scampered off the mound, charged with one run and thankful that it wasn't worse.

With my debut complete, I should have peeked into the stands to find my parents and my siblings and share this moment, but I wasn't even sure where the family section was. I just hustled back to the dugout and exhaled, finally relieved and relaxed. After hundreds of innings in the minors, after all those arguments with coaches, and after all those hours rehabbing my knee, I forced myself to reflect on what I had accomplished. I wasn't a braggart, but I do remember whispering, "You know what? I made it. I did it."

Still so young and so impressionable, I obviously had no clue my career would last for seventeen rewarding seasons. But at that point, my first game was the proudest moment of my life because of the overwhelming odds I had conquered to make it into a major league game. To play in the majors for even one day is a phenomenal achievement, something fewer than thirteen thousand men had done to that point. Actually, I was the 12,782nd major league player. I wasn't always the most mature twenty-three-year-old, but I was mature enough to mentally bookmark that experience. On that short drive home, I smiled because I was content. I was officially a major leaguer.

Yes, my name was now in the *Baseball Encyclopedia*, but that didn't mean I always acted maturely, as I could lapse into being rebellious, reckless, or just childish. On my first road trip with the Royals, a time when I should have been as discreet as possible and should have been willing to shine my teammates' cleats, I behaved like a foolish teenager and someone who was ill prepared for the major leagues. And it involved a pretty lady.

Stationed alongside Saberhagen and Mark Gubicza in the outfield to shag fly balls during batting practice, we saw an attractive woman stroll to her box seats in Anaheim. And we were smitten. Acting like inebriated frat boys, my buddies challenged me to approach her and ask her to lift up her shirt. The easy and appropriate answer would have been a quick no, but, of course, I sauntered off the field and made the request. She didn't oblige, but I did briefly rest my head on her chest. As much as Saberhagen and Gubicza howled, my actions showed a severe lack of maturity. Other players noticed and they weren't pleased with my conduct.

My giggling turned to sheepishness when Dan Quisenberry, a dignified man who was the mustachioed closer for the Royals, wrapped his arm around my shoulder, found a private area near the clubhouse, and offered me some lessons about acting responsibly. Quiz sat across from me, looked me in the eyes the way my father used to, and talked to me like an adult, but he also stressed that I hadn't acted like an adult. He told me the importance of always being a professional because the other players were studying me and evaluating me.

"Everyone is watching you right now," Quisenberry said. "You might not realize it, but they are. They're trying to decide if they can trust you."

If I wanted my teammates to trust me, Quiz said, I had to show that I was serious about the game and I wasn't some silly kid who was more interested in impressing young ladies than actually doing my pregame work. In a stern yet soothing tone, Quiz repeatedly mentioned the word *trust* and how vital it was for players to trust each other and believe that we were all equally invested.

Since I was a rookie who had been in the big leagues for only a few days, Quiz told me I should be the first player on the field for stretching exercises, the first player to finish my wind sprints, and the last player to create a distraction. I should have taken notes on Quisenberry's lecture because his words were profound and necessary. He could sense I had a wild side, and he wanted to remind me that I needed to tame it while also letting my teammates know I had a desire to be successful. Quiz was the first player at the major league level who significantly impacted my career with a lesson I absolutely needed.

Fast-forward to 1996 and to a rookie who was a lot different than me, a rookie named Derek Jeter and a man I often described as the perfect rookie. Recognizing how careless I was as a rookie, I was unbelievably impressed by the way Jeter behaved in his first full season with the Yankees. Even though Jeter was a first-round pick, a prized prospect, and had sat in the Yankees' dugout as an observer for the 1995 Division Series, I hadn't spoken to him much and didn't know him too intimately. He was only twenty-one, and now he was the shortstop for the Yankees, a job that came with hefty expectations. I had made some regrettable choices with the Mets, and I knew the minefields that existed for athletes in New York. Jeter looked like he was going to be a star, so I wondered how he would handle all of the temptations.

Soon, very soon, Jeter showed just how prepared he was to thrive in New York. In our season opener, Jeter ripped a homer and made a nifty over-the-shoulder catch in shallow left field as we beat the Indians, 7–1. I took a no-hitter into the sixth and pitched seven scoreless innings to please George Steinbrenner, who had called me "Mr. Yankee" after signing me to a $19.5 million free agent deal. But, still, I called that game Jeter's coming-out party because he was our youngest player and he looked like the most relaxed and talented player on our team, a team that would eventually win the World Series.

Beyond Jeter's exploits on the field, I noticed how poised he was in dealing with the media and in perpetually discussing the importance of the team over the individual. Teammates are aware of how often a player refers to himself, and Jeter repeatedly stressed how winning games was his sole focus. It was refreshing to see and hear those selfless words from a rookie.

Eventually, I also learned how Jeter's parents, Charles and Dorothy, had been very detailed in preparing their son for life and, ostensibly, for the searing spotlight of New York. When Jeter was in high school, his parents devised a contract that addressed expectations for academics, athletics, behavior at home, and the way he interacted with friends and classmates. Jeter had to sign the contract, and there would be punishment if he violated any of the clauses. I had never heard of parents who did that, but I thought it was a genius approach.

Our 1996 opener was delayed by a day because it had snowed in Cleveland, and that caused an alteration in the Jeter family's itinerary. Because Sharlee, Jeter's sister, had a high school softball game back home in Kalamazoo, Michigan, Jeter's father drove four hours to see her game while Jeter's mother stayed in Cleveland to watch Derek. So Derek's parents applied equal value to both games: a major league game that was attended by 42,289 spectators and a high school game that might have had forty-two fans. I thought that was awesome. Derek's explanation was awesome, too.

"She's just as important as I am," he said.

I don't think veteran players scrutinize rookies as closely now, and I'm glad that first-year players aren't bullied the way they once were. But during the first half of my career, veterans watched the rookies and pounced if they made mistakes, like a police officer with a radar gun poised in a speed trap. But Jeter's behavior was impeccable. He arrived at the ballpark early, he was on time for meetings, and he didn't say anything that was divisive or controversial. And when Jeter did speak, it was instantly apparent how mature he was and that he knew how to handle himself.

Sometimes a rookie might show up in the clubhouse with a bag of chicken nuggets (like I did), and veterans would scold him for not using his meal money and eating steak or salmon like a big leaguer. Sometimes, a rookie might wear a pair of ancient jeans (like I did), and veterans would reprimand him for not buying a crisp suit and dressing like a big leaguer. Sometimes a riveting movie would be playing in the clubhouse and a rookie would talk during a crucial scene (like I did), and veterans would tell him to be quiet. But Jeter wasn't guilty of any of those mistakes.

As much as I said we analyzed Jeter and waited for any miscues, I think most of the veterans on that team quickly realized how special Jeter was and how much he could help us. I consider that season a point in my career where all the senseless bullying of rookies began to wane. When I was a rookie, older teammates thought they needed to break us down in order to build us back up. By the time Jeter was a rookie, the established players were beginning to realize we didn't need to try and embarrass young players to make them fit in with us. In fact, we understood that it benefited us to make a talent like Jeter feel as comfortable as possible.

Let's face it: The 1996 Yankees desperately needed Jeter to be a productive player. I was thirty-three. I wanted to win another World Series title. I didn't want to waste time testing some kid who was clearly an elite player and a major part of our pursuit of a championship. By the end of 1996, Jeter was our leader, a role he would possess for the Yankees for the next two decades.

I've always been interested in the different methods used by leaders. Again, my father was my first coach and the first person who impacted me as a leader, so I was always impressed with anyone who displayed keen leadership skills. One of the most influential leaders I ever encountered was Jamie Quirk, who caught my first outing in the majors after having also caught me at Triple A. When I first worked with Quirk at Omaha, he was making a position switch and was just learning how to become a catcher. He was a light-hitting third baseman who returned to the minors to master the intricacies of catching, a smart move because it added six more years to his career.

As a pitcher, I loved how helpful Quirk was with the mental side of the game because he had such a positive and upbeat attitude. Quirk was the type of enthusiastic catcher who made me feel that he believed in my pitches as much as I believed in them myself.

From a strategic standpoint, Quirk was a refreshing voice because he was the first coach or catcher who told me I could throw my splitter down and in to right-handed batters. I was still refining that pitch and trying to make it a pitch I truly trusted, but I wanted to be able to test it by throwing it in that location to righties. Yet pitching coaches had warned me about doing that, because it could hang in the zone and righty batters would blast it. Quirk dispelled that myth and told me to throw a splitter down and in and almost at a batter's back leg, similar to the way I threw my slider toward a left-handed batter's back leg. I trusted Quirk when he told me that righty batters would swing over my splitter.

If I threw a down-and-in splitter and generated a swing-and-miss, Quirk's face would brighten and he would say, "You see? I told you it would work." For young pitchers, that kind of encouragement is so valuable. Actually, it's valuable for pitchers of all ages. Quirk had a lot of energy, and he implored me to play the game the right way and to ignore my statistics until after the season. If I prepared the way I needed to prepare, Quirk told me my stats would be exactly where they should be.

My stats with the Royals weren't memorable in my rookie season. After four relief appearances in June, I was demoted to Omaha and excelled as the closer at Triple A. I was called up to the Royals in the final weeks of the season and relieved seven more times, finishing with an 0-0 record and a 5.56 earned run average in 22⅔ innings. My role was as the ultimate mop-up man; I pitched in eleven games and we lost ten of them.

Included in those September games was an ugly 18–3 loss to the Angels, a game in which Reggie Jackson smashed three homers, including the second homer I ever allowed in my career. I threw a down-and-away fastball at the knees, and Reggie hit it over the left center-field fence. A scout told me it was a 91-mile-per-hour pitch, but Reggie, who was seventeen years older than me at forty, destroyed it.

"I like to let people know I can still hit," Jackson told reporters.

I was a little wounded and a little speechless after the game, and then George Brett invited me to join him and some of our teammates for dinner. I needed that invite because I needed a distraction, and it was also very cool that Brett, my childhood idol, wanted me to hang out with the Royals. As a kid who grew up in Kansas City and originally dreamed of being a left-handed-hitting third baseman for the Royals, I was in awe of Brett. I think I made Brett feel uncomfortable, at times, because I would study everything he did: the way he hit baseballs off a tee, the way he applied pine tar to his bats, and the generous way he treated teammates, especially the young players. One year, he allowed Saberhagen and Gubicza to move into his house.

Because Reggie had treated me like a batting practice pitcher, I became the target of several jokes at dinner that night, and Brett was the master of ceremonies. It was playful and I expected it, and I didn't mind it at all. In fact, Brett, the savvy veteran, even figured out a way to make me feel better about giving up a homer.

"Hey, look at it this way," Brett told me. "You're in Reggie's book now. There are a lot of really good pitchers in that book."

I always carried that thought with me because it was Brett's way of telling me that good hitters were going to hit homers against good pitchers, and one homer didn't mean my pitching world was destroyed. So what if I gave up Jackson's 545th homer? He hit 563 in his career, and he hit them off 306 pitchers. I was just another victim.

A few baseball chapters and a decade later, I met Reggie in Yankees spring training, and I was so excited to tell him that I was in his "book." I recycled Brett's line and wanted to see Reggie's reaction to the fact that he took me deep in 1986. Reggie stared at me with a puzzled look. While he recalled belting three homers that night, he didn't know I was one of the three men who had surrendered one. I was a no-name back then, and as it turned out, I really was just another anonymous name in Reggie's book.

Throughout that September of 1986, I was mesmerized by the exploits of Bo Jackson, the tremendous two-sport athlete who had won the 1985 Heisman Trophy as a bruising running back at Auburn and who was now my teammate with the Royals. The Tampa Bay Buccaneers had drafted Jackson first in the 1986 draft, but he declined to play for them. A year later, Jackson was drafted by the Los Angeles Raiders and started his NFL career with them.

While I overlapped with Jackson only for a short time, I can unequivocally say this about his athletic talent: The hype was real. Very real. He really was that powerful and that fast, and he really did have an amazing arm, which is something that doesn't get discussed enough.

In those days teams had daily defensive practice, so outfielders would field grounders and fly balls and throw to the different bases. I marveled at how Bo would catch a ball and throw bullets on a direct line to third base. He made perfect throws, the baseball whooshing through the air like a bullet flying toward its target.

Before Bo even had his first major league at bat on September 2, 1986, his teammates were gawking at him because of what he did in batting practice. I've seen some powerful displays during BP, from Darryl Strawberry to Barry Bonds to Aaron Judge, but Jackson's sessions were just as ferocious, a show before the game even started. A few hours before his debut, Jackson drilled a baseball off a set of lights on the back wall of the left field bullpen at Royals Stadium, a ball that traveled at least 450 feet.

With Steve Carlton, a superb left-hander who was near the end of a Hall of Fame career, attacking Bo with fastballs and late-breaking sliders, Bo seemed relaxed in his first at bat. He reached down and clubbed a two-strike slider down the left field line, the ball soaring as if he had hammered it off a tee. The ball tailed foul by a few feet, but that swing showed how quick and how powerful he was, and he received a partial standing ovation for the "foul" homer. Bo later smacked a grounder that eluded the White Sox first baseman, but the second baseman corralled it and threw it to Carlton at first. It was a futile effort. Bo looked elegant and powerful as he blazed down the line and got his first major league hit. He made other players stop and watch what he was doing because he did things we couldn't do. So like I said, the hype was real. I've never seen someone who had the proverbial five tools as a player (hit, hit for power, run, throw, and field), and all five of those tools were insanely good. He was an All-Star in baseball and an All-Pro in football. Amazing.

Trying to play the rookie role of being deferential, even when it involved another rookie, I offered to be a chauffeur when Bo said he needed a ride to downtown Kansas City after a game. The great Bo needed a ride? Of course, I had a car. Of course, I could drive Bo to his hotel. I was excited to do this favor for him, and I viewed it as a way to bond with teammates. I didn't even think about the vehicle I was actually driving, the ugly brown Granada.

Approaching my ridiculous car, Bo was silent. But he didn't have to say a word. His body language told me he realized he would have been better off calling a cab or asking the groundskeeper to borrow a ride-on lawn mower. My $500 jalopy puttered along, navigating Interstate 70 West and delivering Bo to his hotel. Before Bo exited, he spoke.

"I think you need to trade that car in," he advised. "For a bike."

Obviously, Bo knew cars and, apparently, bikes. Every time I saw him do something incredible on the baseball field, whether it was acting like Spider-Man as he actually ran up the center field fence after making a catch or making a 320-foot throw from the outfield to nail a runner at the plate, I always thought about that incident in my car. And I always smiled. He was the greatest athlete I had ever seen.

Meanwhile, I was still trying to become a competent major league pitcher. While I had a lot to learn, there were some Royals policies that clashed with how I wanted to pitch. As much as I focused on attacking hitters and getting ahead in the count, I was exasperated by one rule: Don't throw strikes on 0-2 counts. While the actual rule for minor league pitchers was that we weren't supposed to surrender any hits on 0-2 pitches, I construed that to mean we shouldn't throw any decent pitches in that count. If we gave up a hit on 0-2, we'd be fined, a sad day for the thin wallet of a minor leaguer. The Royals weren't alone with this practice, as teams rationalized that eager hitters might chase lousy 0-2 pitches and hit them feebly or not hit them at all.

I hated the idea of being a passive pitcher at a time when I should have been even more aggressive. It was illogical to ask a smart, creative pitcher—or, really, any pitcher—to work hard to get ahead 0-2 and then take a detour from throwing strikes or trying to secure an out. That shouldn't be in a pitcher's DNA.

Although I heeded that rule in the minors, it was even more aggravating once I made it to the majors and found that ill-conceived policy in effect there, too. As a young pitcher who needed every weapon and every trick to try and negate the best hitters in the world and prove myself in the majors, I didn't want to pitch defensively if I had secured two quick strikes. I considered it a backward mentality, and I ended up getting fined a few times for allowing hits on 0-2 pitches.

In endless conversations I've had with pitchers about 0-2 counts, most of them frown on wasting pitches because they are being asked to throw an extra pitch and being told to throw it with a different mind-set. That one supposedly meaningless pitch can become a disruption because it can distance you from what you're trying to achieve: throwing strikes and getting outs. Throwing one pitch for a ball might seem inconsequential, but it's not. A pitcher can lose his release point because he's suddenly pitching in a defensive mode, instead of continuing to attack. Most pitchers don't practice throwing balls that are way out of the strike zone; throwing a waste pitch could disrupt their rhythm. Suddenly, the count could be 2-2 or 3-2, and you've allowed a susceptible hitter to get into a more comfortable position.

Rather than waste an 0-2 pitch, I liked Gubicza's strategy of throwing a fastball that was about half the width of a baseball off the outside corner. Gubicza called that the perfect 0-2 pitch because he could get the batter to swing at it or because he might get the umpire to call it for a borderline strike. When Gubicza threw an 0-2 pitch that was so close to being a strike, Gubicza believed the hitter probably wondered if he was lucky to have taken the pitch for a ball and didn't know if the identical pitch on 1-2 might be called a strike. That wasn't a waste pitch. It was a purposeful pitch that created doubt in the hitter's mind.

Fortunately, the mentality of fining pitchers for surrendering

0-2 hits isn't prevalent anymore, which probably has a lot to do with control specialists like Greg Maddux. Maddux was adamant about throwing strikes and continuing to attack hitters when he was ahead in the count because he felt that was when they were at their most vulnerable. Furthermore, another reason that current pitchers aren't coached to waste 0-2 pitches anymore is because pitch counts are monitored closely to protect young arms, and every wasted pitch means the pitcher is that much closer to being removed from the game.

Even after relieving in fifty games between the majors and the minors in 1986, I was insistent about needing to pitch some more innings, so I decided to play winter ball in Puerto Rico for the second straight off-season. These days, clubs are militant about guarding how often a pitcher throws during and after the season, but that wasn't true back then. I initiated the idea of returning to Puerto Rico, and I don't remember having lengthy conversations with the Royals about this. But instead of relieving, I went back to starting and pitching from the windup. Thankfully, I felt comfortable and pain free when I landed on my left knee, and I became as confident as I had ever been as a pitcher. In one game, I dropped down to throw a sidearm slider to Ellis Burks, who would go on to hit 352 homers, and he looked hesitant, the kind of reaction that told me how effective that pitch could be. Facing lineups that included major leaguers, I was named the Pitcher of the Year as I led the league in wins and strikeouts and finished with a 2.45 ERA. Rotation, here I come.

Buoyed by what I had done in Puerto Rico, I wasn't nervous when I arrived for spring training in 1987. I was twenty-four, I was tired of lagging behind contemporaries like Saberhagen and Gubicza, and I wanted to show I deserved a spot in the rotation. That determination paid off as I fashioned a 2.25 ERA in sixteen innings and won the fifth starter spot. I was elated. It was another accomplishment that I had chased, and finally I had achieved it. A day after I was told I had made the team, the Royals traded me to the Mets for Ed Hearn, a backup catcher, in a deal that included three other players changing uniforms. I was dumbfounded.

Obviously, history has shown the Royals made a huge mistake, as I went on to win 194 games, a Cy Young Award, and five World Series titles while Hearn managed nine hits with the Royals and was out of the majors in two more years. John Schuerholz, the Hall of Fame executive who made the deal for the Royals, told the *New York Times* the Mets had called the trade "the steal of the century" and he agreed with that assessment. But at the time of the trade, Schuerholz said, "You never like to give up a guy with their potential ahead of them like David."

When I heard that, it angered me because Schuerholz did give up on me, gave up on me just as I had cemented my place in the rotation. I think the Royals were tired of how I squabbled with coaches, tired of how I wrapped my wrist before I threw pitches, tired of how I threw sidearm sliders, and tired of how I fought for my pitching principles.

Years later, when I reflected on this lopsided trade, I wondered, "How could they deal a hometown kid with a power arm for a backup catcher?" And the answer is: Because it was me. I was that crazy kid, that rebel, that hardhead. I wanted to do things my way so I irritated too many power brokers and made it easier for them to unload me. I had also been told that Tom Ferrick, one of the Royals' trusted scouts, thought I was an injury waiting to happen because of my wrist action. Well, I once went 251 straight starts without missing one because of injury.

Anyway, I had never even visited the intimidating city of New York, so the notion of being traded to a talented and arrogant team that had won the World Series five months earlier was more frightening than it was enthralling. Following the trade that blind-sided me, I tried to be glib and told reporters how proud I was to have pitched for my hometown Royals and that my heart would always be in Kansas City. Then I tried to stay cool around my former teammates, too. But, eventually, I retreated to a phone and called my parents. I cried throughout the call.

Chapter 6

LET'S GO METS

IN THE DAYS AFTER I became a Met, I was very anxious because the comfortable baseball world I thought I had found in Kansas City had been upended. I felt I had proven myself as a major leaguer because the Royals had told me I was going to be their fifth starter in 1987. But, a day later, I was unloaded by them and that changed everything. The defending champion Mets had a slew of talented pitchers, and I was worried that I might have to return to the minor leagues.

Confidence was integral to my DNA, but I didn't have a ton of confidence while walking into the Mets' spring training clubhouse for the first time. It was Testosterone City. The Mets had just won the World Series in a seven-game battle with the Boston Red Sox, and they were filled with strong personalities, a wealth of players who performed superbly while acting like they were in baseball's version of a street gang. *Don't mess with us*, the Mets said with their body language and their playing style.

Everywhere I looked, there were stars, stars with swagger. There was Keith Hernandez, the chatty, chain-smoking leader; Gary Carter, the always smiling and always encouraging catcher; Darryl Strawberry, the sweet-swinging slugger; Dwight Gooden, the pitcher with the majestic arm; Lenny Dykstra, the gritty, tobacco-chewing outfielder; Wally Backman, the get-out-of-my-way second baseman; Ron Darling, the smarter-than-all-of-us pitcher; Bobby Ojeda, the mound tactician; Roger McDowell, the prankster and sinker baller, and so many others. As I peered from locker to locker, I saw talent and toughness, and I wondered how I was going to manage to squeeze onto the twenty-five-man roster.

For my first week with the Mets, I was numb and nervous and didn't initiate too many conversations. I listened to my teammates and coaches and I nodded a lot, but mostly I sat by my locker like a kid who was waiting to be called into the principal's office. There was one day where I was fully dressed in my uniform with my blue Mets cap pulled down to my eyebrows, and I suddenly realized there wasn't one other player who was close to being in his uniform yet. What can I say? I was tense because I was obsessed with whether or not I would make the team. So I stayed silent and viewed my pursuit of a roster spot as another test. Actually, I felt as if I was tested repeatedly at the outset of my Mets career.

Passing those tests was critical because that was a way for me to assert myself and prove that I fit in with these elite players. Quickly, I learned how rowdy and resilient the Mets were, but just as important, I learned how much camaraderie existed among the players. Like I said, there were gigantic personalities and huge egos in that clubhouse. And eventually I would do my best to blend in. My oldest brother, Chris, once said he was worried New York would eat me alive. It almost did.

Still getting acclimated to my new surroundings in spring training, the mood of the Mets camp turned sullen when Dwight Gooden checked into a drug rehabilitation center in New York to start receiving treatment for cocaine abuse. It was a startling revelation—at least to me it was—because Gooden, who was only twenty-two years old, was already one of the most dominant pitchers in the majors. Since Gooden had missed the World Series parade a few months earlier and there were whispers about his excessive partying, perhaps this revelation wasn't a surprise to everyone.

Before I had a chance to witness the greatness of Gooden, he was gone. From afar, I had been mesmerized by his overpowering fastball and his falling-off-a-cliff curveball and a smooth delivery in which his leg almost touched his chin. Gooden debuted in the majors at the age of nineteen; at the age of twenty he went 24-4 with a 1.53 earned run average and he won a Cy Young Award. Quite simply, he was as much of a must-see player as there was in baseball. But as I watched televised news reports about Gooden, the intimidating pitcher looked frightened as he walked into the Smithers Center for Alcoholism and Drug Treatment. *Get well, Doc,* I thought.

Around the same time, I was sitting in the office of Charlie Samuels, the Mets clubhouse manager, when Strawberry called. Charlie's twisted face and sharp response told me everything I needed to know. Since it was raining that morning, Strawberry wondered if he still needed to come to the ballpark. Huh? Charlie told him he needed to get to work. I was amused, but I was also flabbergasted. Yes, it was raining, but professional baseball players are expected to come to work, even if it's raining. I guess Straw wanted to sleep in.

As the newbie who was still observing the way the Mets' world turned, it was an eventful opening week. The immensely talented pitcher went to drug rehab and the immensely talented power hitter didn't want to play in the rain. One development was serious and scary while the other one was funny and revealing. But both of those stories were indicative of how the Mets were always creating drama. Some good, some bad, and some mind-boggling.

With each passing day, I witnessed how the Mets were a self-assured team who wanted to own New York City and wanted to own the cities where we traveled to play, too. There wasn't a guidebook for thriving in this macho world, so I did everything I could to try and fit in. Be just as wild and just as crazy as everyone else. I guess my plan worked. Eventually, I was a wild and crazy Met and I relished my status.

My worries about being demoted to Triple A Tidewater subsided when I made the team as a reliever, something that I started to suspect would happen when Barry Lyons, the backup catcher, had trouble corralling my moving pitches. *OK,* I thought, *I'm officially a big leaguer again.* But as I said, being a new guy on the arrogant Mets meant the tests were endless. In my fourth appearance with the team, I was summoned to face the Pittsburgh Pirates with one out in the eighth inning. The plan was for me to record the final five outs and secure the win. I notched two outs in the eighth, but I issued a one-out walk in the ninth, and Barry Bonds followed by socking a two-run homer. Suddenly, our lead was down to one run. Jesse Orosco, who had pitched the night before, replaced me to get the last two outs. We won, although I hadn't done my job.

By the time we huddled in a few rows on the team plane to play some cards, I wasn't thinking about my pitch to Bonds anymore. We usually played Hearts, and there was more banter about movies and TV shows than baseball. At one point, I made an innocuous comment about the way someone had played a hand, and Ojeda pounced on me like a viper snatching his next meal.

"Hey, rookie, you sucked tonight," Ojeda said. "You looked scared. Everybody on this plane feels like you weren't ready to pitch tonight. You let us down. You're messing with our money."

Jolted by Ojeda's remarks, I didn't know how to react. I expected to constantly be tested in the majors, but I didn't think a teammate would challenge me in such a hostile way and in such a laid-back setting. Finally I spoke.

"We're just playing cards," I said. "Is this really the place to talk about the game?"

Ojeda told me it was.

"We're watching you," he said. "You need to prove yourself to us."

I didn't say anything else. I couldn't say anything else. In retrospect, I knew why Ojeda was challenging me. He wanted to know if I was scared, and, of course, I was. Stung by Ojeda's verbal attack and by the fact that none of my teammates defended me, I tried to develop a tougher exterior by becoming much more aware of everything I said and did. The Mets wanted a trustworthy pitcher, not a class clown.

Later in the flight, I returned to my seat, muttered a few expletives, and said to myself, "I will show you who is and who isn't scared." Once I had proven myself to Ojeda and the Mets (yes, more tests), a candid Ojeda explained why he had lashed out at me.

"We didn't know you and we wanted to know what you were all about," he said. "We needed to find out."

I could be flaky, so Ojeda wanted to know if the Mets could trust me or if I would be just as flighty on the mound. The Mets believed they could be in the middle of a dynasty and didn't have time to babysit me. I understood what Ojeda, one of the team leaders, did, but I didn't love his methods. It was something that a rookie had to deal with back in those days, so I accepted it and tried to learn from it.

Soon after that incident, the Mets gave me the chance to make my first start in late April. I was thrilled to start because I had regained my swagger as a starter while pitching winter ball in Puerto Rico for the second straight off-season, and I didn't want to lose that title or lose that swagger. I knew I could succeed in the majors, and it meant a lot to me that the Mets gave me that opportunity after injuries and Gooden's absence created an opening.

But confidence can vanish in a succession of misplaced pitches, a succession of line drives, and lots of doubts, endless doubts. And mine did vanish. My confidence disappeared in my first start because the Astros battered me for ten runs (seven earned) in five innings. I gave up seven hits, including two homers; I walked six; and I threw two wild pitches. I even walked Jim Deshaies, the opposing pitcher, with the bases loaded. He had five hits in fifty-three at bats that season. On a cold night where the temperature dipped into the forties, I felt more and more helpless with each passing pitch.

After the lopsided loss, Manager Davey Johnson referred to our struggling team as hitting "rock bottom." Naturally, I felt as if I had helped us plummet to that point. I finally got a chance to start, and it was brutal. The only reason I even lasted for five innings was because a few Mets relievers were fatigued, so it was easier to just let me keep pitching and take my bruises.

Feeling like a zombie in my hotel room that night, I couldn't sleep because I was worried about being dispatched to the minor leagues and being marooned for months. My pitches were so woeful against the Astros that I presumed I was expendable and the Mets would give my roster spot to a more capable pitcher. There was a newspaper picture of me from that outing with my hands wrapped behind my head and a bewildered look on my face, a picture that told the ugly story of a pitcher who wasn't skillful enough to rescue himself.

Weary, sheepish, and embarrassed, I walked into the Mets clubhouse the next day and kept my eyes trained on my shoelaces, hoping someone wasn't poised to hand me a one-way plane ticket. When I got to my locker, I noticed a softball resting on my chair with a note: "This is what your fastball looked like last night." I picked it up, rolled the softball around in my hand, and chuckled. I peeked around to try and determine who the culprit was and, based on his shrieking, I knew it was Backman. I was laughing, he was laughing, and everyone else in our clubhouse was laughing. Backman did that to lighten me up and to see how I would react, which was at the opposite end of the spectrum from what Ojeda had done. I guess I passed the test because I was relieved that I was still a Met and that my teammates were supporting me.

But as humorous and as calming as Backman's prank was, there was something else that was much more instrumental in helping restore my confidence: the start I made ten days later in a rare regular-season exhibition game against the Red Sox. Although the game had an appealing backdrop because it was a rematch of the 1986 World Series, it didn't count in the standings. For me, it was very meaningful because I needed redemption. After my miserable debut, I pitched five decent innings and earned a no-decision in a loss to the Expos. But it was the game against the Red Sox that was much more memorable because it taught me some important lessons.

It was a bizarre scene at Shea Stadium because the Mets had shocked the Red Sox to win the title on the same field seven months earlier, and now the Red Sox were back in Flushing to soak up all the reminders of that awful experience. The Mets and the Red Sox had previously agreed to play charity games in 1986 and 1987 to support Boston's Jimmy Fund for leukemia research and the New York City Amateur Baseball Foundation. But that agreement was made before Bill Buckner infamously misplayed Mookie Wilson's trickling grounder in Game 6, and the series and the baseball universe was forever altered.

To Buckner's credit, he was self-deprecating on this night and joked around with Wilson about fielding some grounders off Mookie's bat. Buckner also told reporters that the Mets fans should give him a standing ovation. They did. Twice. Still, none of those delightful story lines mattered to me. I wasn't on the 1986 Mets. I was trying to survive on the 1987 Mets.

Across a personally indelible start, I threw a lot of the same pitches that I'd thrown against the Astros, some pitches that missed my location and were obvious mistakes, and the batters were popping them up or swinging and missing. My mistake pitches didn't all get pummeled, and I learned a valuable lesson about how pitchers don't always have to be perfect with everything that zooms out of their hands. There would be games where I grooved a fastball or I hung a slider, but batters wouldn't always smash homers on each of those pitches.

After I generated a swing-and-miss against Dave Henderson on a mediocre slider, I stopped and thought, *Wow, the Astros would have crushed that pitch*. When one of the Red Sox fouled off a misplaced fastball, I told myself, *That's the same pitch that Glenn Davis hit for a home run*. Honestly, I can remember feeling enlightened on the mound and knowing I was in the midst of learning a lesson about pitching, like a high school student who had just grasped the intricacies of trigonometry. That outing told me I didn't have to be perfect with every pitch, and that revelation relaxed me and empowered me.

Those seven scoreless innings against Boston boosted my confidence. Once I stopped trying to be perfect, I could be more aggressive and could take more chances against batters. When a pitcher is aggressive, he's probably going to make mistakes and throw more pitches that will be over the plate and in spots that hitters can capitalize on. But more important, being aggressive allows a pitcher to get away with more mistakes and not feel so panicked on every pitch. That game against the Red Sox, a blip of an exhibition game, was a revelation for me because it taught me that I could be aggressive while being imperfect.

Because of that outing, I was escorted along the narrow corridors of Shea Stadium to a small room to make my first appearance on Kiner's Korner. It was a no-frills postgame show hosted by Ralph Kiner, a Hall of Fame player who led the National League in homers for seven straight seasons and once dated Elizabeth Taylor. Now that's an impressive résumé! Kiner praised my breaking pitches and I told him, "I know I can pitch at this level." As a thankyou gift for doing the interview, I received a weed whacker. Yes, I had officially arrived!

In my next start, I used a lively fastball to pitch a four-hit complete game and squelch the Cincinnati Reds, 6–2, for my first major league game win. Their lineup featured Barry Larkin, Dave Parker, and Eric Davis, but I held the Reds scoreless until Paul O'Neill, my future Yankee teammate, drilled a pinch-hit homer off a fastball in the eighth inning. Not surprisingly, O'Neill remembered the blast.

"I hit it to dead center field at Riverfront Stadium," O'Neill said.

As satisfied as I was with notching my first win, I was also pleased to hear Carter say he knew I was capable of doing this "from the first time" he caught me in spring training. That hefty praise from an All-Star catcher motivated me and stayed with me. I was deliriously happy, but I tried to stay focused on the next game. In the subsequent start, I tossed eight innings to foil the San Francisco Giants and win my second game and increase my confidence even more.

Carter was partially responsible for that confidence because he was so supportive, a walking, talking bolt of energy. I was initially nervous about throwing to Carter, who was one of the best catchers of his generation. But he instantly made me feel as if he was throwing the pitch with me. The typical Carter approach was to wait until the batter had settled into the box, then look at me, then look up at the hitter to make sure he wasn't peeking at Carter's fingers, then deliver the sign. Carter would lower one, two, or three fingers or a sequence of signs, then lift his glove and set a firm target with a determined look that said, *Give it to me right here*. If Carter had had a drum, he would have given me a drum roll. That was how excited he seemed about receiving the next pitch.

Based on the commanding way that Carter gave me signs, he assured me that he was certain about each pitch, and that gave me a psychological boost. If Carter was so emphatic about calling a specific pitch, I thought, then I should be confident, too. Whenever there were runners on base and I wondered if I could get out of the inning, the way that Carter behaved was a subtle yet powerful gesture, a way for me to concentrate on making one quality pitch. *Throw this one!* his body language screamed.

After interacting with Carter, I understood why he was called Kid Carter. He really did love to play, like a kid, and that really came across in the way he acted on and off the field. He was thirty-three going on thirteen. Carter's sunny disposition and spirited actions didn't ingratiate him with everyone; his critics called him Camera Carter and said he was duplicitous and was someone who was always looking for the cameras. I wasn't on the Mets in 1986, but some of my teammates laughed as they told me that before the decisive Game 7 of the World Series, Carter did about five or six one-on-one television interviews on the field. As teammates barked, "Hey, Kid, we've got a game to play," Carter kept bouncing from interview to interview, so maybe he had been Camera Carter on that day. Still, as a pitcher, I loved the guidance and I loved having a catcher who lived through every pitch with me. I can't say the same for all the catchers I collaborated with in my career.

On and off the field, I respected Carter, a very religious man who lived his beliefs and didn't try to force them on any teammates. Religion, at times, brought unusual and humorous contrasts in the clubhouse. The visiting clubhouse in Atlanta–Fulton County Stadium made me feel like I was in a garage, with lockers stacked up next to each other and hardly enough room for twenty-five players. On many days, I remember Carter gathering some of the religious players at one end of the clubhouse and leading them in Bible study. Meanwhile, at the other end of the clubhouse, the rest of us would be cursing, telling off-color jokes, and acting like we were celebrating a bachelor party. It was guys being guys, I guess.

Once Bible study ended, Carter would walk past us, shaking his head and smiling. He never judged anyone. So Dykstra or Hernandez would have some fun with Carter by saying, "What did you pray for today? Hits?" There was actually friendly banter between the players who attended Bible study and the players who didn't, and I think that helps explain why there was such a camaraderie on that team.

Back on the mound, just as I was getting comfortable with Carter and in the rotation, I felt what it was like to be attacked by a two-seam fastball, and what it was like to be uncomfortable. As I turned to bunt in a game against San Francisco on May 27, Atlee Hammaker's fastball buzzed too far inside and shattered my right pinky. I jumped back from the pitch, but I had no time to get out of the way. I slammed my helmet, I shouted at Hammaker, and I even inched toward the mound before I was blocked. I stayed in the game to run the bases and went out to warm up for the next half inning, but the pain was too intense and I didn't throw another pitch. Doctors told me my pinky was cracked in three different places. When I had the surgery, doctors inserted some pins into the lower part of my pinky, which was the part that had been shattered. But they also advised me that they didn't treat the upper part of my pinky, which was crooked from a high school football injury. So the upper part of my pinky is still crooked.

Once the cast was removed from my hand and I began throwing,

I noticed that my pitches had a little more movement. With my pinky tucked beneath the baseball, my wrist position naturally moved a bit, and this created some extra right-to-left movement on my fastball and also helped give my slider some extra bite, too. I'm not claiming I suddenly found cutter-like movement, as Mariano Rivera did while warming up one day in 1997, but there was some extra jump on my pitches.

While I missed two and a half months, the finger injury didn't hamper me in the way my knee injury had stalled me. Besides a circle changeup, a pitcher really doesn't use his pinky much to help him throw his other pitches. Since I didn't throw a circle change, it didn't bother me. I used to make jokes about the injury and called myself Three Finger Brown after Mordecai Brown, a pitcher from the dead-ball era who lost most of his right index finger in a farm-machinery accident and later broke his other fingers in a fall. Brown's damaged fingers resulted in a grip that helped him throw a stellar curveball as he won 239 games in a Hall of Fame career. Well, guess what? Four Finger Cone went from being 5-6 with a 3.71 ERA in 1987, the season where I fractured my pinky, to going 20-3 with a 2.22 ERA in 1988. The injury wasn't the primary reason I improved, but something changed positively with the way my pitches moved. Just don't expect me to provide a firm "great-to-meet-you" handshake, because my pinky always gets caught in the exchange, leaving me as the king of the dead-fish handshake.

Never forgetting the way Ojeda challenged me on the plane, I was always aware of how my Mets teammates perceived me. I could be tough, stubborn, resilient, and reliable, and I wanted them to know that. During a tense game against the Dodgers in May 1988, they saw all of those traits on display as Pedro Guerrero tried to pulverize me in his third at bat of the day.

We didn't know we were on a collision course with the Dodgers to meet in the National League Championship Series, but as a way to combat some of their power hitters, we threw pitches that were up and in to push them off the plate. Since Guerrero was a dangerous hitter who leaned forward in the batter's box, I threw a chest-high fastball that whistled inside and backed him off the plate. His head snapped back and his blue helmet flew off his head and landed in the dirt. It was a high-and-tight pitch, a pitcher's pitch, but he was so comfortable that he didn't even try to get out of the way. There was nothing wrong with trying to tie up a hitter with that kind of fastball. His comfort level in the batter's box a little less secure, Guerrero glared at me for several seconds.

The normally staid Dodger Stadium became a little more restless as I threw a second inside pitch, a pitch that wasn't as close to him as the first one. Still, Guerrero was annoyed again, glaring at me some more. I stood on top of the mound and stared right back at him. This was a test and I was going to pass it. On the third pitch, I threw a fastball down the middle and Guerrero took a mighty swing and fouled it off. And then he stared at me some more. Again, I stared right back. I refused to let him intimidate me with his staring, his antics, his mumbling, or anything else he did. I knew my teammates were studying me. I could hear Hernandez yelling, "Good pitch, good pitch" from first base, a euphemism for *Don't you dare back down.*

After throwing three straight fastballs, I wanted to change Guerrero's eye level and tossed a curveball. But the ball didn't break properly; it floated toward the inside corner and hit Guerrero in the left shoulder. He almost leaned into it, as opposed to trying to avoid it. And then an enraged Guerrero flung his bat at me, the dark-stained wood helicoptering to my right and skidding toward shortstop. Was he delusional?

"It was a curveball," I shouted, snapping my right wrist to amplify my point.

Guerrero shed his helmet like a boxer taking off his robe and barreled toward the mound, but I didn't budge from my spot and kept telling him it was a curveball. After about three strides, Guerrero stopped and turned his body back toward the plate, almost waiting for Lyons to intercede. I thought the entire incident was a power play by Guerrero, a flashy show to try and get some kind of reaction after he was offended by my first high-and-tight pitch. Gooden had drilled Alfredo Griffin with a pitch in the previous game, and I know the Dodgers were irritated about that. Still, that didn't give Guerrero the license to whip a hunk of wood at me. He was ejected and was later suspended for four games. I pitched six solid innings and we won the game.

Another test with the Mets, another passing grade. I stood up to Guerrero, a muscular player who might have snapped me like a toothpick. But I was just pitching him tough. I didn't do anything wrong in that situation, so I stood my ground and stood tall on the mound, just the way my teammates would have expected me to react. Many of the tests with the Mets were a simple question of "Were you tough enough?" On that day, I was.

I will always despise the 1988 season for how it ended, for how we lost to the Dodgers in the National League Championship Series. I will always believe we should have won that series because they beat us only once during the regular season. As I've detailed, I will always regret my decision to ghostwrite a newspaper column that impacted the way I pitched in Game 2. On that day, I wasn't as tough as I needed to be, and it turned into one of the most debilitating experiences in my career.

But, despite the depressing ending, that was the season where I won twenty games and finished third in the Cy Young Award voting and tenth in the Most Valuable Player Award voting. That was the year in which I secured my position as one of the best pitchers in the majors, a place I had been longing to be in since those days on the backyard mound with my dad in Kansas City.

Unfortunately, those Mets teams of the mid- to late '80s are viewed as underachievers because they won only one championship. It's painful to call those teams underachievers, but I understand it. One ring is one ring, and I wasn't even with the Mets for that ring in 1986. We went 87-75 in 1989 and finished six games behind the Cubs in the NL East, never getting closer than two and a half games in September. We were in first place as late as September 3 in 1990, a season in which Bud Harrelson replaced Johnson as manager. But the Pirates zoomed past us and won the division by four games. Ninety-one wins wasn't good enough that year. We were a disappointment in 1991 and went 77-84, finishing 20½ games behind the Pirates.

Did we fail to reach the height of our potential in those seasons? With the talent we had, it's easy to make a compelling argument that we did underachieve. There were some late nights, some excessive partying, and some reckless behavior, so it's reasonable to theorize that our off-the-field behavior could have adversely influenced how we performed on the field, at least to some extent. Once a team gets the reputation as being rough and rebellious, you can either get upset about it or you can embrace it. We embraced it. I know I embraced it. A lot of the joking I've done about my behavior over the years is me trying to own it and then defuse it, because it's something that's always going to be there.

In evaluating my time with the Mets and wrestling with the seasons where we could have done so much more, 1988 resonates even more painfully. That was the defining year for us to make the leap from being a great team to being a greater team. If we could have conquered the Dodgers and then won the World Series, that would have bolstered what the Mets did in 1986, and it would have been so meaningful to the team's legacy. I equate it to how the Yankees won a title in 1996, lost in the first round in 1997, then rebounded to win it all and become one of the best teams of all time in 1998. To me, that historic 1998 helped validate what the Yankees did in 1996 and also had a springboard effect as we won championships in 1999 and 2000 (over the Mets). If the 1988 Mets hadn't disintegrated and had secured another ring for the organization, the rest of the decade might have unfolded differently, and we would definitely be viewed otherwise. Maybe a team with another ring would have had better finishes in 1989 and 1990. But that didn't happen, and that was why it was a devastating loss for the organization. Just devastating.

Despite the heartache of an agonizing ending, my achievements in 1988 resulted in invites to a series of off-season banquets and I happily made the rounds. At Mickey Mantle's, a now-defunct restaurant near Central Park, I was introduced to the great Joe DiMaggio. As you would expect, DiMaggio was impeccably dressed with a gray sport coat, a black vest, and a purple tie while I was wearing a white long-sleeved T-shirt, blue jeans, and what I called a Brady Bunch belt, a bulky brown belt that looked like something Bobby Brady would wear. It was pure class meeting pure novice, and I cringe every time I see the picture of us. Why did I wear a T-shirt?

When DiMaggio said hello and congratulated me on my season, I was gratified that he even knew who I was. I was intimidated by DiMaggio, so I let him guide the conversation. He told me, "I've seen you pitch and, sometimes, you look unhittable." Unhittable? Did the great DiMaggio really just say that about me? But, after a few seconds, he added, "And, sometimes, you look pretty hittable." I think I nodded. He dispensed his opinions in his typical Joe D. way, a mixture of intelligence, arrogance, and aloofness.

Our exchange lasted a few minutes. Then he went to his table and I retreated to my table. It was a positive experience because it was classic DiMaggio, similar to the stories I had heard about him from his teammates. Now that three decades have passed since our interesting encounter, I appreciate the meeting even more because, in that sliver of a conversation, I got to know Joe D. a tiny bit. His comments to me were the perfect passive-aggressive DiMaggio remarks. The fact that he called me "unhittable" left an indelible impression. The fact that he said "pretty hittable," too? Well, I could live with that because that was also accurate.

It must have been "Meet the Yankee Legend Month," because I also met Mickey Mantle at the restaurant with his name on the marquee and he acted the way I would have expected him to behave. Clutching a Bloody Mary in one hand and patting me on the back with the other, Mickey lauded me for excelling with the Mets. Then he turned toward my girlfriend at the time, smiled, and said, "Oh, yeah, I can see why you're doing good." It was a typical Mickey comment, and as politically incorrect as it was, we loved it. Again, like with DiMaggio, it was flattering that such a legendary player even knew who I was.

Everything moved fast in 1988. Real fast. In my final start of the regular season, I beat the St. Louis Cardinals, 4–2, to win my twentieth game of the season. After a groundout finalized the win, I shook my head and I exhaled, trying to comprehend what had just happened, trying to comprehend everything that had happened that season. First baseman Dave Magadan asked me if I wanted the baseball from the final out, and I eagerly grabbed it from him, knowing I would give the milestone baseball to my parents. It was my most exhilarating moment in baseball, and I wanted to slow it down and absorb every detail, even acknowledging the dedicated fans who I spotted wearing Coneheads on that splendid night.

When I descended the first base dugout steps, I was surprised to be met by Richard Nixon, the thirty-seventh president of the United

States and the only president who ever resigned from the office. The Mets had ushered Nixon into the dugout because he was a devoted baseball fan, and he wanted to congratulate me. We shook hands and he told me he had attended many games, so I thanked him and told him, "You have to keep coming then," trying to make a former president feel fulfilled about being a good luck charm. I really didn't know what to say. I can be glib when I need to be, but I was out of my element for that conversation. I had just become the fourth Met to win twenty games, and I was trying to put that in perspective. I come from a family of Democrats, but Democrat or Republican, I was uncomfortable with seeing Nixon in the dugout. I wanted to be respectful, but I wanted it to be a quick chat. It lasted about thirty seconds.

Nixon wasn't the only fan who was watching me closely. Before an early season start, I noticed fans wearing bald cones on their heads while standing behind a sheet that said "Cone's Co'ner." Were they serious? Dwight Gooden, a Cy Young Award winner with a sizzling fastball who was nicknamed Doctor K, appropriately had a legion of fans who hung out in the K Korner. After each Gooden strikeout, the fans hung up cards with Ks on them. But how did a fledgling pitcher like me end up with the Coneheads in the left field upper deck? I can thank Andrew Levy.

Levy is a passionate and knowledgeable fan who attended grammar school with my ex-wife. During the 1988 season, Levy and some fraternity brothers from Lehigh University donned Coneheads, bought $12 tickets for all of my starts at Shea Stadium, and became my personal cheering section. Obviously, their pointed headwear was patterned after the comedy sketches from *Saturday Night Live*, which was about an alien family and featured Dan Aykroyd, Jane Curtin, and Laraine Newman.

As a pitcher who was still trying to prove himself in New York and at the major league level, I was motivated when I saw those

Coneheads gathered in the stands. I didn't want to disappoint them. My dedicated fan base even traveled to road games, and the Conehead theme followed me for the rest of my career, no matter where I pitched. There was one game in which a couple of Phillies wore Coneheads in the dugout in order to, I guess, try and distract me. When my no-hitter reached the sixth inning, I noticed they had ditched their headwear. The Coneheads journeyed to Los Angeles and witnessed my debacle of a start in Game 2 of the 1988 NLCS, which resulted in Dodgers fans serenading them with "Go home, Boneheads!"

Before Andrew started the Coneheads craze, I didn't know him too well, but he has become a close friend and my business agent. Levy is the owner of Wish You Were Here Productions in Manhattan and represents me and other athletes in appearance and memorabilia deals. Somewhere in Levy's office, he still has his Conehead. Very few players are fortunate enough to have their own devoted fan group, so I considered myself a lucky player.

The players I was comfortable hanging out with were leaders on the field, the men who would curse at you and scold you if you missed a meeting or missed a sign. That was a world I cherished, and the leader in that world for the Mets was Hernandez. A former MVP with the St. Louis Cardinals, Hernandez spoke more than any of us and was a fiery player who challenged himself and challenged his teammates to be better. I've never played beside another first baseman who was more immersed in the game than Hernandez, a man who challenged pitchers from his perch and who elevated bunt defense to an art form.

To have Hernandez at first base and Carter behind the plate was reassuring, especially since Keith always seemed to be one pitch ahead of everyone else on the field. While Carter was hands-on with directing the pitchers and took the lead in that department, he deferred to Keith in terms of being in charge. Gary was pious and Keith was the prince of darkness, but they respected each other and they coexisted for the betterment of the team. And Hernandez never hesitated to offer opinions about pitch choices, either.

"Throw the Laredo!" I once heard Hernandez yell. "Throw the Laredo now!"

During one of my earliest starts with the Mets, Hernandez shouted those words, and at first I had no idea what he meant. An uncomfortable hitter is a vulnerable hitter, so as a way to unsettle hitters, I liked to lower my release point below my waist and throw a sidearm slider. After seeing the southern location from where I released the ball, Hernandez actually dubbed it my "Laredo" slider, after the city in southern Texas.

Since batters aren't accustomed to seeing a slider from that angle, I knew it could surprise them so I usually saved it for two-strike situations. After I threw my Laredo slider to Todd Zeile and he watched it break by him for a strike, he told me he was so puzzled by the flight of the ball that he thought the pitch had sailed between his legs and somehow curled into the strike zone. That was the epitome of being perplexed, which was what I wanted to do to every batter.

Seconds after I rebounded from the worst start of my life to defeat the Dodgers in Game 6 of the 1988 NLCS, Hernandez pounded my chest, leaned into my face, and said, "You did it. You're a man now." He was so animated, screeching at me as if we were crawling out of a foxhole together. That happened more than thirty years ago, and that interaction, so brief yet so powerful, stayed with me. Maybe it was all macho nonsense, but that was the way the Mets played it. They were going to push you and test you, and that time I had passed the test. In 1991, I switched my uniform number from 44 to Hernandez's 17 as a way to honor my ex-teammate.

With some helpful advice from Hernandez and Darling, I embraced New York City, a place I'd never even visited. I lived there, I played there, I partied there. In my earliest days with the Mets, Darling recognized that I was intimidated by the Mets and I was struggling to fit in, and he welcomed me and helped me get adjusted. I was a high school graduate from the Midwest, and he was a French and Southeast Asian History major from Yale who was born in Hawaii, but we were kindred spirits who loved pitching and loved to discuss pitching. Darling taught me how to behave like a New Yorker, advising me on everything from restaurants to bars to clothing stores to neighborhoods. My first apartment was a studio on Forty-Seventh Street and Second Avenue for $600 a month, but it felt like a mansion because it was mine and I was in the big leagues. It was rent stabilized. I wish I had kept it.

The first time I ever visited Montreal with the Mets in 1987, Darling took me to a men's clothing store and bought me a navy blue blazer to wear on our charter flights. I didn't have an extensive wardrobe, and players were required to wear a sport coat or a suit on the flights. Darling was the first person who ever told me, "A blue blazer goes with everything," and he advised me to match it up with some slacks or some jeans to stretch my wardrobe. It might seem like a small thing, one navy blazer. But it wasn't to me. That was a big deal, and I appreciated how Darling guided me and taught me how to be a professional.

Of course, as much as I tiptoed around and tried to find my place in the early days with the Mets, I did show a little bit of my personality once I knew I had made the team in 1987. After I pitched three scoreless innings and struck out five in my Mets debut that spring, I felt comfortable for a few days. So, as our plane was about to land in New York to begin the season, I decided to have some fun. I took a plastic safety card from my seat, stood on it, and used it to help me surf all the way down the aisle as the plane descended. That was the first time the Mets saw my looser side and saw that I was trying to fit in.

"With the way he had pitched against the Cardinals, who were a really good team, we were all asking, 'How did we get this guy?'" Darling recalled. "And then we saw him shooting down the aisle and we all said, 'Oh, that explains it. That's how we got this guy. He's one of us.'"

I once told a magazine writer from *Esquire* that Darling and Hernandez had shown me the ropes in New York. When he asked what the ropes were, I said, "The East River and the Hudson River. Anything in between is fair game."

Beyond the life lessons, Darling and my fellow starting pitchers also gave me terrific pitching lessons, some of which I learned through osmosis. I felt we had the most formidable rotation in the major leagues because of our skill level and our diversity. Our starters were all distinctive, so opponents never saw the same type of pitcher on consecutive days.

Gooden pumped fastballs that looked like Tic Tacs and also threw a curve that danced as high as a batter's head before plummeting into the strike zone. Darling was a technician, an intelligent pitcher who used his splitter to make his fastball even more effective. Ojeda was the master of changing speeds with his sneaky changeup, a pitch that made his fastball a better weapon. Sid Fernandez had a fastball that exploded, and he also was adept at hiding the ball before he released it. Meanwhile, I threw four pitches: a fastball, a slider, a splitter, and a curve, and I threw them at different speeds and from different arm angles. In my zeal to be as much of a mystery as possible, I tried to poach ideas from all of the other pitchers. But I learned the most from Darling.

Watching Darling throw his splitter and stay with it when it failed him impacted me to do the same thing when my splitter sputtered. I was amazed at how stubborn he was with the pitch and how he refused to abandon it if hitters weren't swinging at it. Darling could have thrown two splitters in the dirt to get to a 2-0 count, and everyone in the stadium would expect him to come back with a fastball because that was considered the more reliable pitch for getting a strike. Instead, he would throw another splitter. That approach allowed Darling to remain unpredictable, even on days when it looked like he would be predictable because he couldn't command the splitter.

By 1989, I was as comfortable as any other player on the Mets, so I mimicked what I saw Ojeda and Darling do in the dugout. They were smart and talented pitchers who didn't possess over-powering fastballs, so they followed games very closely and used their eyes and their brains to help themselves succeed. Because of their influence, I analyzed every pitch like a pitching coach and offered up nuggets of advice to our pitchers.

My first mission was to read the batter's swings and detect how they were reacting to certain pitches. If I noticed a batter was late swinging at a hittable fastball and had fouled it off to the opposite field, I would remind a pitcher that the batter was probably waiting for a slider or a curve, and that was why he was tardy at getting to the fastball. During tension-filled games, not every pitcher is equipped to read a batter's swings and assess that information, so I tried to do it for them. Since I typically started about thirty-two games per season, I desperately needed to find a purpose and be involved in the other 130 games. As much as I was trying to help my buddies, I always felt I was benefiting from assisting them. If I helped my teammates thrive, the information I had collected would help make my job a little easier when I followed them in the rotation.

Even Gooden, who had been a prodigy and an overwhelming pitcher who seemed to have all the answers he needed, occasionally asked me for some pitching advice. Initially, that development shocked me. The brilliant Gooden wanted to pick my brain? Even though our rotation was diverse, Doc and I had some similarities as right-handers who relied on breaking pitches (his was a curve and mine was a slider). So it was natural for us to share our thoughts about the different ways to attack hitters.

But Doc was curious about my splitter because he didn't really have a reliable third pitch. As a pitcher with an over-the-top motion, Gooden couldn't drop down and throw sidearm sliders like I did, so he quizzed me about the splitter. Mostly, Doc was just poking around for information, because as far as I know, he never did throw a splitter. The splitter can be a difficult pitch to master, and it can also cause a pitcher to lose some velocity on his fastball, so it's not something everyone should try.

Since Gooden was so dominant with a fastball and a curve at the outset of his career, he never needed a third pitch. Later, Gooden would occasionally throw a changeup. After Gooden lost a little power on his fastball, he became interested in how to be more of a pitcher and not just a thrower. As a power pitcher, he didn't need to be creative, so our conversations revolved around different ways to attack hitters in different counts and when to change speeds.

Doc and Darryl, Darryl and Doc. Those two talented players and friends of mine are forever intertwined because of everything they did on the field and because of all the things they did off the field, too. It's impossible to review the 1980s Mets without dissecting the careers of Gooden and Strawberry, two phenomenal talents who were destined for the Hall of Fame. But both struggled with drugs and alcohol, and those demons interrupted that narrative and that potential path to Cooperstown.

To this day, I have never seen two more talented youngsters than when Strawberry debuted with the Mets as a twenty-one-year-old in 1983 and when Gooden followed a year later as a nineteen-year-old. I know there are arguments to be made for players like Mike Trout, Ronald Acuña Jr., and several others who were incredible players at the age of twenty-one or younger. But as a fan who watched the young Doc and the young Darryl, I have to say their talent level was remarkable. There was a powerful arm from the East Coast and a powerful swing from the West Coast, and those two players—two players who were just babies—performed in a strong and electrifying way that left me flabbergasted. It was almost as if Doc and Darryl jumped out of a video game and burst to life in New York.

Strawberry was a fearsome presence from the moment he stepped into the batter's box, tall and lean and capable of terrorizing pitchers. That presence started on his first day with the Mets and persisted until his final day with the Yankees. Trust me, there wasn't a pitcher in the world who wanted to face Strawberry, the young version or the old version. When Brian Cashman, the Yankees' general manager, mentioned the value of Aaron Judge's mere presence in the box in 2018, he cited Alex Rodriguez and Strawberry as players who had that type of presence, the type that makes pitchers sweat before they have even thought about throwing a pitch.

I relieved Gooden in our season opener against the Montreal Expos at Olympic Stadium in 1988, but what we did in a 10–6 victory was irrelevant. What Strawberry did was phenomenal, loud, and boisterous. Strawberry clubbed two homers, including one that was the longest homer I have ever seen. He took his usual effortless swing to hammer a fastball from Randy St. Claire, and he really did send the baseball into orbit, depositing it off the bank of right field lights that lined the roof of the stadium. Yes, I said the roof of the stadium, a crash landing for the baseball that hit about 160 feet up from the right field fence (just picture hitting a ball as high as a sixteen-story building) and about 350 feet from the plate. It was estimated that the ball would have traveled 525 feet if it hadn't hit the lights. A physicist determined that distance, but, frankly, I was there and that distance seemed short. I would have added another 100 feet.

"You know, it scares me a human being can have that much talent," Magadan, my teammate, told reporters. "I mean, is there anything Darryl can't do?"

When I shagged fly balls in the outfield during batting practice, it was mostly idle time to chat with other pitchers. But I would stop talking when Strawberry batted and I would just watch and listen to the way he crushed a baseball. His bat speed was amazing, and the baseball had a different sound when it rocketed off his bat, a sound of fury and a sound that I've rarely heard before or after Strawberry's career ended.

Drama followed Straw, all kinds of drama, and some of it was self-created. On a sunny day that should have been a nothing day in the spring of 1989, many of the players were sweating because of what happened at Photo Day. Yes, freaking Photo Day! What team has an issue on Photo Day? We did. Kirk Gibson won the 1988 NL MVP in a narrow vote over Straw, while Kevin McReynolds, our teammate, finished third. During the summer, Hernandez was asked who our team MVP was, and he sided with McReynolds because McReynolds had a better second half. That pissed off Strawberry because he thought it hurt him in the MVP voting, and he chose an awful time to challenge Hernandez, with all the photographers poised to take pictures of us. I was in the middle of the scrum as Strawberry lunged at Hernandez and threw a punch at him, and I remember thinking how stupid the whole thing was. We hadn't even played a spring training game yet and our best player and our leader wanted to pummel each other.

Like Strawberry, Gooden made his peers stop what they were doing to observe him because they didn't want to miss the fastball that evaporated into a mist of white or the curve that caused a batter to spin his head around like a cartoon character. Unfortunately, I wasn't Doc's teammate during his first three seasons with the Mets, which were his most dominant years. After Doc returned from drug rehab, he was still an elite pitcher with a superb repertoire, but we didn't see the same electrifying stuff that he had exhibited in one of the best three-year starts to a career.

But on some magical days and nights, Gooden would remind everyone why he was such a special pitcher, and even as a peer, I would be in awe of him. Since the next day's starting pitcher would chart the pitches from that day's game, I kept track of the pitches for many of Gooden's starts and I would end up scrawling F, F, and F, as I chronicled another batch of fastballs.

Looking for the warmest spot in the dugout on a raw day in April 1991, I had a sly grin on my face because I wondered how the Expos were going to manage to hit Gooden's fastball. Connecting against Doc's fastball was a challenge when it was sunny and eighty degrees, but hitting it on a day when a misty rain was in your eyes and your hands were freezing from the chilly weather? Well, good luck with that.

As I charted pitches that day, my confidence in Gooden increased even more because he was throwing like he threw in his early days with the Mets. Gooden threw a whopping 149 pitches in the game and he was still throwing 94 miles per hour in the ninth inning. Those velocity readings came from the old ray gun, which were about three to five miles slower than the current radar readings, so that means he was actually throwing between 97 and 99 miles per hour. With so many of today's pitchers now throwing 99 miles per hour or better, we've become accustomed to witnessing a succession of ferocious fastballs. While that might make Gooden's velocity readings seem ho-hum, it shouldn't. I was watching Gooden throw, and that version of Doc's fastball was as intimidating as any I had seen in 1991. He struck out four-teen in a complete-game win, an amazing performance that I called "inhuman." I told reporters a radar gun wasn't necessary to know how hard Doc was throwing because I could hear the ball whooshing through the air and then crashing into the catcher's mitt.

Those memories of one of Doc's games and one of Darryl's games are just a couple of snippets that detail why they were supreme talents, a couple of examples from careers that were filled with memorable moments. Whenever there's a discussion about Gooden and Strawberry and the Hall of Fame, I become defensive because there's too much focus placed on what they didn't achieve as opposed to what they did. It's very, very hard to make it into the Hall of Fame. Of the nearly twenty thousand men who have played in the majors, about 1 percent have been enshrined into the Hall, so we shouldn't act as if Doc and Darryl forfeited an invite to the neighborhood block party.

Did Gooden and Straw have the talent to get to the Hall of Fame? Yes, they definitely did. But both of them still had out-standing careers, careers that would place them in the Hall of Very Good. Darryl had substance abuse problems and battled colon can-cer, but revived himself and finished with 335 homers, four World Series rings, four top-ten finishes in the MVP voting and a Rookie of the Year Award in a seventeen-year career. Doc, who missed the entire 1995 season because of a drug suspension, won 194 games, pitched a no-hitter, won a Cy Young Award and a Rookie of the Year Award in his sixteen-year career.

After Yankees owner George Steinbrenner showed confidence in them and signed both former Mets, they had second acts to their careers and I had the opportunity to be teammates with them again. We were all a little older and, hopefully, a little wiser. I was part of four World Series championships with the Yankees; Strawberry was on three of those teams and Gooden was on two of them. A second act, indeed.

With the Mets—the arrogant, successful, and imposing Mets— it was commonplace for fifteen of us to cruise into a bar after a game, open our wallets, order enough surplus drinks so that last call wasn't an obstacle, and clink our glasses until it was time for bacon and eggs. Straw and me were close, so we would almost always be together when the team had those massive "We are the Mets and we are here to commandeer your bar" kind of gatherings. This happened in pretty much every city where the Mets' schedule took us.

Obviously, there were times where too much alcohol was consumed and someone spilled a drink or bumped into another person or someone was disrespectful and, inevitably, Straw would be in the middle of a scuffle. I can remember a handful of times where we would be guzzling beers and someone would say, "Oh, crap, Straw is in a fight. Let's go help him." We would all converge and try to usher him out of the bar safely and make sure these skirmishes never got publicized. Fortunately, none of the ones I participated in ever received any media attention. Thank goodness there were no iPhones back in those days, or we might have been YouTube stars for all the wrong reasons. Straw didn't start the brawls, but he was a lightning rod because of his stature and because he wouldn't allow someone to insult him. He was six foot six and from Compton. Who would be silly enough to mess with him?

Believe it or not, there was always another clown who wanted to challenge Strawberry. One night, we were at a bar in Manhattan, and a woman kept pestering Strawberry and trying to get closer to him. I witnessed the entire incident, and I know that Straw didn't initiate the conversation. He was just trying to hang out with his teammates. It turned out that the woman was the bouncer's girlfriend. All he saw was his girlfriend cozying up to Straw, so he rushed over and threw a punch at Straw. It happened so fast and then there were bodies, big bodies, pushing and shoving and flailing, and somehow I was one of the Mets who helped push Straw out of the middle of this melee and into the street. From watching out for each other in those kind of messy situations, Straw and I developed a strong bond.

But as I have reflected on how Strawberry battled substance abuse problems and whether there were warning signs, I remember he had a secret side to him off the field, and there were times where he didn't let any of us in on where he was going. Like I said, we were attached at the hip for many nights, but he had a different set of friends apart from the team, and I think that's how he got caught up in some of his cocaine issues.

Cocaine scared me, frightened the heck out of me, because I had tried it as a twenty-year-old with the Royals, and I was fortunate that my brief usage didn't cause more dire circumstances in my life. Since I was rehabbing my knee injury with the major league team in Kansas City, some of the players invited me to parties at Willie Mays Aikens's apartment near Royals Stadium.

Two years out of high school, I was a follower, not a leader, at these parties. When I saw the lines of cocaine being offered and I saw the older and cooler Royals doing it, I did it, too. I shouldn't have done it, but I tried it and I learned a very valuable lesson along the way. The lesson was: *Don't do it. Your life could be ruined.*

Four members of the 1983 Royals were ensnared in a federal cocaine investigation, and they were all sentenced to three months in jail for trying to buy coke from federal agents. Those players were Aikens, Willie Wilson, Jerry Martin, and Vida Blue, the same players who were at the parties I attended. Talk about getting scared straight. I was frightened for a long time, upset at myself for what

I had done, and concerned that the Feds might want to question me. But that never happened. I had avoided a serious stain on a baseball career that was just beginning.

So by the time I got to the Mets in 1987, and I heard about Gooden's cocaine use and heard rumblings that other players might have done it, too, I knew there was no chance I would ever do that again. Hernandez, who had testified about his cocaine usage during what became known as the Pittsburgh drug trials in 1985, called coke "the demon" in him and estimated that 40 percent of major leaguers had tried coke. Unlike some of my teammates, I never became addicted.

I know there were players who used cocaine on the Mets because they've admitted it, but that wasn't something I ever witnessed. Maybe I was shielded from it because I was one of the new guys who showed up in 1987, or maybe I just missed it. I heard it was rampant in 1984, 1985, and 1986, but after my Kansas City experience, I would have fled the room if I did see it. I saw some teammates smoke pot, which I tried in the minor leagues. But, to me, there was a big difference between smoking pot and using coke.

While I hung out with Straw more than with Doc, I was still friends with Doc because our pitching staff was a proud and close unit. On the nights where I saw Straw strictly have some drinks, he would become a happy drunk and someone you could easily hang out with. Doc was different. When Doc drank excessively, there was a distinct difference in his demeanor. We would encounter an inebriated Doc in a bar and he would be much more aggressive, and that would cause us to say, "Who is that guy?" He was an affable guy when he was sober, but when he drank, his eyes rolled back in his head and he became belligerent.

There were so many rough and reckless nights with the Mets, but there were a lot of lighthearted moments, too. Fernandez was a quiet, portly left-hander, a pitcher with a moving fastball and a pitcher who was sensitive about his weight. He was listed as 220 pounds, which seemed a few pounds too light. After Fernandez pitched an exceptional game for us, he boarded the team bus and Straw shouted, "Hey, Sid, great job. You pitched your ass off tonight." Then he paused and added, "You pitched both of your asses off."

Damn, I loved those teams and loved my teammates. At times, I loved the mayhem and the chaos and the noise a little too much. Yes, I was combustible. Yes, I was always searching for an edge and I was always living on the edge. I was always the pitcher with the veins popping out of my neck. I wanted to be King David, but too many times I was Crazy David.

The Mets were hard-living and hard-partying and I followed that path, making some dubious decisions and having to live with the embarrassing consequences. Before the final game of the 1991 season, the Mets told me a woman had accused me of rape. Furious and nervous, I still made my start against the Phillies, struck out nineteen, and was vindicated when the police called the charges unfounded seventy-two hours later. That incident was followed by a rape investigation involving three of my Mets teammates in the spring of 1992. I was implicated because I had been briefly involved with the woman at an earlier time. The investigation was eventually dropped. There was a lawsuit charging me with verbal battery in September 1991, in which three women claimed I threatened to kill them. Later, they charged that I had allegedly masturbated in front of them in the Mets bullpen in 1989, causing the *New York Post* to run the front-page headline WEIRD SEX ACT IN BULLPEN. Try explaining that headline to Mom and Dad. The indecent-behavior charge was dropped, while the harassment charge never made it to trial. By the way, I was actually defending Fernandez's wife against verbal abuse. I called the women "groupies." That's a long way from threatening to kill them.

Listen, I have acknowledged I wasn't an angel, but I definitely didn't rape anybody and I definitely didn't perform any weird sex act in the bullpen. Those allegations were found by a court of law to be baseless. But whether I discuss it or refuse to discuss it, I perpetuate it. As I was enduring all of this, I remember taking a baseball bat and pounding it into the dirt over and over, then telling a reporter that pile of dirt was what had become of my name. Now I just concede it's part of my past—way in the past— and move on.

On the field, I led the NL in strikeouts in 1990 and 1991 and won fourteen games in each of those seasons, my competitive streak endlessly pushing me to be smarter and better. Actually, based on a composite ranking that assessed wins, winning percentage, earned run average, innings, and opponents' batting average, I was rated the best pitcher in the NL from 1987 to 1991. At that time, we didn't yet have WAR (Wins Above Replacement), the sabermetric statistic that summarizes a player's total contributions to a team. But I was still proud of being rated number one in that statistical analysis, even though I've since learned and preached that a starting pitcher shouldn't be judged merely on wins and losses. There are too many factors that a starting pitcher doesn't control, like how many runs his team scores, what kind of defense his team plays, and how the relievers pitch after he is out of the game.

Before the 1990 season, I won an arbitration case against the Mets and was awarded a salary of $1.3 million. ONE POINT THREE MILLION! I wanted to scream when I won, but I waited until I turned on the shower and then I screamed in the bathroom. The reason I was so excited was because of what this salary would allow me to do for my parents. I called my father and told him he wouldn't have to work the graveyard shift anymore. It was time to retire. To this day, that's as proud a moment as I've ever had in my life.

Along the twisting path of my career with the Mets, I never stopped fighting for what I believed in as a pitcher, even if I defied the manager. I thought I needed a pair of glasses when catcher Charlie O'Brien signaled for a pitchout against the opposing pitcher in June 1991. I knew pitchouts were called from the dugout by Manager Bud Harrelson, who had replaced Davey Johnson, and Doc Edwards, Harrelson's bench coach. but I refused to throw it. I wanted to attack Cincinnati's Kip Gross in the fourth inning, not overthink the situation about whether he might try and bunt the runner to second. In addition, I was also reluctant to throw the pitchout because some players had a suspicion that Edwards, not Harrelson, was running the show.

Upon returning to the dugout, I bolted straight toward Harrelson, spewing profanities, and told him what I thought of his bleeping pitchout. Harrelson, furious with my insubordination in front of the team, snapped at me, poked his finger in my chest, and pushed me. Teammates intervened and separated us, but all of my rage and our chest-to-chest dispute was captured by the television cameras. As the pitcher who was trying to determine the best way to get through an inning, I felt I was well within my rights to bypass the pitchout. Harrelson and I met for fifteen minutes, and he told me to just pitch and to let him just manage. I understood why he was mad, but I let him know why I was aggravated, too. The incident didn't impact my performance as I notched thirteen strikeouts and we silenced the Reds.

Sometimes, being too much of a fighter sabotaged me and even made me look foolish. While facing the Braves on April 30, 1990, I thought we had collected the third out of the inning when second baseman Gregg Jefferies fielded a grounder and flipped the ball to me, and I grazed first base with my foot. But Mark Lemke was called safe. I was livid and kept pointing at the base as I marched into foul territory to confront Umpire Charlie Williams about the call. With my back to the plate, I continued bickering with Williams and inexplicably allowed two runners to scamper home. I ignored the runners for about ten seconds, but Jefferies said he felt as if it took "seven or eight hours" for me to turn around and realize what was happening. We lost, 7–4.

"I'm a human being and an emotional person," I said after the game. "I snapped emotionally and I have to live with it. It's an embarrassing moment that might have cost us the ball game. For two minutes, I snapped. I was in my own little world."

That little world became a little darker. After the loss, my fiery eyes were bulging more than usual, my cropped hair was more unkempt than usual, and my typical posture was more wobbly than usual as I berated three Mets reporters across the bar. It could have been any bar while I pitched for the Mets, but it was a nondescript sports joint on Peachtree Street in Atlanta. I had sent some shots to the reporters, but they didn't drink them and they were also ignoring me.

"Retaliate," I screeched, waving my hand at the bar to indicate I wanted a return shot. "Retaliate."

After an awkward standoff, they responded. I grabbed the shot glass, raised it to the dusty ceiling, and gulped the drink. I don't know what it was, but it was toxic. Instantly, I hustled toward the door and barely reached the sidewalk before vomiting. It was a good, old-fashioned blowout, one of many in my Mets career.

Did my off-the-field actions ever adversely impact my pitching? I guess it's possible to say that. But I still poured every ounce of energy into becoming an ace for the Mets. My desire to be an accountable and productive pitcher was displayed when I threw a 166-pitch complete game and won, 1–0, over the Giants in July 1992. One hundred and sixty-six pitches! Someone would be fired if a pitcher threw 166 pitches nowadays, and that dismissal would be for a legitimate reason. But that game was the ultimate sign of a pitcher who was saying, *Give me the ball. It's my game. I don't care how many pitches I have to throw to win this thing.* That was my bullheaded attitude for most of my career, even if I now know that was sometimes detrimental.

How rare was a 166-pitch outing? That was the most pitches I have ever uncorked in a game and it was also the most any pitcher threw in a game in 1992. Actually, since then, the only pitcher who has exceeded that hefty total in a game is Tim Wakefield, a knuckleballer. Wakefield did it twice, including one game in which he pitched ten innings.

Six weeks after that marathon performance, the Mets traded me to the Blue Jays for Jeff Kent and Ryan Thompson. I was more confused than offended and told reporters it was "an abrupt and rash decision." The Mets had offered me a four-year, $17 million deal in February, but with free agency pending after the season, I didn't accept it. They claimed I insisted on a five-year deal, which wasn't true and was just a way for them to continue purging one of the remnants of the arrogant Mets.

Truthfully, I never wanted to leave New York, but the Mets forgot how difficult it is to find players who are tough enough and talented enough to thrive in the adversity and pressure that exist in New York. To me, there's no city where the expectations and the scrutiny from owners, fans, and reporters are as intense as in New York, and it's something that the players feel every day. I had proven that I could survive and thrive in the toughest city in the major leagues and the Mets ignored that intangible trait, a trait I was proud to possess.

Then and now, I believe the Mets were careless to trade a gutsy player like me. I was a nervous Kansas City kid who fell in love with New York during my six years with the Mets. All these years later, I still live in Manhattan. My love affair with New York didn't end, but my association with the Mets did. I was a hired gun, a pitcher who the Blue Jays wanted to help them pursue a World Series title. New York didn't eat me alive after all.

Chapter 7

THE DANCE WITH CATCHERS

M‌Y EYES ARE STRAINING, MY face is dripping sweat, my heart rate is accelerating, and my right arm is poised to throw a pitch, but I can't because I am waiting. Pitchers stand on the mound, peer at the catcher, and wait for him to put his fingers between his knees and lower one digit, two digits, or a sequence of fingers. Until the catcher offers those signs, pitchers must wait. I hated waiting.

When I was pitching and plotting, I wanted to throw the baseball almost as soon as the catcher returned it to me. Delays were aggravating because I was a better and more comfortable pitcher when I had an expeditious approach, an approach I controlled. While pitchers can dictate the pace, catchers can influence the timing, too, because they first must give the signs that free us up to actually throw the ball.

The flashing of a catcher's fingers leads to head nods or head shakes from the pitcher and is a game of communication within the game, a nonverbal exchange that determines every pitch that is thrown. If the catcher shows one finger and motions toward the inside corner, that means he wants an inside fastball. The pitcher will say yes or no to that sign. If it's a no, the process continues until the pitcher and the catcher agree.

For the majority of pitchers, that simple act of shaking yes or no represented an easy swap of information, the simplest way to decide on a pitch. But I was different and was a pitching rebel, of sorts. I didn't like to shake off pitches all the time, because I thought that gave batters a better chance to decipher my plans. I preferred to stare at the catcher, stoically or solemnly, if I didn't approve of the suggested pitch, and wait until he offered another sign. I didn't want batters to see me shaking to get to a specific pitch, believing the less they observed, the better.

As I waited on the catcher, I could get fidgety and breathe a little heavier or fiddle with the baseball or even give him my version of the hurry-up-and-give-me-the-sign glare. Not only did working quickly benefit me, but batters told me a fast-working pitcher made them more uncomfortable, too, because they had less time to think.

In the most memorable and most successful start of my career, I was a quick-moving and a quick-thinking pitcher because I was in such a seamless collaboration with Joe Girardi. Naturally, I'm talking about the steamy and historic afternoon in July 1999 when I pitched a perfect game against the Montreal Expos, a game in which Girardi and I were perfect dance partners. I always thought the relationship between a pitcher and a catcher needed to be like a beautiful and balanced dance in which the partners feed off each other, help each other, and improve each other.

As that game evolved and I felt stronger and more confident in the way my pitches were confounding the Expos, I barely left the pitching rubber between pitches. I was eager to throw the baseball because I could almost predict what was going to happen with my exploding fastball and my elastic slider. Girardi swiftly delivered his signs, I accepted his suggestion for all but a few of the eighty-eight pitches I threw, and we retired twenty-seven straight batters. Not me, we. Everyone says I pitched a perfect game, but Girardi pitched it with me.

As quick as I was that day and as I tried to be in my career, I was never able to master the strategy of throwing a quick pitch to a batter. Because I had a drop-and-drive delivery with a long stride, I couldn't speed up the process with my legs, and I failed the few times that I tried to incorporate a quick pitch. It's a sound and legal approach for pitchers who can execute it, with the crucial element being an awareness of who to use it against. For instance, a hitter with a big leg kick or a lot of movement at the plate would be susceptible to a quick pitch because it would foul up his timing.

Some pitchers are methodical, stepping off the rubber between pitches, cautiously reviewing their choices and not objecting if the catcher moves deliberately, too. That's an acceptable approach because pitchers need to be comfortable, and if moving at a modest pace is their preference, that's fine. Most pitchers I've known were more interested in moving at a faster pace because it helped them create a rhythm and it made their fielders more alert.

Before a pitcher releases the ball, any seemingly benign movements could be slivers of evidence for the batter to know the pitcher has more confidence in a specific pitch. Paranoia was my constant companion and I thought some head shaking about signs could lead to batters knowing I was ready to throw a slider, a pitch that generated swings and misses. Obviously, batters could have been guessing I was about to throw a different pitch, but that's the anxiety I felt. I was obsessive about protecting any information, even if that information had to be dissected by batters.

Honestly, a lot of pitchers I played with and against didn't share my fear of potentially giving away information and would shake their heads up and down like bobblehead dolls, refusing to believe those actions revealed any insight. Over and over, I reminded some of my teammates about how protective they needed to be of the sign-giving process. Pitchers would never let a batter peek at their grip, which is the equivalent of shouting out which pitch they are about to throw, so they should be equally cautious about not giving batters any evidence about what pitch is looming.

While the exchange of signs between the pitcher and the catcher is the most important form of communication on the field, the notion of reading different signs stretches beyond that relationship. There are obvious signs for a starting pitcher to assess after a seething manager stomps to the mound. Again. Guess what? Perhaps he's miffed that you keep allowing hits with your fourth-best pitch. There could be equally obvious signs from one teammate to another, like a frigid stare when one of them spends too much time gushing about himself, not the team, in an interview.

And those signs don't end when the games end. There could even be signs from a wife or a girlfriend, bored expressions as the player recounts the gory details of a loss for the seventh time. That significant other's eye rolling and silence are ways of informing the player it's time to move forward and attack the next challenge. Of course she is correct. Reviewing the game for the seventh time isn't going to change the outcome, but if we don't recognize and understand the signs, we might review the game for an eighth time.

Some catchers listened to me explain my philosophy for receiving signs and easily adapted to the timing of this method. If the catcher flashed a sign and waited for a beat—think of one tap of your foot—and I hadn't begun lifting my hands to start my delivery, then he had to be speedy enough and savvy enough to advance to the next sign. He couldn't wait two or three beats or stare back at me quizzically. The process needed to be sign, stare, sign, stare, sign, pitch. And it needed to happen as quickly as you read that last sentence.

Obviously, it's easier for a catcher when a pitcher shakes or nods because the catcher can see the pitcher's reaction and counters. It's a natural exchange. When your phone rings, you answer it. When the traffic light turns green, you put your foot on the gas. When the pitcher shakes no to a sign, the catcher gives another sign. But with staring, the catcher must be more aware of a pitcher's body language and must react to a nonreaction. A pitcher who stares makes the catcher's job tougher, but pitchers can't be obsessed with what makes anyone else's job easier. They need to be focused on what makes them the most productive because that's what most benefits the team.

Shaking off signs was something I still did, but there were important situations where I wanted to have the option to stare in for pitches. Pitchers who were more apt to pitch backward, which means they would throw off-speed pitches in fastball counts, are the type of pitchers who would benefit more from staring. Those pitchers don't want batters to see them shaking off signs in fastball counts, a potential clue they were pondering throwing something other than a fastball, so they opted to stare. With a power pitcher who relies on a combination of a fastball and a slider or a fastball and a changeup, staring versus shaking isn't as much of an issue.

The catcher who was most comfortable with my mound behavior was Girardi, who was so familiar with my pitches and my preferences that he seemed as if he were reading my mind. If I didn't like his first sign, I barely exhaled before one finger followed another and he advanced to the next sign. Girardi's ability to react to me allowed me to maintain my rhythm and increased our comfort level with each other, even though I was one of only two pitchers he ever caught who were adamant about staring in for signs. Orlando Hernández was the other.

The cerebral and square-jawed Girardi caught me more than any catcher. He understood I was flaky and understood the panicked look I would get in my eyes when my pitches were ineffective. When Girardi noticed my deteriorating pitches and my suspect body language, he offered reassurances that he would help get me through a game and made me feel as if we were taking this dangerous ride together. He did it with a few words of encouragement about my mechanics or my pitch selection, and he didn't flinch when I sometimes cursed and ordered him to get off the mound. Unless a catcher is the reincarnation of Johnny Bench, he had better be immensely supportive of pitchers.

In my evaluation of Girardi, I would say he had decent skills as a thrower and at framing pitches on the corners. But in terms of his baseball intelligence and working with pitchers and diagramming game plans, he was well above average. Girardi would absorb the information in the scouting reports, evaluate it with me, then implement our ideas during the game. I knew he would retain the information and make shrewd adjustments about attacking batters, so I was free to focus more on my execution. As I noted before, pitching to Girardi was like dancing; he would lead and then I would lead and we would remain in sync with each other. He picked up on what I was thinking and reacted. *OK*, Girardi's actions would say, *I see that you want to go back to the fastball now.* Instead of being offended by me navigating toward certain pitches, he embraced that. Since the effectiveness of my pitches could change each inning, I reveled in having a catcher who adjusted with me.

"David was probably the most enjoyable pitcher for me to catch because he was so creative," Girardi said. "Obviously, he had great stuff, but he also used different arm angles. That enabled him to have deception and that gave him the ability to show so many different looks. Not many pitchers can drop down and change arm angles and still throw pitches accurately. David could do that and he could do it with more than one pitch."

With Jorge Posada, Girardi's successor, our collaboration wasn't nearly as flawless. Jorge caught me a lot at the beginning of the

2000 season, which was my worst year ever, a year in which the quality of my pitches diminished almost overnight and I felt helpless. My slider, a pitch that had been reliable throughout my career, was hanging, and I couldn't come up with a grip that restored it to some level of dependability. I kept trying different grips, but nothing worked. I was tense, and Posada, who was stellar at receiving the ball and throwing the ball, became the recipient of my simmering frustration.

An angry veteran pitcher who is struggling can be very intimidating to a young catcher, which was how Posada said he felt when he caught me. At times, I would scream at myself after a dreadful result and Posada, a fierce sort with a take-charge voice, thought I was screaming about his pitch selection. As much as I told catchers not to take my words and my antics personally, I know that wasn't so simple. I could be very challenging to catch because I was headstrong and because I would keep searching for a pitch that worked, even chastising my catcher along the way.

Sometimes politely and sometimes not so politely, I stressed to Posada that he needed to be quicker with signs, especially with runners on base. If I didn't concur with the pitch Jorge called, it was because I had experience against the batter and I had a plan for navigating my way to a certain pitch or sequence. If I overruled him on a decision, I could see how it bothered him in the way that he would pause and wiggle his fingers, which was his own stalling tactic before he got to the next set of signs. By the time he reset himself to give another sign, even if it was two seconds, I had become antsy. Every time we collaborated, I was anxious because of our disconnect. Jorge was a proud catcher and he craved being the leader on the field, which I respected and which was a trait that helped him have a superb career. But I know he didn't like me to shake him off, because advancing to the next set of signs was not his greatest strength. It was almost an affront to Posada if I shook him off, which, again, is the opposite of the way a catcher should react.

With my frustrated expressions almost slapping him in the face on every pitch, Posada met with Joe Torre in April and told the manager that I seemed exasperated with him. We had partnered for my first three starts of the season. Torre told Posada there were conflicts with pitch selection and started Jim Leyritz in my fourth game, but I was still abysmal. Both Posada and I kept trying to mesh, but, eventually, Torre separated us. Posada, an All-Star catcher who hit twenty-eight homers that season, only caught me in four of my last seventeen starts.

Posada knew I was obsessed with the rhythm of getting the ball, getting the sign, and throwing, but since he hadn't caught me much before 2000, he had doubts about what to call. And once Posada saw me pause or take my cap off and wipe away the sweat, all indications that I was frustrated, he was thinking, *What the heck does he want me to call now?* If I had declined to throw a fastball or a curveball earlier in the count, Posada was hesitant to call those pitches again, which slowed the process even more. We were a pair of stubborn players who didn't mesh as well as we should have.

"Coney kind of scared me," Posada has said. "He was a veteran and he knew what he wanted to do. I had ideas, but I was scared to go to them. He was very challenging to catch. It was very challenging for me. I'm a hardheaded guy. He's a hardheaded guy. We didn't click."

Discouraged and searching for any solution, I tried to align with Posada by making him the boss and telling him I would throw whatever pitch he called against the Expos on June 5, 2000. We had tried to do it my way and failed, in large part because my pitches weren't doing what I wanted them to do. So I decided to see if letting Posada lead the dance would be a positive compromise and change my fortune. It didn't. I hurt myself by getting behind in counts, allowed a couple of homers on 2-0 pitches, and was bruised for six runs in six innings. Orlando Cabrera's three-run homer off a fastball was the decisive hit. Eleven months earlier, I had retired Cabrera on a pop-up to third base and collapsed into Girardi's arms after completing my perfect game. Those contrasting at bats with Cabrera showed how things had definitely changed for me as a pitcher.

Depressed, defeated, and unable to reinvent my slider or find a solution by switching sides of the rubber, I needed to laugh. At myself. After that loss, I had a hideous earned run average of 6.49, so I sauntered past reporters and said, "Anybody got any suggestions?" I was joking, mostly, but I was desperate enough to listen to anyone because my confidence in my pitches had almost disappeared.

How perturbed did I get with Posada? After one miserable game in 2000, I scolded him in a corner of the clubhouse, with witnesses saying my face was as red as a fire hydrant and my voice was as booming as a gunshot. It's unfortunate this ever happened, but I don't even remember shouting at him. I was so bewildered that I must have blocked it out. But Posada and Derek Jeter insist that it happened and have repeatedly and playfully reminded me about how I chastised Posada.

"Every time I see him, he tells me he's sorry for giving me a hard time," Posada has said. "I've told him not to worry about it. At that moment, I knew he wanted what was the best for him. I don't think he was tough on me. I think he was tough on himself because of the way he was struggling.

"I don't hold anything, any grudges, against him," Posada added. "He's one of the most creative pitchers I ever caught. I have big respect for him. I think he made us a better team. He made me a better player. You need people like that to make you stronger and make you a better player."

My experiences with Posada are a reminder that the smartest advice I could give any catcher is to not get offended when a pitcher wants to throw something different from what you suggested. Instead of dwelling on the fact that the pitcher disagreed with his sign, the catcher should be willing to make the adjustment and move on to the next sign.

"The reason I was able to work really well with David is because I didn't take anything personally," Girardi said. "I didn't react to his intensity and didn't take his intensity personally."

As dogged as I was in trying to shield my reaction to the signs, it occasionally became an afterthought because I was in such a challenging position with my catcher. Having Mackey Sasser catch me on the Mets meant routine starts could turn into adventures because he had trouble with one of a catcher's most basic responsibilities: throwing the ball back to the pitcher. Exchanging information via signs became secondary to simply getting the ball back from him.

Like every kid who receives early pitching lessons, I was taught to throw strikes by aiming the ball at the catcher's target. Nice and easy. I never envisioned I would get to the major leagues, where I needed to be consumed with countless elements to be able to throw an effective pitch, and I would also have to be uneasy about the catcher tossing the ball back sixty feet.

Shaggy-haired and round-faced, Mackey was a stellar hitter, a solid teammate, and a friend, but during the 1990 season, throwing problems from earlier in his career resurfaced, and he began tapping the ball into his glove and double- and triple-pumping before he could send the ball back to the pitcher.

After virtually every pitch, the pitcher would have to walk about five steps toward Sasser and Sasser would walk toward the pitcher and either flip or underhand the ball to him. When a pitcher has to descend the mound after every pitch just to retrieve the ball, it's a distraction and it becomes impossible to establish a rhythm.

Behind the mask, tension blanketed Mackey's face as he cocked his arm back to throw the ball, because he didn't know what was going to happen. I had a lot of sympathy for Sasser, but there were games where I wondered if he would have helped me avoid a damaging inning if he hadn't been preoccupied with delivering the ball to me. In the forty-two games Sasser caught me, I had a better-than-I-thought earned run average of 3.82, but there was a lot of heartburn in many of those games. I tried to encourage Sasser and promised I would work with him, but I wasn't a sports psychologist and I couldn't crawl inside his head, so I'm not sure any of my words helped him.

Catchers are a pitcher's best resource on the field, sherpas to help guide us through a game, and most of my other catchers gave me sound advice about using certain pitches in certain situations. I appreciated those strong partnerships and yearned to always have that kind of relationship with my catcher. But Sasser was so consumed with his own issues that he wasn't able to suggest, "Let's use a slider early in the count here," or "Let's go back to the splitter here because he won't be expecting it."

An empathetic figure on the Mets because of his acute struggles, Sasser became a verbal target for opponents. During one of my starts against the Montreal Expos, I heard strange noises coming from their dugout, noises that sounded like a bunch of college students yelping as their buddy tried to guzzle another can of beer.

After a few more pitches, I surmised that the Expos had synchronized their howling to match the cocking of Sasser's arm as he tried to throw the ball. If he cocked his arm once, they howled, "Whoop." If it took Sasser three tries before he finally released the ball, they howled, "Whooop, whoooop, whooooop" in an annoying and singsongy way. I was livid about this juvenile behavior, so I marched toward their dugout and said, "That's enough." I threw the next fastball under the batter's chin and scowled at their dugout once again and said, "No." That finally silenced them. It was my responsibility to defend my teammate, a likable player who really tried but who was so discombobulated behind the plate.

Whatever I experienced with Sasser, I must emphasize that I believe in accountability from all pitchers. Execution was the most important part of being a pitcher, so despite the awkwardness of the situation, it was my obligation to throw a quality pitch. Yes, there were days where I groused to myself about how I wasn't getting any help from my catcher. But, as I've said, the pitcher throws the baseball and he is responsible for the results.

As paramount as it is for a pitcher to be confident in himself, he needs to have a catcher who shares that unwavering confidence. Most pitchers can sense when a catcher believes in him or his pitches, and as he's standing alone on that mound, having that support matters. If a catcher lacks creativity and repeatedly calls the same sequence of pitches, if he tosses the ball back to the mound as if he's throwing a Frisbee on the beach, or if he doesn't even bother questioning the umpire on borderline calls, the pitcher knows he's grouped with someone who is simply catching the ball, not someone who is acting like a copilot.

There is a sacredness to the pitcher-catcher relationship, a world where "we" and "us" has to replace "I" or "you," and that relationship must be sincere, not counterfeit. Sometimes, a pitcher will say, "We tried to throw the two-seam fastball on the inner half in that at bat," or "We didn't have a great curveball in the first few innings." Obviously, the pitcher is the one throwing that fastball or that curve, but, by describing the experience as "we" in postgame interviews, the pitcher is emphasizing how linked his performance is with his catcher. It's an intentional tethering that strengthens the pitcher-catcher bond, a bond that many managers, players, and team executives insist is the most important of any in baseball.

Ten seconds into a conversation about the value of a strong pitcher-catcher relationship, the incomparable Mariano Rivera said, "It's the whole game. It's how you win games." That relationship was so pivotal to Rivera that he also described it as "a marriage. A good marriage." Each partner needs to have an innate feeling for what the other is doing, hour to hour, inning to inning, minute to minute, and pitch to pitch. And if they are disconnected, they need to continue making adjustments. It's a relationship where they must overcome the disagreements, dodge the potholes, relish the achievements, and do it together, always together.

As a pitcher prepares to make a pitch, there are so many factors swirling around him that the catcher will never fully know. The pitcher has more knowledge about himself, from the ache in his shoulder when he throws a fastball to the blister that is beginning to form when he throws a curve, and that insight enables him to make the most informed choices about what pitch to throw. At times, the seams on a baseball felt higher to me and I knew that could help me get a better grip to throw a sharper slider. The catcher isn't privy to that information, which is another reason the pitcher should make the ultimate decision about what to throw.

When I was in my first full season in the rotation with the Mets, Barry Lyons, who was in his third season with the team, became the first catcher who ever thanked me for shaking off his signs and pursuing alternatives. We were close friends and roommates, and we talked a lot about the intricacies of pitching, so I figured Lyons would be receptive to me doing that. And he was.

In an unforgettable game against the Phillies on Father's Day in June 1988, I countered some of Lyons's early suggestions because

I wanted to throw my slider. After I did that a few times, Lyons followed my lead, and when we experienced the same type of situation, he called for the slider. We agreed on pitch after pitch, and that rhythm helped carry us through hitless inning after hitless inning after hitless inning. With two outs in the eighth inning, I was still clinging to a no-hitter and we were still agreeing on our pitch sequences.

On one pitch, that harmony was disrupted as Steve Jeltz, who would finish with a puny .187 average that season, hit an 0-2 fastball for a looping single over the glove of shortstop Kevin Elster and into shallow center field. I thought Elster might corral it, but he missed it by about a foot. The soft hit and the soft hitter combined to make it an excruciating way to lose my no-hitter. Afterward, I didn't disguise my disappointment, because it was one of those magical games where I really thought my pitches were dynamic enough to guide me to a no-hitter.

Still, as frustrating as it will always be to narrowly miss the no-hitter, one of my fondest memories from that game is how Lyons and I worked together to decide on the pitches. Lyons was responding to me and what I wanted to throw, and he didn't get agitated when I shook him off to request another pitch. And, man, we almost rode that strategy to a no-hitter. Instead, I settled for a two-hit shutout.

"I'm glad you shook me off because you showed me a pattern that I can go to with you," Lyons said to me. "I can tell what you're looking to throw, and we can go with that and that can alleviate some of the pressure."

The desire to be the ultimate decision maker was always with me and should be with every pitcher, but, as a young pitcher, I understood why it was logical to trust veteran catchers like Jamie Quirk and Gary Carter. They had much more knowledge and insight about the hitters and understood their tendencies better than me. Carter had more than ten years of experience over me and Lyons. In addition to being a great catcher, Carter was a great teacher, too, dispensing sound advice on how to attack certain hitters. The Mets had an intense rivalry in the late 1980s with the St. Louis Cardinals, who were fueled by players like Ozzie Smith and Vince Coleman, a couple of speedy slap hitters. My plan was to throw sliders and curveballs to them because I thought that slap hitters wouldn't make robust contact against softer pitches.

Aggravated from seeing too many grounders slither along the Astroturf and turn into singles in St. Louis, Carter calmly and expertly explained why my approach was flawed. If I threw breaking pitches, I was giving Smith and Coleman a better chance to make contact and smack grounders, grounders that could become annoying hits because of their speed. Throw fastballs and throw them up and in, Carter stressed.

So I did. I threw high and inside fastballs, pitches that pesky hitters like Smith and Coleman were more likely to hit in the air and therefore negate their greatest advantage: their speed. Since neither player had the power to routinely hit deep fly balls, Carter and Mel Stottlemyre, the Mets' pitching coach, were insistent about having me throw shoulder-high fastballs and forcing them to swing at those pitches.

Always alert and always studying hitters, Carter would monitor Smith's and Coleman's swings to see how they were reacting to the fastballs and whether they were getting frustrated. Sometimes, by their third at bats against me, Carter would theorize that they were desperate to see anything other than a fastball, and he'd signal for a breaking pitch to exploit their edginess.

Suddenly, my breaking pitches were my new weapons against the Cardinals, but not just any breaking pitches. Make them shoddy pitches, Carter said. Because Coleman and Smith seemed antsy, Carter ordered me to bounce my curves and sliders right on or near the plate to make them chase those low pitches, more pitches that they couldn't hit with authority. For most of my career, Carter's strategy worked wonders as Smith was 7 for 46 against me while Coleman was 12 for 55. Neither player hit a homer.

Whether or not the catcher is a true collaborator, pitchers are considered solo artists in a team sport because their performances amount to one-on-one fights against each batter. In those duels, it would be logical to absorb every shred of information, no matter how innocuous, that the batter, wittingly or unwittingly, gives you. As soon as the ball left my fingertips, I turned into an investigative reporter. I would look at the batter's eyes to see how he had reacted, I would study the speed of his bat to see if he had been ahead or behind the pitch, and I would notice if his knees had wobbled on a curveball. If I detected anything, like a left-handed batter leaning across the plate to try and cover the outside corner on a backdoor slider, I would log that information in my mental notebook and use it for making future decisions. If I saw the batter leaning again, even if it was something as subtle as his right shoulder bending closer toward the plate, I'd throw a fastball that was designed to nip the inside corner and fool him.

While David Wells studied the batters intently, too, pitchers are sixty feet away. So he wanted his catcher, who was only inches away from the batters, to watch their feet and be aware if they moved to a different position in the box. If the batters moved forward or backward or sideways, Wells wanted to know because he could strategize against them. If the batter inched forward in the box because he was protecting against a breaking ball, Wells would throw a fastball up and in. If the batter crept closer to the plate because he wanted to guard against an outside pitch, Wells would pump a fastball on the inside corner.

Thoroughness in studying a batter was a prerequisite for me, as I think it should be for all pitchers, so I acted as if every batter was scrutinizing me just as closely. Pitchers should constantly quiz themselves: Am I throwing too many first-pitch fastballs? Am I taking too much time to establish a grip in my glove and hinting about throwing off-speed pitches? Not every hitter guesses pitches, and there were surely hitters who weren't analyzing me as keenly as I was analyzing them, but it helped to make that presumption because it forced me to hide my pitches and disguise my emotions.

Stay with me. That's what pitchers should tell catchers who are bothered when their decision clashes with a catcher's suggestion. In addition to a catcher's essential responsibilities, he needs to be a psychiatrist and a cheerleader, too, because with every pitch the pitcher becomes restless. This might sound optimistic, but the savvy catchers understand pitchers can be needy and can experience dramatic mood swings, and part of a catcher's responsibilities include keeping them calm and even inspiring them.

As much as I wanted to lead in making the decisions about pitch selection, there were countless times where I let the catcher lead me and wanted the catcher to lead me. In the hectic and tense relationship between a pitcher and a catcher, it's sometimes OK for a catcher to lie to a pitcher. Actually, sometimes, it's imperative. Charlie O'Brien was a master at playing mind games with pitchers, telling them whatever he felt they needed to hear to make them believe they could succeed. O'Brien would say things like "Your curve is starting to break a little more" and "Your fastball had more life in that inning." If O'Brien needed to lie to a pitcher across several innings, he did it and he did it convincingly.

Not all pitchers are comfortable with a catcher doing what O'Brien did, but I wanted him to occasionally lie to me because we all need that positive reinforcement. I knew when my fastball felt like I was throwing a shot put and when my slider was hanging, but it was still reassuring to hear O'Brien say that I was getting closer to pitching like myself. "Keep working and pushing," he would say.

There were times where we worked and pushed our way through seven decent innings, even with ordinary pitches. And sometimes I pushed myself through nine innings.

On a stagnant Friday night in April 1992, my pitches were as flat as a placemat, not moving or exploding or allowing me to get the swings and misses that were so essential to my success. It took me 101 pitches to navigate through five innings, and even though we had a 4–1 lead, I felt like I was about to crumble. I struck out one batter in the first five innings and that was the opposing pitcher, an obvious indication that my pitches weren't fooling anyone.

But O'Brien kept encouraging me, kept calling for all my pitches, and kept telling me to look at the scoreboard because we had the lead. "You don't have to strike everybody out," he said. "Keep pitching this way." I listened, even as I allowed eight base runners in the first five innings and even as I threw at least five pitches to eleven of the first twenty-one batters. I listened to O'Brien and finished a 145-pitch complete-game win. It wasn't a masterpiece, but it was a win.

And, when a game like that was over and O'Brien didn't have to try and trick me anymore, he would be candid about how I had pitched. "You really didn't have your best movement on your pitches tonight," he would say with a smile. Even that honesty was O'Brien's way of cultivating a pitcher's psyche; it reinforced to me that I could be effective in games where I wasn't at my best. The lies led to the truth and a bit of genius by my catcher.

The truth. We should all be able to handle the truth, right? Of course, I wanted the truth from my catchers, too. But a catcher's timing in delivering the truth is incredibly important. Upon exiting the bullpen for a start, I wanted to trust that I had all my pitching options: fastball, slider, splitter, and curve. Even if one or two of my pitches were inept in the bullpen, I didn't abandon hope about using them, because I knew I could revive them during the game. That was why Doug Mirabelli infuriated me in August 2001 when we finished a bullpen session for the Red Sox and he said, "Your slider didn't look too good. Maybe we should think about going with something else."

Suggesting that I ditch my valuable slider a few minutes before my first pitch of the game was horrendous timing by Mirabelli, like a surgeon discussing insurance coverage as a patient is being wheeled into the operating room. Those words surprised me and stung me. We're all human. Since the man who was catching my slider in the bullpen told me that it looked weak, that appraisal was foremost in my mind as I faced the Cleveland Indians.

I will acknowledge that I pitched poorly against the Indians, giving up four runs and lasting only four innings. I shook Mirabelli off a lot, sometimes to get to a slider that he was hesitant to call. I needed to throw that pitch to try and resuscitate it, but it seemed as if Mirabelli stopped thinking along with me in trying to deceive batters, because his body language screamed of disinterest after the second inning.

Fuming on the inside, I couldn't let Mirabelli's performance go unchallenged when Joe Kerrigan came to the mound to remove me from the game. I gave him the baseball, but then I turned to Mirabelli and said, "So you just quit? You quit trying back there?" I'm sure that he was stunned by my bluntness, especially in front of the manager, but I was furious. I had never called out a catcher on the mound like that, but Mirabelli's indifference ignited me.

After the game, Mirabelli and I had a forehead-to-forehead discussion about what happened. He was upset that I criticized him on the mound, which is something I knew was harsh and something that would have angered any catcher. But I explained that we were in trouble as soon as he told me my slider was shabby. We both apologized for our poorly timed comments.

Still, I reinforced to Mirabelli that I needed him to be even more of a copilot when I was shaking off pitches and laboring. In those situations, I needed a confident catcher to help me make adjustments, not a catcher who left me stranded. I thought Mirabelli got flustered and quit on me. In Kerrigan's session with the media, he conceded that we were out of sync all game and noted how I repeatedly shook off Mirabelli's signs. When I spoke to reporters, I accepted the blame for the failure to execute and said, "It was my fault all the way. It wasn't Doug's fault." But, in private, I thought Mirabelli shared some of the blame.

In the demanding and dizzying world of pitching, everything gets more complicated when there are runners on base. The pitcher slows his pace because the strategy gets more complex, and every pitch, which means every sign, becomes even more pivotal. With the anxiety level that exists for every pitcher, those levels rise when there is a runner dancing off second base with an unobstructed view of the catcher's signs. In those situations, it's imperative for the catcher to be even quicker in delivering the signs.

Most pitchers would probably disagree with me, but it was more important for me to have a catcher who consistently gave the signs quickly than it was to have a catcher who consistently shielded the signs from the runner. Obviously, no pitcher or catcher wants signs to be stolen. But I was much more concerned about my timing and what I was trying to do than I was about a runner deciphering our code and adeptly delivering the intelligence to the batter.

Stealing signs and then passing them to the hitter is an intricate process and requires rapid communication among multiple people. There are some batters, like Paul O'Neill, my old Yankee teammate, who don't even want to be told what pitch might be coming, so any stolen insight wouldn't help them. And, even if a runner successfully relayed a signal to the batter, there's no guarantee the batter is going to get a hit on that pitch, either.

Of the hundreds of players who reached base against me, Paul Molitor and Robin Yount were among the very few players who were exceptional at picking off signs and exploiting a pitcher. It was up to the catcher or the players in the dugout to study a runner and notice if he was doing something different that indicated he was stealing our signs. There are numerous ways the runner could send a sign to the batter, from touching his helmet with his left hand for a fastball or with his right hand for a breaking pitch. Since my back was to the runner on second, I didn't want to worry about any of this, because that would detract from what I was trying to accomplish.

Every time a runner advances to second, pitchers and catchers use multiple signs to camouflage what they are doing. If a catcher flashes a combination of fingers and the pitcher doesn't want to throw that pitch, the pitcher needs him to move to the next set of signs, with little interruption. The final finger from the first set of signs has to almost bleed into the first finger from the next set. Girardi understood that and moved like a pianist. Since he never hesitated, I never, never, lost my rhythm. When a catcher is uncertain, the way Posada was with me, it can create doubt for a pitcher.

These days, paranoia is at an all-time high regarding sign stealing because the advancements in technology have made it easier for teams to analyze everything pitchers and catchers are doing. In 2017, the Yankees filed a complaint with the Commissioner's Office and accused the Boston Red Sox of using an Apple Watch in the dugout to steal their catcher's signs. With the proliferation of cameras throughout the ballpark and cameras in everyone's hands, teams have become much more vigilant about trying to protect every sign they deliver. When I pitched to Girardi, we never used a second set of signs with no runners on base. Nowadays, pitchers and catchers do that a lot. Catchers often peek into the dugout to get signs from coaches and some catchers also stare down at their information-filled wristbands, developments that make pitchers wait a little more.

To help disguise signs during my career, pitchers often used a system called the first sign indicator. So if 1 is a fastball, 2 is a curveball, 3 is a slider, and 4 is a splitter, they would know that the first sign the catcher gave is the numerical indicator for what pitch he wants. If he first flashed a 2, that means the pitch he wants was two signs after the first sign. If the sequence is 2-3-1-2, that means he is calling for a 1, a fastball. If the second sign is the indicator, it was the same premise. So if the catcher flashes 1-3-2-1-3, he wants the third sign after the second sign indicator: a 3, a slider. Using these different indicators or series of indicators and switching them from inning to inning or at bat to at bat creates additional protection.

Of the many ways to hide signs, one of the easiest for pitchers to remember is to let the number of outs help dictate which signs will be used. For instance, if there's one out, the pitch the catcher wants is the first sign. So 1-2-3-2 means a 1, a fastball. If there are two outs, the second sign is the pitch he wants. So a sequence 1-3-1-2 would be a 3, a slider. Again, it's a way to make sure the signs are protected because the sequence for the signs is constantly evolving. And, again, the layers of protection are much stronger in 2019 than they there were in 1999.

During Andy Pettitte's career, exchanging signs could be as simple as him telling the catcher what was coming next. The sneaky Pettitte would often place his glove just below his chin, would make sure the batter wasn't looking at him and would mouth what pitch he was about to throw. He warned his catchers to always keep their eyes on him because he might mouth *cutter*, therefore eliminating the need for a sign.

In addition to mouthing specific pitches to his catchers, Pettitte also used other basic actions to communicate signs with them. If

Pettitte touched his belt, that meant he was throwing a fastball. If Pettitte nodded his head, that meant he was going to throw the same pitch he just threw. If he shook to the left or to the right, that told the catcher whether the pitch was going to be inside or outside. Having those quick ways to communicate allowed Pettitte to keep the flow of the game moving and kept him from waiting for signs.

While shaking yes or no to the signs is the most popular way for the pitcher and the catcher to communicate, a small percentage of pitchers essentially call their own games by wiping their gloves across their bodies as a signal. Once the catcher gives a sign of two fingers for a curveball, the pitcher can wipe his glove on his chest to represent a "plus one" to what was offered, meaning that he will throw a 3, a slider. Or the pitcher can wipe his glove on his leg to refer to a "minus one," meaning he will throw a 1, a fastball. If the pitcher wipes twice on his chest or his leg, that means a "plus two" or a "minus two" to the number sign that was offered. If the pitcher likes the first sign, he won't wipe and will simply throw the pitch.

In principle, this approach appealed to me because of how much control the pitcher has, but in practice, I couldn't implement it in the frenetic atmosphere of a game. Although it might sound simple to add or subtract one or two to get to my desired pitch, I didn't want that extra pressure. I could understand slider over fastball better than I could comprehend a 3 needing to turn into a 1.

Forty thousand fans are yelling, I'm jittery as I search for the right pitch, and now I'm supposed to brush my glove across my chest or my leg to indicate what I want to throw? No way. Most pitchers were as hesitant as me about even trying this approach because if a pitcher isn't quick and confident, it can lead to confusion with the catcher.

Pitching intelligence was something I prided myself on having, except when it came to using wipes. I was awed by a cunning pitcher like Jimmy Key, who was so smart and so swift that he could control the rhythm of the game by calling his own pitches. As soon as Jimmy received the sign from the catcher, he began to wind up, or he wiped and then began to wind up, totally controlling the pace of the action.

Because of the way Key orchestrated the calling of the game, he needed a catcher who was quick and sharp. If a catcher gave Key the sign and then was distracted for a second, he could have missed Key's glove motions. Suddenly, the catcher wouldn't be sure if Jimmy wiped once or twice or not at all, so he wouldn't be sure about what pitch was coming. "Sometimes," one catcher told me, "I get lost." But a catcher couldn't be lost for long or he wouldn't be catching Key for long.

Wiping is more protective than shaking yes or no because fewer pitchers do it, and that adds to the mystery of what a pitcher is doing. When Al Leiter did it, he sometimes brushed his glove across his body as a decoy to simply confuse the hitter. If the catcher showed Leiter three fingers for a cutter, Al would wipe his glove across his chest as a "plus two" and follow that by wiping his glove across his leg as a "minus two," meaning that those actions canceled each other out and that he was going to throw the cutter all along. With those extra movements, Al felt that he could baffle the batter or cause the batter to lose concentration.

Leiter's decoy moves were prompted by a recommendation from Cito Gaston, a former major leaguer who managed me and Al with the Toronto Blue Jays. Gaston told Al it unnerved him when a pitcher moved his glove across his body a few times or shook his head a lot before throwing the ball, because it gave Gaston extra time to think about the pitch. After Gaston's admission, Leiter would use some phantom shakes or phantom wipes to try and puzzle hitters.

Even if a catcher is single-minded about how to communicate

signs, a pitcher needs to be more stubborn because his comfort is the priority. After I was traded from the Mets to the Blue Jays in August 1992, Pat Borders caught me, and at first he couldn't comprehend why I refused to shake off pitches. We had awkward standoffs where I wouldn't shake off a pitch and he would wait for me to shake and wouldn't advance to the next sign.

In my first start for Toronto, I saw a line of triple 7s, and that wasn't a comforting sight. It would have been refreshing if I'd spotted those numbers on a slot machine in Las Vegas, but my 7s were under the columns for hits, earned runs, walks, and stolen bases off me in a dreary 7–2 loss to the Milwaukee Brewers. I was a little tired, a little tense, and while I didn't know it then, I was in desperate need of a mechanical adjustment on the mound. Many of the 50,413 fans who attended my Jays debut probably said, "This is the guy who is supposed to help us win a World Series?"

Since I was accustomed to not shaking off, I didn't want to make a change as I was adjusting to a new team in a new league. I spoke to Pat about the timing of sign giving and how it made me more comfortable and more confident to stare. If he gave a sign and I didn't budge from my spot on the rubber, he needed to see that and be quick with the next sign.

Borders was a hard worker and a solid receiver. After he listened to my explanation and sensed how crucial this approach was to me, he agreed to study me and adapt to my preference. While we experienced some awkward exchanges, we graduated to the point where he read my expression and fast-forwarded to a new sign.

On a stressful and emotional night in Kansas City, my collaboration with Borders came together. It had been five years since I had pitched a game there, five educational and successful years since the Royals traded me to the Mets and decided they wanted a backup catcher named Ed Hearn more than they wanted me. In my third start with the Jays, I left tickets for more than thirty relatives and friends, who all crowded together in a few rows and shouted my name and made me feel like I really was at home. There were three weeks left in the season and George Brett, a player whose swing I copied while playing Wiffle ball as a Kansas City kid, was 22 hits away from 3,000. And we were trying to increase our two-and-a-half-game lead in the American League East. There were potential distractions everywhere, but I focused on one thing: getting in sync with Borders.

With Borders watching me and delivering the signs, we made strides toward allowing me to just stare in for a sign, so I didn't have to worry about shaking my head. Once I achieved that comfort level, my slider, my splitter, and my fastball were the best they had been in my time with the Jays because I had more confidence with my execution. I fell two outs short of a complete-game shutout, tiring a bit in the ninth as we won, 1–0. I pitched very well to end the regular season (allowing four earned runs in the last 40⅓ innings) and that was related to two factors: how comfortable I felt with Borders, and an adjustment I had made with my positioning on the rubber.

In a year where I pitched in my first World Series and helped the Blue Jays win it all, I was calm amid the intensity because I could stare at my catcher and not do anything to potentially help the batter. That relaxed feeling is pivotal for pitchers, a much better feeling than being restless or anxious as we wait for the next sign.

Pitchers can be moody and they can be divas. Sometimes pitchers need advice. Sometimes they need to be scolded. Sometimes they need to be left alone. But, all of the time, they need someone who is a serious partner, not just someone who is worried about his next at bat. Even the most dominant offensive catchers will acknowledge that a catcher can be much more valuable to a team because of how he influences pitchers.

While a major league pitcher needs to be mentally strong, with or without his catcher, even the toughest pitchers want some support. Memo to catchers: Pump your fist a few times. Thrust your mitt toward the pitcher to show that you liked the pitch. Call a time-out and offer some encouragement. As modest as those actions might sound, pitchers will admit that they are welcomed.

The best catchers understand that pitchers can be needy and selfish, and they also understand their advice might be shunned by the same pitchers who long to be in a partnership. But those catchers keep trying to make the pitcher feel comfortable because that's their job and that's the best script for trying to win games. They keep dancing with the pitcher. One leading, one following, both of them working in unison.

Chapter 8

THE MAN IN BLUE IS LURKING

Two BATTERS INTO THE GAME and I was already furious with the plate umpire, my cheeks turning different shades of red and the blue veins bulging out of my neck. I had thrown a 2-2 curveball that bent so neatly over the outside corner and I knew, I absolutely knew, it was strike three to Darren Daulton. But Fred Brocklander, the umpire, didn't raise his right hand. Huh? Unsettled by the call, I sailed my next pitch out of the strike zone and walked Daulton.

Livid and stunned, I trudged toward the plate to ostensibly ask for a new baseball. I couldn't ask for a new umpire. But, in reality, I took that sixty-foot walk because I wanted to ask Brocklander how the heck he had missed that call, although I planned to use a more explicit word for *heck*. Fortunately, Orlando Mercado, my catcher with the Mets, knew my temper was bubbling and he smoothly steered me away from Brocklander.

My anger wasn't simply about Brocklander missing one pitch, because every ump can miss one pitch and pitchers need to adjust. More than the one pitch, I was worried about the ramifications of such a dreadful call and envisioned Brocklander repeatedly refusing to call any similar breaking pitches for strikes. The fear of the future was further motivation for confronting Brocklander and reminding him about the missed pitch against the Phillies on a sun-splashed day in August 1990.

Like all pitchers, I wanted answers about the umpire's tendencies in the first inning, wanted to know just how much I might be able to stretch the strike zone and pilfer some strikes. Was it two inches? Could I steal a strike with a pitch that was three inches off the plate? I tried to get those answers by tossing pitches on the edges of the outside corner to see if the umpire's zone would grow a bit. Discovering that information was essential because having additional space off the plate was akin to having extra ammunition, and it gave me more options, like targeting a slider a few more inches off the plate and forcing the batter to extend to try and hit it.

Before the first pitch of every start, a pitcher has studied scouting reports, met with his catcher and his pitching coach, and maybe even changed the grip on a pitch or adjusted his delivery. But, regardless of how much preparation he's done, even the most prepared pitcher can become unsettled if the umpire is inconsistent. The pitcher wants to be in control, but he can't control how the umpire performs. If he feels the umpire has an erratic strike zone, it can make him hesitant to throw a specific pitch to a specific spot.

As I breathed deeply and tried to remain calm about Brocklander, my mind flashed back to the game from three months earlier in which I had inexplicably argued with an umpire in foul territory and allowed two Atlanta Braves to sneak home. As I was pondering that previous brain cramp, Harry Wendelstedt, the second base ump, ambled over to give me a vital piece of information. Sensing my frustration with Brocklander, Wendelstedt confided in me that Brocklander had received some disturbing personal news before the game and it might have been weighing on him. Basically, Wendelstedt, who was an ump for thirty-three seasons, was asking me to give Brocklander a mulligan on the pitch. When I heard Wendelstedt's straightforward and honest story, my animosity toward Brocklander morphed into sympathy. *Hey*, I thought, *he's in the middle of a bad day. I get it.*

Wendelstedt defused the situation, and it actually disarmed me and even relaxed me. I did throw my next pitch over Von Hayes's head because I was excitable, not because I was trying to make a point. And I got a baseball thrown over my head in the second for what I did to Hayes. But I forgot about that one missed call, I kept throwing my curves and sliders to the outside corner successfully, and I pitched into the eighth inning as we prevailed, 8–4. If only all umpires had Wendelstedt's savviness and tact.

"I am an emotional player," I told reporters about the animated first inning. "That's the package you get with me. I wouldn't be a good poker player."

I wish I had a better poker face, especially when it came to dealing with umpires. The man in blue is lurking behind the plate, always lurking and always hovering. Watching everything you do, watching every pitch you throw, and getting prepared to judge you because that's his job. The plate umpire, who is dressed in blue and whose face is covered by a mask, is peeking through it to grade your performance. Pitch after pitch, the grading is endless.

Every precious pitch is the equivalent of taking another quiz, and the only meaningful grade will be rendered when the umpire determines whether it's a ball or a strike. After a pitcher unleashes a baseball, he is concerned with the speed and the movement of the pitch and how the batter reacted, but he is also concerned with the umpire. The pitcher is hoping the umpire clenches his fist and lifts it up, a sign that he passed the latest quiz by throwing a strike.

The width of a baseball is about three inches—a measurement that seems small, but it's large when a pitcher can exploit that extra territory outside of the zone. Even if I didn't always get a called strike with pitches that were slightly off the corner, getting even one strike called in that area might entice the batter to swing at the next pitch that is thrown there.

The challenge is different for current pitchers than it was for me and my peers because they have to deal with the Zone Evaluation System, which was installed in every stadium in 2009 and uses cameras to track the location of every pitch. The pitch tracking data is then used to determine how successful an umpire was at calling strikes, so the umpire is now judged on every pitch, just like the pitchers they are judging. Big Brother, or Big Umpire, is watching.

Obviously, with the umpires being more closely monitored than at any time in baseball history, the ability to widen the zone isn't as prevalent as it was when I pitched. Umpires receive a detailed evaluation of their performances after every game; among other things, the evaluation tells them if a pitch they called a strike was actually outside. If an umpire's evaluators reported that he incorrectly called six low pitches as strikes, that would naturally be on his mind for his next appearance, and he would be less likely to give a pitcher a larger zone. However, there are still some strikes to be mined on the outside corner, strikes that a pitcher can snatch by being impeccably consistent with his location and by having a catcher who is adept at framing pitches.

Umpires are taught to expect and even demand respect, something that is ingrained in their heads from their first day in the minor leagues. Sometimes, even a perceived lack of respect toward an ump can be detrimental to pitchers and catchers. Four outs from winning my first major league game, I had a 6–0 lead over the Cincinnati Reds, so I wanted to be aggressive and delivered a fastball down the middle to Paul O'Neill. It was called a ball. I later learned that Gary Carter and plate ump Ed Montague debated the call. The count drifted to 3-1, and O'Neill crushed my fastball for a homer. Would the at bat have been different if the first pitch had been called a strike? Possibly.

Soon after that curious first-pitch call to O'Neill, I found out why it might not have been called a strike. After Carter popped out in the top of the eighth, he told Montague that a slider during the at bat nearly hit the ground and shouldn't have been called a strike. Apparently, Montague was bothered by the criticism because, after my first fastball to O'Neill, Carter said Montague screamed "Ball" in Carter's ear. Then Montague walked around Carter to seemingly assert his authority some more.

"Is that weak or what?" Carter said to me and to reporters after the game.

It was weak. But, fortunately, I didn't know about it at the time, and it didn't prevent me from getting the final outs and notching the win. Strangely, Montague spoke with me before the ninth and told me to overlook his verbal sparring with Carter. At that point, I didn't know what he meant because I was consumed with getting the victory. Still in the formative part of my major league career, I filed that away as an example of how some umpires might react to being challenged and how they always want to emphasize that they are the sole arbiters on the field.

O'Neill was just a bystander in my experience with Montague, but he was much more than a bystander in so many other incidents with umpires in his career. I thought Paul had as much passion for the game as any teammate I've ever had, and I also thought the Yankee teams from our dynastic streak fed off of his emotion and his competitiveness. But O'Neill was ornery, and if he felt an umpire missed a ball-strike call by one-eighth of an inch, he would become enraged. O'Neill's distaste for umpires was legendary when he was bashing watercoolers as a player, and it's still easy to hear the disdain in his voice for umps when he broadcasts games with me on the YES Network.

If O'Neill felt he was wronged, he would always react and would always have something to say to the umpire. So he reacted in animated fashion when he hit a baseball off his right foot against the Expos in June 2000 and it was ruled a groundout to first. Once a batted ball hits a player's foot in the batter's box, it's a dead ball. But plate umpire Rich Rieker didn't think the ball struck O'Neill's foot, and he called the play as the third out of the inning. I lost that game as Orlando Cabrera hit a three-run homer off me, but I think O'Neill, who was clutching his bloody sock in the clubhouse, was much angrier than me.

"I'm going to lose my big toenail," O'Neill said. "I'm going to send it to him."

Players grade umpires the same way we grade other players, and the best umpire I ever saw was Steve Palermo. Palermo was in an elite class because of his polished approach in running the game, the authoritative style in which he called balls and strikes, and the way he commanded respect. From the moment he appeared on the field, Palermo was so active and so involved with the game that there wasn't an ounce of doubt about who was in charge. He made eye contact with the pitchers and batters, he was willing to have a back-and-forth conversation with players and, long before pace of play became such a significant discussion point in baseball, he even encouraged it. Palermo would tell batters, "Get in the box," and he would bark out to pitchers, "Time to throw some strikes." I loved his body language and professionalism, and I even loved the fact that he knew he was exceptional at umpiring. In my seventeen-year career, there wasn't another umpire like him.

The great Rickey Henderson learned just how much of a commanding umpire Palermo was. With rain threatening before an Oakland A's game, Palermo sought out Henderson, their leadoff batter, to tell Rickey about the weather and that he wanted to start the game as soon as the National Anthem ended. Rickey nodded. When the anthem was completed and the pitcher finished his warm-ups, Palermo looked at the A's on-deck circle and it was empty. Palermo waited and waited some more. Finally, Henderson slowly climbed the stairs to the dugout. Rickey put a weighted donut on his bat, took a few practice swings, did some stretching, and strolled to the plate. Throughout Henderson's histrionics, Palermo was staring at the man who ignored his pregame message. Once Henderson reached the batter's box and settled into his crouch, Palermo hollered, "Play ball." The first pitch sailed a few inches off the outside corner, but Palermo raised his right arm and called it a strike. The next pitch was even farther outside, and Palermo called it a strike, too. A confused Henderson turned around and asked Palermo what he was doing. "Just making up for lost time, Rickey," Palermo said.

When Palermo passed away from cancer at the age of sixty-seven in 2017, he was remembered as more than just an outstanding umpire. While having dinner in Dallas in July 1991, Palermo saw two restaurant servers being mugged after they left work. He intervened to chase the attackers and was shot. Palermo was paralyzed from the waist down, and the emergency room doctor informed him that he would probably never walk again. From his hospital bed, the feisty Palermo told the doctor he would walk again and predicted he would be back on a major league field before the season ended. Three months later, Palermo used a cane to walk to the mound and threw out the first pitch in Game 1 of the World Series in Minneapolis.

From my conversations with Palermo, I was able to get inside the mind of an umpire, and I appreciated his insight because it helped me as a pitcher. According to what Palermo told me, umpires are taught to never let a manager or a player take advantage of them or they won't be respected as someone who is in control of the game. In the days of combustible managers like Billy Martin and Earl Weaver, umpires might hear complaints from the dugout on every pitch. Although the advent of instant replay review has minimized a lot of the hostility between managers and umpires, there are still umpires who have thin skin and sensitive ears. If the umpires don't look and act like they're the dictators of the calls, they fear that they will be trampled.

That umpiring mind-set reinforces how fragile the pitcher-umpire relationship can be. If the pitcher shakes his head, kicks at the dirt, shouts some profanities, or shows any type of emotion, even if it's not intended for the umpire, it might ignite the ump. While I was pitching for the Royals in May 1994, that happened with me and umpire John Shulock.

I walked two, hit a batter, and threw a wild pitch in the first inning against the White Sox, my attempts to throw pitches on the outside corner fizzling and my patience evaporating. I wasn't getting any close calls, so, out of exasperation, I flung my arms in the air. Umpires hate those demonstrative gestures, but I didn't care because I was in my own chaotic world. Shulock removed his mask and glared at me, but he didn't say anything. Upon returning to the dugout, I hurled my glove against the bench and screamed some more.

Before I reached the pitching rubber for the next inning, Shulock intercepted me and said, "If you were a younger pitcher, I would have thrown you out for what you did." I knew he was right. He could have ejected me for my actions, so it was cool to receive some leeway.

But as much as I appreciated Shulock giving me a longer leash, I also wanted him to know why I had behaved that way. It was a windy night with temperatures in the forties, and I told Shulock my pitches were wayward and I was trying, desperately trying, to pinpoint them on the edges. When I couldn't do that, I felt helpless and I was frustrated at myself and at the situation, not at Shulock.

"I wasn't arguing balls and strikes with you," I said. "I was all over the place with my stuff and I'm busting my ass out there on a cold night and trying to get better. I just want you to know that I'm working hard out there and there's going to be emotion."

Shulock just looked at me, but it was an understanding look. I think my words resonated, because I invited him into my chaotic world and explained how and why a pitcher can suddenly feel crazed and powerless. With my explanation to Shulock complete, I continued to throw some of those same pitches on the outside corner and I started to get some of them called as strikes.

I persevered and ended up getting the win, an ugly 6–5 win as I lasted seven innings, allowed five earned runs, and walked five. But, after walking five of the first nineteen batters, I didn't walk any of the last fourteen batters. A lot of that was because I simply pitched better. But some of that was because I received some of the calls I hadn't been getting earlier. And on a night where my emotions escalated, where I was almost thrown out of the game, and where I appealed to an umpire and reached an understanding, I also notched my one hundredth career win.

Whenever there's a confrontation between a player and an umpire, I think the umpires should always remind themselves that it's natural for players to be emotional because they are competing and trying to win. Of course, players are going to be intense. But the umpires don't have anything invested emotionally in winning or losing the game, so they should be calmer than the players. Because of that, I have always felt that umpires should give players some latitude to vent at themselves or even engage in some dialogue with the umps. The pitcher's performance will help determine if he leaves the ballpark as a loser that night, but the umpire never has to be concerned about leaving the park with a loss attached to his name. The umpires are perpetually undefeated.

Some umpires walk toward confrontation when they could just as easily walk away from it. Don't take your mask off. Don't yell back at the player. Some players just want to scream for five seconds. But if the umpire responds aggressively, that situation has a chance to escalate. Again, I also understand why the umpires feel the need to respond and why they don't want to be disrespected.

I never saw an umpire preen, pose, and shout like Dutch Rennert, who always pumped his volume up to 11 and who might have had the most entertaining strike call in baseball history. When Rennert spied a pitch that was a strike, he would turn his body ninety degrees, take a step toward the first base dugout, lunge forward, then lift up his right arm like a music conductor and scream, "Striiiiiiiike one!" He was the ultimate showman, an umpire whose boisterous strike call made pitchers feel as if they had just won an Olympic gold medal and made batters feel as if they should go hide in the bathroom. Do yourself a favor and look Rennert up on YouTube. I guarantee you will chuckle.

With Rennert styling and screeching behind the plate in April 1992, I almost pitched a no-hitter against the Houston Astros. Once catcher Todd Hundley and I realized that Rennert was partial to calling pitches off the outside corner, Hundley kept setting his target there, I kept throwing fastballs there, and Rennert kept doing his strike dance. Between innings, Hundley and I laughed about how some of the strike calls were on pitches that were six inches outside the zone.

Do you know who wasn't laughing? The Astros. Craig Biggio and Jeff Bagwell, two Hall of Fame players, were in the lineup and were ticked off with Rennert's questionable calls. The Astros didn't collect a hit off me until Benny Distefano, a .228 lifetime hitter, cued a slow roller along the third base line for an infield single with two outs in the eighth. I thought the ball was going to trickle into foul territory, but it stayed fair. It was a disturbing way to lose a no-hitter. But with all the generous calls Rennert gave me, I'm sure the Astros would have argued that the baseball gods were being fair in causing me to lose my no-hitter on a dribbler of a single. I finished with a complete-game, two-hit shutout and eleven strikeouts.

If an umpire showed me he had a liberal strike zone, I would seize that extra space and exploit it for as long as I could. Like I said, I always tried to discover in the first inning if the umpire was willing to call strikes on pitches that were off the plate. In a game against the Twins in August 1993, I struck out the side in the first, ending it by getting Kirby Puckett on a slider. It was only one inning, but I could tell it was going to be a productive game because of the way the pitches were soaring out of my right hand.

The Twins had seven right-handed batters in the lineup, so I used my split-finger fastball down and in and also used my slider down and away, a superb combination of pitching to both sides of the plate. As soon as umpire Vic Voltaggio began calling strikes on some pitches that were a few inches outside of the zone, I peppered that area with fastballs and sliders.

Danger was looming with the bases loaded, two outs, and a 1-0 count on Puckett in the third, but I managed to push the count to 3-2 before whiffing Puckett on a slider. In the sixth, I struck out Jeff Reboulet and Puckett on pitches that were off the outside corner. After Puckett's strikeout, he placed his bat adjacent to the plate as a way to tell Voltaggio that the strike zone didn't extend that far. An agitated Puckett also spun his helmet in the dirt on a day where he went 0 for 4 with four strikeouts, three of them against me. I understood Puckett's frustration because there had been many days in which an umpire's strike zone infuriated me, but Voltaggio worked to my benefit as I struck out eleven in seven scoreless innings. Incidentally, in a Hall of Fame career that spanned 1,783 games, Puckett only struck out four times in a game one other time.

On the days when I wasn't pitching, I was restless, so I would study every aspect of the game, like a law clerk analyzing every development in a courtroom. My routine included studying how the ump was calling pitches, and I would verbally tweak them if their strike zone was inconsistent. And if the ump spent too much time glaring into our dugout, I would accuse him of having "rabbit ears."

One month into my second stint with the Royals in 1993, my teammate Félix José was called out in a tight play at home. Manager Hal McRae was perturbed and screamed at Durwood Merrill, the plate umpire, so, with nothing else to do, I chimed in and lambasted Merrill, too.

Eventually, Merrill grew weary of us flogging him. He ejected McRae, then pointed at me, and said, "And you, too. I don't even know who you are, but you're out of the game, too." It was a priceless and comical moment. At that point, I was the highest-paid pitcher in the majors on an average annual basis ($6 million a year) and Merrill was clueless about my identity. Since the umpires were still divided between the two leagues at that time, Merrill, an American League umpire, hadn't seen much of me and didn't recognize the pitcher who had spent almost all of his career in the National League.

More amused than angry by the ejection, I said, "Come on, Durwood. Why do you have to be like that?" As Merrill approached the dugout, I could tell that he was still mystified about who I was. Mike Macfarlane, our catcher, noticed Merrill's baffled expression and said, "Durwood, don't you know who David Cone is?" As stone-faced as umpires usually are, Merrill laughed at himself for the oversight.

Interestingly enough, Merrill and I were cordial with each other after that incident, and we joked about it whenever he umpired my games. Merrill wrote a book about his career called *You're Out and You're Ugly, Too!*, and he referred to me as a "junkyard dog" in it because of my competitiveness. For Merrill, my competitiveness started when he heard an unknown player screaming at him and he tossed that no-name out of the game.

There are ordinary pitchers and then there are artists, pitchers who can place the ball precisely where they want. Of all the pitchers I competed against, Tom Glavine was the best at extending the zone and getting umpires to call strikes on pitches that looked like balls. With his fastball-and-changeup combination, Glavine had amazing control and always seemed to know just how far he could stretch the zone. He would tantalize the ump by throwing a pitch that was a fraction off the plate, and if he got a strike call, he'd try to steal another inch and another and another.

Home plate is a five-sided slab of whitened rubber that is seventeen inches wide at its widest point and is framed in black, which is why pitchers talk about throwing pitches on the black. If pitchers can target their pitches on the black, they can get called strikes and they can make it more difficult for batters to square up a baseball and hit it with authority. That's why pitchers are obsessed with working the black, living on or just off the black, or, when they are struggling, simply finding the black. Glavine lived on the black. He had a house on the black.

As Glavine contemplated how he was going to attack each hitter, he also had a scouting report on the umpire and knew who was considered a "pitcher's umpire" or a "hitter's umpire." While Major League Baseball has become much stricter about trying to enforce a regulation strike zone through its radar system these days, Glavine theorized that no two umpires are going to see every pitch exactly the same. There will be different interpretations of the strike zone, so Glavine studied umpires and knew their tendencies and then tried to take advantage of them.

In Glavine's universe, the catcher had to set up off the outside corner, his body sometimes closer to the opposite batter's box than to the plate. The catcher would be positioned two inches off the plate or four inches off the plate and, each time, Glavine kept hitting him in the mitt. That smart, steady routine made it tougher for the umpire to avoid calling those pitches as strikes because the ump saw that Glavine was hitting his spot again and again. If the umpire saw the ball hit the catcher's mitt and didn't see any extra movement with the glove, his inclination was to call it a strike.

Just as there is an art to pitching, there's an art to umpiring a game, an art that includes the human element. The pitchers who exhibit the best control are going to get the benefit of the doubt from the umpires, which is the way most pitchers believe it should be. The extra inch or two off the corners or those extra strikes during a game are a reward for having pinpoint control and mastering your craft. That distinction becomes even more pronounced because the umpire is a living, breathing human, not a robot simply calling pitches that land in a rectangular box.

Once QuesTec, baseball's first pitch-tracking technology, began in 2001, Glavine noticed the strike zone became more uniform and most of the umpires became similar strike callers. Having a legion of umpires who call the same strike zone is a positive, but that disappointed Glavine, a pitcher who had dutifully analyzed how conservative or liberal each umpire was with his strike zone. When that cat-and-mouse game with umpires faded, some of the excitement about pitching lessened for Glavine.

Those changeups on the outside corner, the types of pitches that had made Glavine so successful, weren't called for strikes as much because of QuesTec. Batters recognized that and stopped chasing them, which impacted one of Glavine's edges. Glavine's plan was to throw his pitches away from right-handed batters, but he had to adjust by throwing all of his pitches on the inside part of the plate, too, something he had never done. Glavine still wanted to entice batters to chase his outside pitches, but if he didn't mix in more inside pitches, batters wouldn't sniff at his outside offerings.

It's important for pitchers to pitch to both sides of the plate, but the challenge of getting an umpire to widen the zone is always fought on the outside corner, never on the inside. With a pitch that's thrown to the outside, the umpire has an unobstructed view and that might coerce him to extend the zone. But, with pitches on the inside, it's more improbable for an umpire to give the pitcher any additional room, because those pitches are pushing batters off the plate.

Pecking away at the outside corner and trying to learn which umpires might call some balls as strikes was a significant part of my strategy, but I didn't like it when the strike zone was a mystery. Some pitchers say they merely want an ump to call a consistent strike zone for both teams and then the pitchers should adjust, a philosophy that I considered ludicrous. I don't think the strike zone should change based on which umpire was behind the plate. A strike should be a strike with every umpire, understanding, of course, that there will always be some very close pitches that are going to be judged differently by different umpires.

As insistent as I was about wanting a consistent strike zone, it was Wade Boggs, a seven-time batting champion with a precise command of the zone, who strengthened my thoughts even more on this topic. Boggs was a perfectionist and was adamant about swinging only at strikes. In the games where an umpire had a float-ing zone and was calling pitches that were balls as strikes, Boggs would be incensed because he felt that umpire was undermining his years of diligence in learning the zone. Even if Boggs knew an umpire might call a certain pitch as a strike because that was the way the ump was calling the game, Boggs wouldn't swing because he didn't want to ruin the batter's eye he had cultivated.

At least Boggs and other batters could ask the umpire about the location of a pitch. The sixty feet and six inches that separates a pitcher and an umpire creates an adversarial moat that doesn't exist between the umpire and the batter or the umpire and the catcher. One of the advantages that catchers or batters have is that they can converse with the umpire because they are so close to each other. It happens often, and as long as it's done respectfully, it's something umpires are willing to do.

As I stood alone on the mound, with that invisible barrier be-tween me and the umpire, it was frustrating because I couldn't have that dialogue. Catchers can help their pitchers by having non-confrontational conversations with an umpire. If a catcher thinks an umpire missed a call, he can say, "We need to have that pitch," or, "Am I setting up wrong? Because I think that was a strike." Carter was shrewd and would stand up between batters, never turn around and chat with the umpire to try and make sure we were getting as many calls as possible. Sometimes I had to remind my catcher to prod the umpire about pitches.

It's acceptable for a catcher or a batter to ask an umpire the lo-cation of a pitch, but pitchers aren't given those same liberties. If a pitcher takes a few steps forward and asks an umpire about the location of a pitch, the ump might get irritated because it's not as subtle as when a batter does it. A batter's question seems benign and might go unnoticed by most. But, when a pitcher asks about a pitch, it could be viewed as second-guessing the ump.

As someone who thrived on having as much information as possible, I was jealous of the access that batters had to umpires. That sixty-foot distance is one reason there will always be an antagonistic aspect to the pitcher-and-umpire relationship, a lingering feeling of distrust. In every game, there will be pitches that the pitcher and the umpire see differently. And the only opinion that matters is the umpire's opinion. And, as always, he's watching you.

Chapter 9

UNDER PRESSURE

I can't remember if I first heard it on my car radio, in a minor league clubhouse, or in a random bar, but I do remember "Under Pressure" was a powerful song that resonated with me and seemed to be playing everywhere in the early 1980s. I was drawn to the collaboration between David Bowie and Queen because of the opening lyrics: "Pressure, pushing down on me, pressing down on you, no man ask for."

Those lyrics reflected my feelings when I was traded to the Toronto Blue Jays because there was immediate and intense pressure to help them win their first World Series. It was a pressure that hovered over every pitch and every decision I made. Did this man ask for it? No. But it was pushing down on me.

The first-place Blue Jays had just lost fourteen of their last twenty-three games when they acquired me in late August, so their message was obvious: They considered me the final piece on a club that could and should win it all. Why else would they have obtained me after the non-waiver trade deadline and with five weeks left in the regular season? There was tremendous pressure on the Jays, a franchise that played its first game in 1977, to climb to the next level and win a championship. After all, the Jays had finished at least ten games over .500 for nine straight seasons and had been to the ALCS three times, including the previous season, without ever reaching the World Series.

From the moment I pulled the number 11 jersey over my head and became a member of the Jays, I sensed that the entire country of Canada was rooting for us and treating us like an extended part of their family. But as warm and fuzzy as that support was, there was an accountability that came with receiving that passion. Despite what I had accomplished in my six seasons with the Mets, I also felt as if I had to prove myself to my new teammates in Toronto. Following a trade, every player feels that way. Suddenly, I was the new kid on the mound and they were relying on me to be one of their instrumental players. I relished this opportunity, walking around the mound like an assassin and trying to pass the latest set of baseball tests.

There wasn't any time to search for an apartment so I stayed in the SkyDome hotel, which was attached to the stadium. It was convenient because I walked to work with one of the shortest commutes in the history of Major League Baseball. But there were times where it felt a little like Groundhog's Day. Outside my window, I could see train tracks, and that made me think of traveling, and that made me think of New York. As I tried to acclimate to my teammates and my surroundings and be one of the lead actors in Toronto, I still missed New York.

Unlike the first time I was traded, from the Royals to the Mets, this trade was much different. I wasn't an unproven and nervous kid anymore, a kid who had been worried about even making it into the Mets rotation. Now I was the electrifying pitcher who would lead the majors in strikeouts that season—twenty more than runner-up Randy Johnson—so there was an expectation that I would succeed. Again, I wasn't unnerved by that pressure. Being called the hired gun was appealing because I had been widly competitive since I was a kid playing at Budd Park in Kansas City.

My reckless mantra as a young pitcher was always, "I'm going to go until I blow," and my arm validated every word of that mantra in my last few months with the Mets. In one stretch of games, I had the following pitch counts: 134, 136, 142, 134, 166, 132, 115, and 140. In those eight starts, I averaged 137 pitches per game. For some perspective, the durable Max Scherzer of the Washington Nationals led the majors in 2018 with an average of 106 pitches per start. His season high was 121. Yes, I was stubborn and I wanted to pitch in those games. I even joked with some Mets coaches that they were trying to bleed everything out of me before I left for free agency. Maybe it wasn't a joke. I continued pitching on the days where my arm felt like it had a vice attached to it, and my body rebelled and turned me into a less coordinated pitcher.

After a pitcher releases the baseball, his front foot or landing foot should be aligned with his back foot. If a pitcher stopped in the middle of his delivery and used a tape measure, he should be able to extend the strip directly from one foot to the other. Since the rubber is parallel with the plate and the pitcher is moving toward that target, it would seem fundamental that his feet would be aligned. But it's not always as simple as walking a straight line along the curb of the sidewalk, because pitchers can become sluggish. Sometimes, like all pitchers, I dug myself holes on the mound, literally and figuratively.

In that draining summer with the Mets, I grew weary and stopped lifting my front leg as high as I usually did, and my landing foot created a hole about six inches from where it should have been, which meant all my pitches were scattering. The mission was to extend my front foot forward as much as possible to power a baseball from Point A to Point B and to have my back foot in line with the lead foot. But I was landing six inches to the left of where I should have landed, so my pitches emanated from a wayward release point. And foolishly, I didn't even detect how erratic my landing was.

Picture a marksman who is readying to shoot at a target and, just as he pulls the trigger, he gets pushed. He will miss the target. That's similar to what happened to my pitches. In my first start with the Blue Jays, I struggled to throw strikes and had an ugly pitching line of seven runs, seven hits, and seven walks. There was nothing lucky about those numbers as the Milwaukee Brewers also stole seven bases with me on the mound in their 7–2 victory. I was supposed to be the big, bad pitcher who would help the big, bad Jays have a memorable October, but I looked feeble and lost.

Thankfully, Galen Cisco, the silver-haired pitching coach for the Jays, studied videotape of my recent performances and discovered what was awry. In a subsequent bullpen session, Cisco asked me to throw some pitches before stopping me, pointing at a hole in the dirt, and saying, "Do you always land there?" Cisco noted how my aimless front leg was not in line with my back leg and was hampering me from consistently throwing strikes. On virtually every pitch, my sloppy approach created a six-inch complication, so my pitches didn't reach their intended locations.

I was puzzled and furious about my mistake, but Cisco had a solution. He instructed me to switch from the right side of the rubber (third base) to the left side (first base), a change that forced me to keep my right shoulder closer to my body and helped my feet stay in a straight line. Since I was already spilling over toward the left, it might have seemed strange to shift to the left side, but it was a smart move because a right-handed pitcher who is on the left side isn't likely to drift even farther to the left—it would be too awkward.

If I drifted even a few inches to the left after starting from the first base side of the rubber, my landing leg would have been so far to the left that I'd almost be tossing the baseball into the dugout. Obviously, that's an exaggeration, but being on the left side forced me to keep my hips closed and helped rectify my alignment.

Cisco's advice offered me a new pitching device, and it was something that I used for the rest of my career. Unlike most pitchers, I easily gravitated toward different spots on the rubber, even switching in the middle of an inning. Whatever adjustment I had to make in throwing a slider from a more challenging arm angle, I gained in forcing the batter to deal with a pitch that was coming at him from an unusual angle. I've known pitchers who were hesitant to move one inch on the rubber because they felt that it disoriented them, but I viewed it as a way to make quick mechanical fixes, to give me more options, and to deceive hitters.

I'm forever grateful that Cisco diagnosed my problems so quickly because every start was precious in this dash to the post-season. The Blue Jays were a confident team, a team with players like Dave Winfield, Joe Carter, John Olerud, Jack Morris, and Roberto Alomar, an old buddy from the Puerto Rican winter leagues, and they were a team that had been assembled to win that season. Now I was part of the construction. Once I switched spots on the rubber and convinced catcher Pat Borders to let me stare in for signs and not shake him off, I became very comfortable with my new baseball home. In my last six appearances of the season, I had a 0.89 ERA in 40⅓ innings. No doubt I was ready for October.

We had a serene and reassuring manager in Cito Gaston, and I connected with him because of the mature way he handled players and how he trusted us to perform. Gaston commanded respect by the way he treated people, and he wasn't hesitant to let the veterans take the lead in certain situations. He didn't undersell my role with the Jays, either, and spoke about my importance at the top of the rotation. I liked that and appreciated his confidence. After we lost to the A's in Game 1 of the American League Championship Series and felt edgy as a team, I started Game 2 in what was one of the most nerve-wracking starts I've ever had. I was weary, but I tossed eight solid innings in a 3—1 win and made sure we didn't fall behind 2-0 in the best-of-seven series.

I've already discussed the pivotal at bat in that game and how I used a backdoor slider to surprise Walt Weiss and strike him out with two runners on base in the third and followed that by whiffing Rickey Henderson. Not only did I stop the A's in that inning, my nifty slider to Weiss confused them for the rest of the game because they couldn't be certain about what pitches I might throw.

The A's weren't confused when I pitched on three days' rest and faced them in Game 5. There was a distinct difference in the effectiveness of my pitches, probably because I was worn down and needed the extra day of rest. I knew how tired I felt, but it was October and I had to compete. I tried to throw a fastball by Ruben Sierra in the first inning, but he attacked the pitch like he was expecting it and rocketed a two-run homer. We lost the game, 6—2. Fortunately, we won the series in six games.

By the time we made it to the World Series against the Braves, I was trying to figure out how many bullets I had left in my right arm. I'm not making excuses. I'm just being honest about how taxing a long regular season and a postseason can be on a pitcher. I faced John Smoltz in Game 2 and the most positive aspect of my game is that I somehow slapped two hits off Smoltz. I'm still not sure how that happened. I walked five batters, three of whom scored, and I was out of the game in the fifth inning. Still, the Jays rallied to win.

On the night of October 24, 1992, I was pitching in Atlanta—Fulton County Stadium with the opportunity to win the decisive game of the World Series. But actually, I had pitched this game many times before. I had pitched this game in my mind in my back-

My father was my first pitching coach and my forever pitching coach. Without his support and his instruction, I wouldn't have become the pitcher that I became. *(Courtesy of David Cone)*

I was nervous and thrilled when I made my major league debut with my hometown Kansas City Royals in 1986, exactly five years after they drafted me out of high school. *(Courtesy of the Kansas City Royals)*

Before being traded to the Mets in 1987, I had never even visited New York. But I did my best to quickly fit in with my rowdy teammates and I also fell in love with the city. *(Focus on Sport via Getty Images)*

Gary Carter and Keith Hernandez congratulated me after I pitched the final inning in our 8–4 win over the Los Angeles Dodgers in Game 3 of the 1988 NLCS. That was a relief because I had pitched miserably in our Game 2 loss. (*Heinz Kluetmeier*/Sports Illustrated *via Getty Images*)

I was flattered to have the Coneheads, my personal fan group, cheering for me at games. As a pitcher who was getting acclimated to New York, those dedicated fans helped motivate me. (*Courtesy of Andrew Levy and the New York* Daily News)

When Keith Hernandez left the Mets, I switched to his uniform number 17 to thank him for his guidance and to honor him, too. (*Bruce Bennett Studios via Getty Images*)

I was sweating and I was concerned after I was bruised for seven runs and lost my first start with the Blue Jays, who had acquired me from the Mets in August 1992. Fortunately, I rebounded, pitched effectively, and helped us win a World Series title. (*Dick Loek*/Toronto Star *via Getty Images*)

I put my hands on my knees and felt like collapsing after my 147th pitch of Game 5 of the 1995 ALDS resulted in a game-tying walk to Seattle's Doug Strange. I threw a split-finger fastball that bounced. Guess what? I would throw it again. (*Stephen Dunn/Staff via Getty Images*)

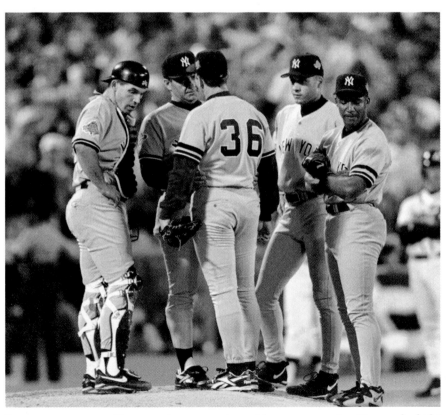

In my most memorable mound conversation with a manager, Joe Torre asked if I could pitch through the sixth inning of Game 3 of the 1996 World Series. I told him I could, and I did. (*Doug Pensinger/Allsport via Getty Images*)

I pitched six strong innings to help us defeat the San Diego Padres in Game 3 of the 1998 World Series. I won twenty games for a club that might have been the best team of all time. (Sporting News/Sporting News *via Getty Images*)

On this monumental day at Yankee Stadium, I hugged Joe Girardi after becoming the sixteenth pitcher in major league history to pitch a perfect game. What an amazing memory. (*Linda Cataffo/New York* Daily News *Archive via Getty Images*)

With my perfect game complete and the fans showing their appreciation and adulation, my teammates lifted me up on their shoulders and I waved my cap to the crowd. Literally and figuratively, I felt as if I was on cloud nine. (*Vincent Laforet/Allsport via Getty Images*)

Joe Torre was a pillar of strength and stability during my years with the Yankees and was someone I deeply respected. We enjoyed several celebrations in the clubhouse, including this one during the 1999 postseason. *(Paul Buck/Stringer via Getty Images)*

I trusted Joe Girardi as much as any catcher because of his ability to study scouting reports and retain the information and because of the way he understood my intentions. We were true dance partners, with each of us knowing when to take the lead. (Sporting News *via Getty Images*)

I admired Jorge Posada's passion and desire and his take-charge attitude, but we were disconnected for much of my dreadful 2000 season. My slider vanished and that helped turn every start into a challenge and many conversations into chores. (*Jeff Kowalsky/Stringer via Getty Images*)

Following five and a half seasons with the Yankees, it was time for my career to take an interesting detour. I rediscovered my slider and found some redemption by having a solid 2001 with the Red Sox, which was my last full season in the majors. (*Courtesy of the Boston Red Sox*)

This perfect picture was taken before the final game at old Yankee Stadium on September 21, 2008. It features the three pitchers and three catchers who combined on the only perfect games in franchise history. Left to right, it is Joe Girardi, me, Don Larsen, Yogi Berra, David Wells, and Jorge Posada. (*Jim McIsaac via Getty Images*)

Golf was my savior after my career ended because I was searching for a competitive outlet. And some of my most rewarding days on the golf course were when I played in Yogi Berra's charity tournament. (*Courtesy of the Yogi Berra Museum and Learning Center*)

yard while playing Wiffle ball, so I tried not to let the moment be any bigger than it already was. As Morris, my Jays' teammate, said before some of his starts, "I'm going to have to trick my mind today." That meant Morris was going to have to convince his mind that his arm felt better than he actually did. I adopted that philosophy and tried to trick my mind in Game 6.

Mental tricks or not, my fatigued arm told me this game was going to be a grind. And it was. My most important sequence occurred with two on and two out and Terry Pendleton batting in the fifth. With Braves fans standing and wailing, I threw two straight balls to Pendleton on fastballs. I pitched backward and snuck a slider in for a called strike, but then I missed with another fastball to push the count to 3-1. My shoulders were sagging, I was gassed, and I had no command of my pitches. As I've subsequently seen replays of that game, I can see how much I was searching for any pitches that would work. Pendleton fouled off a low fastball to get me to a 3-2 count.

On the mound, I was breathing heavy and talking to myself. I remember asking myself, *Do you have one more good slider in that arm?* After Borders gave me a series of signs, Pendleton called time-out, so Borders had to give me the signs again. I knew I was going to throw a slider, so I would have waited an hour to get that sign. Finally it came. I broke off a sweet slider. Pendleton swung over the top of it and tipped it into Borders's glove, and the wailing stopped. It was the best pitch of the at bat and allowed me to rush back to the dugout, totally relieved that I had escaped.

I left the game with a 2–1 lead after six innings, and I was in line to be the winning pitcher in that clinching game. But I lost that opportunity when the Braves scored a run in the ninth inning and the game went to extra innings. I was thrilled to see Winfield, one of the greatest all-around athletes of my generation, rip a two-run double in the eleventh inning to help catapult us to a 4–3 win. It was a shining moment for Winfield, who went 1 for 22 for the Yankees during the 1981 World Series. Four years after Winfield's disappointing performance, owner George Steinbrenner called him "Mr. May." I was elated for the gentlemanly Gaston, the first African American manager to win a title, and for the entire city of Toronto as the Jays won their first championship. And naturally I was excited for myself, too, for handling the intense pressure that was pushing down on me. I had a World Series ring after a wonderful two-month experience with a classy organization that treated me warmly, and now I could journey to my next baseball address.

Throughout October, the postseason was my focus, but I'm human, so I also knew I was pitching for my future beyond October. Before every postseason game and workout, reporters asked me about my impending free agency. I mentioned the Yankees, the Orioles, the Blue Jays, and the Royals as teams that might pursue me. The Yankees were an appealing destination to me, but they made an offer, then withdrew it, then made another offer, and that caused me to describe their front office as "chaotic." Honestly, I also felt they were more interested in Greg Maddux, the premier free agent pitcher who was once managed on the Cubs by Gene Michael, the Yankees' general manager. I thought the Yankees might wait on Maddux's decision, and I didn't want to lose out on a seat in this game of musical chairs for free agent pitchers.

On an otherwise bland night in Louisville, Kentucky, I walked into the Galt House Hotel for the 1992 Winter Meetings and didn't know how my life was about to be altered. After me and Steve Fehr, my agent, were ushered into the suite of Ewing Kauffman, the billionaire owner of the Royals, it was impossible not to gawk at the prominent bed in the middle of the room. At first, it was all I noticed. Kauffman was seventy-seven years old and was fighting cancer, and there was no disguising how much he was ailing. But Kauffman had traveled from Kansas City to Louisville because he wanted to present me an offer in person. While Steve and Herk Robinson, the Royals' general manager, were in the room, Kauffman was so riveting and so convincing that I really felt as if he and I were the only people in the room.

Meeting with the ailing owner of my hometown team in this setting was dramatic and memorable, and it had a profound impact on me. One of the first questions Kauffman asked me was whether or not I was interested in returning home. I told him I was and he said, "Then we're not leaving this room until we nail down a deal." I thought about how much Kauffman had done in bringing Major League Baseball to Kansas City, how much the community meant to him, and how much strength it required for him to make the trip to Louisville, and I could feel my compass pointing back toward home. Kauffman mentioned the possibility of a future players' strike, which we both knew was looming, and he offered me a three-year, $18 million deal, which included a record $9 million signing bonus. It was a tremendous proposal because it would enable me to earn more than half of the money in the first year. With a potential work stoppage hovering over the sport, that signing bonus was an extremely enticing part of the offer because players wouldn't receive their salaries if we were on strike.

But Kauffman was a smart businessman, and the offer included a pivotal caveat in that he wanted me to decide quickly. As we negotiated with this man, this giant of Kansas City, and studied how aggressively he pursued me when he would have probably preferred to be resting in that bed or any bed, I was transfixed by his passion. I accepted the deal and went back home. By the way, one day later,

Maddux signed with the Braves for five years and $28 million, $6 million less than the Yankees offered him.

My historic Royals contract was phenomenal because it brought me and my family so much security, but it also brought me a lot of pressure. There's that P word again. Every time I pitched, I was viewed as the $18 million man and I felt as if I had to justify my enormous salary. Confidence is so vital to pitching, and the contract spooked me into asking myself, *Am I really worth this much money?* Mentally, that was a problematic place to be.

In my second start of the season, I faced the Yankees in their home opener at Yankee Stadium, and my temper flared during a 4–1 loss. Paul O'Neill had three hits off me that day, including a line drive triple into the left center-field gap. Brian McRae, a speedy center fielder, made a valiant effort to catch the ball, but he had been shaded toward right field and couldn't make up the ground. I was ticked off that O'Neill's shot wasn't caught. I wasn't upset with Brian, but I was annoyed with our coaches for positioning him there. Why were we playing O'Neill to pull to right field when I was pitching him away and he was more likely to hit it to left?

I didn't have to wait long to ask someone that question as pitching coach Guy Hansen decided to visit me on the mound. I think Hansen just wanted to have a quick chat and get me to regroup after the run-scoring triple, but I wasn't interested in idle conversation. I pointed my finger at Hansen and yelled at him and basically said, "What the heck are you guys doing in the dugout? Is anyone paying attention?" The fans noticed my anger because they started to cheer, a rarity for an opposing team's mound meeting. Hansen didn't have much of a response for an enraged pitcher, and he turned around and returned to the dugout.

My mood didn't get much better in the early part of the season. I wouldn't change my decision about accepting that contract for anything, but it did become a psychological burden for me. When I started 1993 with an 0-5 record, I heard a lot about my salary and I let that get to me. I was pitching well with a solid 3.38 ERA, but the Royals scored a whopping nine runs in those five losses, so I couldn't secure a win. I put tremendous pressure on myself to chase that first win and to show that I was a formidable pitcher.

Kauffman died that summer, but a few months before he passed away, he called me and reassured me that he was pleased with my performances and said I had done everything the Royals had expected me to do. "You're not getting any run support," he aptly said. That call meant a lot to me, especially because I knew how much Kauffman was struggling with his health.

I went 11-14 with a 3.33 earned run average and 191 strikeouts in 254 innings that season—which, oddly enough, was one of the best statistical seasons I have ever had. I was a relentless and durable pitcher for the Royals as I averaged 7½ innings per start. Since my losing record garnered a lot of attention and seemingly indicated I was unsuccessful, that season later inspired my interest in sabermetrics. I knew I had pitched well, and the statistics that I could control verified that. I couldn't control my run support. My Wins Above Replacement (WAR), which, again, is a statistic that measures a player's total contributions to a team, was the highest in my career in 1993, higher than in either of my twenty-win seasons with the Mets (1988) or the Yankees (1998).

Serendipity isn't a word that is used much in baseball clubhouses, but it described my relationship with Bruce Kison, who was a bullpen coach and then a pitching coach during my second stint with the Royals. Kison was a versatile pitcher on two World Series championship teams with the Pittsburgh Pirates in 1971 and 1979, and he was known for being feisty and for pitching inside. There's a famous picture of Mike Schmidt tangling with Kison on the mound after Kison drilled him in the back with a pitch, a picture that always makes me smile because it showed Kison's scrappy side. In a slice of pitching serendipity, I found someone who was more obsessed with throwing pitches to both sides of the plate than me and someone who was as competitive as me. When Kison spoke, I listened, listened and absorbed the lessons, and became a more competent and better-prepared pitcher.

Kison was a walking, talking pitching expert, a coach who preferred to discuss pitching over virtually any other topic. Whether we were standing together in the bullpen, sitting in the clubhouse, or sharing a meal, conversations with Kison focused on the intricacies of pitching. "Pass the salt and pepper," Kison might say, and without pausing, continue to add, "and let's talk about how you're gripping your slider."

The barrel of the bat, which is the thickest part of the bat and the sweet spot where the batter wants to make contact, is your enemy. That is essentially what Kison said when he counseled me about throwing pitches that would "run away from the barrel of the bat." It's something every pitcher knows, but Kison said it so often and said it with such fervor that it resonated. Of course I wanted a batter to hit the ball off the handle of the bat or off the end of the bat because he wouldn't hit it as robustly, but I couldn't simply wish for that to happen. I needed to throw the pitches that caused that to happen, something that became easier to comprehend and execute when Kison introduced me to his plan: X-Games.

After Kison told me how he loved the explosiveness on my fastball, the movement on my slider, and the way my splitter dropped out of the strike zone, he gently added that he didn't think I was using my pitches as efficiently or as collectively as I could. Kison suggested a revision of my repertoire in which I focused on having pitches that crisscrossed on both sides of the plate.

Imagine having a pitch that broke right to left and a pitch that broke left to right on both the inside and the outside corner, Kison said. Imagine how those contrasting pitches could confuse batters because there would be varied movement and no predictable patterns, he added. I was very intrigued because disrupting a batter's timing was the essence of pitching, and Kison's method seemed like a perfect prescription for doing that.

Since I already had a splitter, which dived down and moved from left to right against left-handed batters, I needed a complementary pitch that broke from right to left to complete the X on the outside part of the plate. That pitch was my backdoor slider, which was a breaking pitch that I wouldn't grip as tight; it started off the plate and then dipped into the strike zone, through the backdoor. On the inside part of the plate, I had a two-seam fastball that broke from left to right, invariably looking like it might plunk the batter before bending into the zone, and I also threw a cutter that broke from right to left, so that helped me form another X. I also threw my four-seam fastball to both sides of the plate and up and down, which gave me more options and provided more ways to stymie the batter. Kison was a genius, I thought.

The batter's eyes provide pieces of evidence, something pitchers can study to see how the batters react to their pitches and whether they seem unnerved or confident. One of the benefits of X-Games was the ability to change a batter's eye focus by making them look for pitches that were located on both sides of the plate, forcing their eyes to look in and out and in again. Pitchers often try to change a batter's eye level by alternating between north and south by, for example, throwing a high-and-tight fastball and following that with a slider that was down and away. It's an effective way to trick hitters, but it's also smart to change the batter's eye level from side to side by pitching in and out, a notion that isn't discussed enough.

Attacking a left-handed hitter with a pitch that begins outside and curls to the left to nick the corner and following that with a pitch that starts out on the inside and bends to the right to brush that corner forces him to be wary of both sides of the plate. Some batters pick a location like "middle and away" and focus on that spot because it's a less complicated way to hit. But if the batter is anticipating a pitch on the outside corner and suddenly there is a pitch zooming toward his hip, he will be flustered, and X-Games will have worked. The theory with throwing to both sides of the plate is that the batter won't know which areas of the plate to protect, making him uncomfortable. Several catchers told me that they despised facing pitchers who threw to both sides of the plate because they couldn't accurately predict what pitch was coming and that could lead to perplexing at bats.

Implementing what Kison taught me about my pitches helped make me a pitcher who was more efficient and, honestly, made me lament why I hadn't used this approach a lot sooner. Before connecting with Kison, my résumé included five 200-strikeout years, a 20-win season, and a World Series ring on my finger, but playing X-Games was the equivalent of shifting from algebra to calculus. It was an advanced form of pitching and it was liberating, too, because I had a definitive plan for pitching to left-handed and right-handed batters.

Aided and abetted by Kison's advice, I followed up my stronger-than-it-looked 1993 season by going 16-5 with a 2.94 earned run average and 132 strikeouts in 171⅔ innings to win the 1994 Cy Young Award in the strike-shortened season. I edged out the Yankees' Jimmy Key, my former teammate with the Jays and someone I'd been connected with before, for the award. As I said, I started Game 6 of the 1992 World Series and pitched six reliable innings, and it was Key who came into the game in relief and notched the decisive win. Now we were linked again, and we would be linked one more time when we both pitched for the Yankees.

Being a major leaguer was always my dream, but winning the Cy

Young? That was beyond my dreams. Remember, there was a time in my life where I thought it would have been cool to simply make it as high as Double A in the minor leagues.

In the moments after I learned I had won the award, I first thought about my father and all the sacrifices he had made as my first pitching coach, and I thought about my mother and all of the games she attended and how I always heard her voice encouraging me. I also thought about Kauffman. I wished he would have been alive to see me win the award and confirm his belief that I was worth the investment. When we negotiated the $18 million deal, there were no bonus clauses for winning any awards because he told me, "I'm paying you to win the Cy Young Award." Two seasons later, I did. I gave the plaque to my father.

As humbling as it was to win the prestigious award, I would have traded in a Cy Young for the opportunity to compete in a World Series with the Royals. We actually had a fourteen-game winning streak that season and were only four games out in the AL Central when the players went on strike on August 11. The last fifty-two days of the regular season were never played and there was no post-season for the first time in baseball history.

Since Steve Fehr was my agent, I also became friendly with Donald Fehr, his brother and the general counsel of the Players Association, and they educated me about what was at stake for the players' futures and how we couldn't allow the owners to enforce a salary cap. I've always felt indebted to the players who came before me and who sacrificed for the next generation of players, and I felt an obligation to look out for the future players.

As one of the higher-profile players in the game, I felt the call of duty to fight for the players' rights and to be one of the faces and the voices of the players during this impasse. The less established players were concerned about being outspoken because they were fearful of backlash from the owners. There was a need for someone to take the heat, and I didn't mind being that person because I felt very strongly about the issues. Instead of worrying about sliders and splitters, I was the AL player representative for the union, and I spent months worrying about salary caps, revenue sharing, and being locked out by the owners.

Four days after the players returned to work in March 1995, the small-market Royals traded me to the Blue Jays. It was strange, to say the least, for a team to trade a reigning Cy Young Award winner, but I wasn't surprised. Kauffman had passed away, and the new owner had a different vision for the future. The Royals slashed payroll as they stressed the need to build around younger players, and they considered my $5 million salary too expensive for them.

Although the Royals said they didn't trade me because of my union activism, any sane person had to wonder if that was a factor. The new owner was David Glass, the chief executive officer of Walmart, and Glass didn't share Kauffman's affinity for me. Just like that, I was dispatched by the Royals again.

When I arrived in the Jays' spring training complex in Dunedin, Florida, Joe Carter, my old teammate, gave me a humorous welcome by getting down on his knees and shouting, "The savior, Coney!" I didn't feel like a savior of baseball or the Blue Jays, but it made me smile. It was much easier to return to the Blue Jays the second time, and I pitched reasonably well with a 9-6 record and a 3.38 ERA, but we didn't have the same success as we did in 1992 (or as they had in winning another title in 1993) and we were in last place in July. And suddenly, the Yankees came calling and acquired me for three minor leaguers for their own postseason push in 1995.

Shortly after I was first traded to the Jays in 1992, I made a start against the Yankees. I stood by my locker at Yankee Stadium and said, "New York gets in your blood. Once it gets in your blood, you miss it." The quote received a lot of attention because many observers believed those words meant I would end up signing with the Yankees as a free agent. I didn't. But now I was a Yankee and I was happy I wouldn't have to miss New York anymore. I felt like I was going back to my second home, back to try and help the Yankees win a championship. New York was in my blood. This was about to get very interesting. Again.

Chapter 10

NO TIPPING ALLOWED

To be a pitcher is to be a liar. Pitchers are accomplished liars or, at least, they should be consummate concealers of the truth. They are deceivers on the mound, utilizing every pitch and every trick to fool the batters. But it's complicated and maybe even impossible to mislead batters if pitchers become careless and reveal clues about what type of pitch will soon soar out of their hands.

As pitchers grasp the baseball, endless sets of spying eyes are studying how and where they are holding their glove, are analyzing how their hands are moving in and around their glove, and are gauging what every blink, grimace, and idiosyncrasy might mean, including, sometimes, what they are doing with their tongue. Yes, even a protruding tongue can be a telltale sign about a looming pitch.

If pitchers suddenly or subtly do something different, whether it's widening their glove before a split-finger fastball, tapping the ball in their glove before a curve, or speeding up their delivery before a changeup, those nuances will eventually be detected by opponents and exploited by them. No one is scrutinized more than a pitcher, who is one slipup away from surrendering precious information.

Pitchers are instructed to be careful and consistent with their mannerisms to avoid offering any inadvertent clues about the next fastball or slider. The preparation before tossing a pitch can be almost as pivotal as the pitch itself because if a pitcher is tipping pitches, he's basically shouting what to expect and giving that batter the capacity to hone in on one pitch.

Anytime a pitcher has the baseball, he should behave as if there are fifty thousand pairs of high-powered binoculars focused on him, studying him and dissecting him. The most likely way for a pitcher to tip pitches revolves around how he gets a grip on the baseball in his glove. If a pitcher puts his hand in the glove and then dawdles as he gets his fingers into position on the ball, that may indicate he's about to throw a split-finger fastball or a circle changeup because establishing those grips is usually more time-consuming. With a splitter, a pitcher needs to spread his index and middle fingers on the outside of the horseshoe seam and tuck the ball deep into his palm. With a circle changeup, a pitcher places his thumb and his index finger on the side of the ball and presses them together to form a circle, and he puts the ring and the middle finger along the seams and uses the pinky finger as a stabilizer. Those grips must become automatic so a pitcher can have a consistent timing with his pre-pitch routines.

There are many smart hitters who are searching for any kind of movement with the glove and, if the pitcher spreads the glove wider (which is called fanning the glove), those batters will assume he's changing his grip because it's taking him longer to get ready. The batter might not know if the pitch is a changeup or a slider, but, as soon as he sees the pitcher do something different with his glove, he can make an educated guess about the identity of the next pitch.

Hitters rely on recognizing pitches to help them thrive because the sooner they know what pitch is coming, the sooner they can react, try to generate bat speed, and make contact. Whether it's by spotting the red dot from the spinning red seams that some batters see in identifying a slider or by the upward tilt of a curveball, the smartest hitters recognize pitches the quickest. But when a hitter has detected a pitcher's tell, possessing that information eliminates the guesswork and has the potential to make hitting that much easier.

When batters are in the box and don't have any idea what the pitcher is about to throw, they are trying to prepare for pitches that are thrown on the inside and the outside corner and pitches that might be up or down in the zone. The batters aren't sure if the pitcher is throwing a 95-mile-per-hour fastball on the inside corner of if he is about to float a 75-mile-per-hour curveball across the outside corner.

But once a batter uncovers a tip and, for instance, knows that a pitcher is getting ready to throw a fastball, he can make adjustments that enable him to hit while eliminating concern about a pitch that could break. Not only is that a significant physical advantage for batters, many batters have told me it's a significant mental edge, too. If batters are able to determine what pitch will be next, their confidence increases because the pitcher has fewer ways to attack them. When the pitcher tips his pitches, it's the equivalent of giving a batter a multiple choice quiz with only one answer.

From the first hopeful pitches of spring training, every starter dreams about having the opportunity to pitch in the potential clinching game in the World Series. But if a pitcher is ever fortunate enough to get to that place and he unwittingly informs batters about his pitches, that's a devastating development. And that was what happened to Andy Pettitte.

It's been eighteen years, and Pettitte is still distraught when he recalls how he tipped pitches to the Arizona Diamondbacks in Game 6 of the 2001 World Series. Pettitte's voice trails off as he recounts the experience and then he starts meandering around the topic, almost as if talking about it makes it seem even more painful than it was. With the Yankees needing one more win to secure their fourth straight title, the Diamondbacks humiliated Pettitte for six runs and seven hits in two innings, in large part because his glove placement gave them an inkling about his pitching plans. Arizona battered the Yankees, 15–2.

Focused and determined, Pettitte was renowned for holding his glove in front of his face as he awaited a sign, his eyes burrowing ahead like someone inspecting the smallest line on an eye chart. After a runner reached base and Pettitte began his motion from the stretch position, he lifted his hands above his shoulders and lowered his glove to his belt as he was about to throw a fastball. When Pettitte was throwing a breaking pitch, his mechanics would be identical, except he would only drop his glove to a spot slightly above his belt, probably because he was a little more anxious to throw his breaking pitches. It was a modest difference of only a few inches, but it was noticeable to someone connected with the Diamondbacks, someone who was studying Pettitte intensely.

Pettitte doesn't know who first discovered his tell, but he does know his actions doomed him. Shortly after the Diamondbacks won the championship, Todd Stottlemyre, one of their injured pitchers, told Mel, his father and the Yankees' pitching coach, that their players knew what Pettitte was throwing by the positioning of his glove.

A depressed Pettitte blamed himself for how the Yankees lost the World Series, but he also vowed that he would never tip another pitch. In the spring of 2002, Pettitte solidified his motion so that his hands would always be in the same spot when he came to the set position. Out of the windup and out of the stretch, Pettitte became incredibly cognizant of never letting his hands settle in a different place before he was about to throw a pitch. He lowered his hands to his belt buckle, not a quarter inch above the belt or below it. It was a painful lesson to learn in the World Series, a reminder of the perils of giving the hitters any kind of assistance.

Pitchers are constantly fearful about tipping their pitches or telegraphing their pitches, a slightly different version of dispensing information to the batter. Sometimes, a pitcher will slow his arm down on a changeup because he thinks he needs to throw that pitch slower, or he will do the same for the curveball because he is focused on snapping his wrist to create a greater break on the pitch.

By reducing his arm speed, the pitcher has alerted the batter that something is different in his delivery and that action could cause the batter to not swing. The batter doesn't necessarily know what pitch is coming, but the pitcher has telegraphed that there is something different, so the batter freezes and doesn't swing at a chase pitch that is designed to leave the strike zone. In that sense, telegraphing can be just as damaging as tipping because the pitcher's sloppiness with his arm speed can cause a valuable swing-and-miss pitch to be wasted.

There are different reactions pitchers experience upon learning they have tipped their pitches, usually wobbling from being surprised to dumbfounded to enraged. After the Mets acquired Tommy Herr from the Philadelphia Phillies in August 1990, I discovered I wasn't as protective of my pitches as I had thought. I knew the switch-hitting Herr well because he had previously played with the St. Louis Cardinals, the Mets' nemesis for much of my six seasons with the team from Flushing. Within a few weeks of becoming my teammate, Herr told me something I probably should have suspected.

"You tip your pitches," he said, which jolted me like a line drive to the shin.

I was half perturbed and half perplexed because I had been

effective, at times, against the Cardinals. But there were also confounding starts in which I felt as if I had FASTBALL or SLIDER tattooed across my forehead because they were taking such confident swings against very good pitches.

As Herr explained the specifics of my mistake and how batters exploited me, I felt as if I was driving the same vehicle into the same wall, over and over. Before I started my windup, I would have a four-seam fastball grip on the ball in my glove, and my hands would be positioned near my belt. When I threw a breaking ball, I would lower my hands beneath my belt to give me an extra second or two to change my grip, then raise my hands above my head and continue my motion. But, when I threw a fastball, since I already had set up my four-seam grip, I started my delivery by moving my hands directly from my belt to above my head. I never dropped my hands before throwing a four-seamer, a recognizable difference that served as an embossed invitation to batters.

"When you drop your glove below your belt, you throw a breaking pitch," Herr told me. "When you go straight from your belt to over your head, you throw a fastball."

I cringed. He was right. It was a simple flaw that was easily detectable, but it went unnoticed by me, my catchers, and the rest of my team. Pitchers can grow comfortable on the mound, and, within that comfort zone, they can become oblivious to the development of some poor habits. Because it can take years for pitchers to advance to that comfort zone, it can also be challenging to change what they're doing, even if those habits involve tipping.

While I wasn't haphazard with my glove on every pitch, I did it frequently enough that Herr told me the Cardinals and, later, the Phillies had conversations about how often they accurately guessed my pitch choices. This harmful information made it into multiple scouting reports about me and, honestly, the entire National League was probably aware of it.

A pitcher's protective shield must be reliable because he only needs to tip one pitch to potentially alter an at bat and decide a game. If a pitcher tips off that he's throwing a slider or a splitter on a 2-2 pitch, the batter can anticipate it and he might not swing at the type of two-strike pitch that often produces a strikeout. The pitch is designed to tantalize the batter before narrowly dropping out of the zone by a few inches, but since the batter is expecting it, he gazes at it as if it's a pitch that floated five feet away from the catcher. If the batter follows with a hit on the 3-2 pitch, the pitcher will be haunted by the previous pitch.

On the final day of the 2014 season, there was a message scrawled on the railing in the visiting dugout of Nationals Park in Washington, DC, a message that was presumably meant to be passed on from team to team. "Zimmermann tips. Watch glove." That message referred to Jordan Zimmermann, then a Nationals pitcher. Ironically enough, the *Washington Post* and *Miami Herald* cited the presence of the message after Zimmermann had pitched a no-hitter against the Marlins. Maybe it was a dated message or maybe it was written as a ploy. But, whatever it was, it emphasized that someone is always analyzing the pitcher and is eager to share their knowledge about his behavior.

For any skeptical pitchers who doubt that the opponents are watching them, they need to hear the intriguing story of what batters noticed with Mark Gubicza. Gubicza didn't tip pitches with the way he gripped the ball in his glove. No, that would have been too basic. Instead, Gubicza tipped in a much more unusual way, a way that would seem impossible to uncover.

Gubicza would throw sliders, pitches that would spin from right to left and, at the last moment, would dive several inches. They were terrific pitches. They were pitcher's pitches. But several members of the Baltimore Orioles studied the pitches and then they wouldn't swing. They were the same types of sliders Gubicza had often used to fool these same batters, but, suddenly, the batters who had been quick to attack these tricky sliders had little inclination to swing.

Just like with my tipping revelation, Gubicza received an explanation about Baltimore's approach when a new teammate arrived in Kansas City. Bob Melvin was traded from the Orioles to the Royals after the 1991 season, and he told Gubicza that the Orioles somehow realized that Gubicza's tongue dangled out of his mouth on almost every slider. It was OK for Michael Jordan to do that when he was slashing to the basket for a dunk because he was pretty unstoppable. But it wasn't acceptable for Gubicza because his seemingly benign action diluted the strength of one of his best pitches.

After Gubicza watched videotape of his antics, he still wondered how the batters uncovered this quirk and was grudgingly impressed that they had enough time to locate his tongue and react.

"Eventually, after Bob Melvin told me what I did," Gubicza has said, "I made sure to keep my tongue in my mouth."

When Gubicza threw his slider, he was cognizant of making sure that his arm was in a higher position so that he could really snap his wrist and get the most break on the pitch. Since Gubicza was fixating on elevating his arm and getting that extra snap, he thinks he poked his tongue out as he exerted himself, his version of a tennis player's grunt on a serve. Gubicza's innocuous action wasn't innocuous at all, because it became an indication to batters, a way for them to bypass his deadly slider.

Once Herr told me about my clumsy approach, I became obsessed with hiding everything that I was doing and, at the time, I felt unnatural because I was so worried about the possibility of tipping. Slowly but surely, I grew comfortable with disguising my pitches again and was confident I wasn't tipping them anymore. While I was pitching for the Royals in 1993, I told Bruce Kison how I had tipped my pitches with the Mets. Kison had a brilliant pitching mind, and he was the first person who suggested I go on the offensive and try to trick batters into thinking that I was still tipping. If batters thought I was still doing it, it could be an opportunity to unsettle them.

"Wiggle your glove," Kison said, "and then hit them in the neck with the pitch."

Kison was old-school, so his advice didn't surprise me. Later, Kison amended it to say I should wiggle my glove and then "knock them down." I took part of Kison's advice as I continued to lower my glove below my belt to act as if I was establishing a grip on the splitter or the slider, but then I would throw a fastball and disrupt the approach of anyone who used that now-dated scouting report about my tipping. I don't remember the specific batters I used this against, but I lulled them into believing I was throwing off-speed and then pumped a fastball by them. To me, getting the strikeout was a lot more effective than knocking a batter down.

Besides tipping pitches, a pitcher can also telegraph his pitches. Sometimes, a pitcher will do something different in his delivery, usually right at the release point, and the hitter notices the difference. The batter doesn't necessarily know what pitch is coming, but he sees something different, so he won't swing and he won't chase any pitches that are designed to leave the strike zone. This can happen with changeups because some pitchers have a tendency to slow their arms down when they throw that pitch. If they do that and the batter notices it, he might freeze and not swing because the pitcher has telegraphed that there's a difference.

Throughout our careers, a smiling Roberto Alomar used to intimate that I was tipping or telegraphing my pitches to him. I first met Alomar when he was about seventeen years old and we both played winter ball in Puerto Rico, and I was immediately struck by how talented and how smart he was. We were teammates on the 1992 Toronto Blue Jays, who won a World Series title. Alomar would study my movements more than anyone and, since we were friendly, he would always tell me that he had detected something.

"I see what you're doing with your glove," Alomar would say. "I know what you're going to throw."

I must admit that Alomar did get inside my head because I knew how intelligent he was and, if I was tipping or telegraphing, he would be the type of player who would have noticed it. But Alomar never told me exactly what he uncovered, and perhaps it was just gamesmanship. He was a lifetime .300 hitter, and he's in the Hall of Fame, but Alomar was 18 for 82 (.220 average) with 2 homers, 11 runs batted in, and 11 strikeouts against me. If Alomar really knew what was coming, I must have thrown some phenomenal pitches to get him out so often.

With everything that a pitcher is reminding himself to do on the mound, from deciding on the right pitch and the right location to remaining balanced and in sync, it's not uncommon to get distracted or lackadaisical and forget about being so guarded. Tipping pitches can happen to anyone, even the greatest of pitchers. It happened with Dwight Gooden, who debuted in the majors at the age of nineteen and was one of the most talented and overpowering pitchers of his generation. At Gooden's pinnacle, teammates joked that he should have to reveal to batters what pitches were coming to make it a more equitable confrontation. In a way, he did.

Herr, the full-time baseball player and part-time sleuth, gave Gooden the same sobering news that he had given me. When Doc held his glove in front of his chest to get the sign, if it was for a curveball, he would look down into his glove to adjust his grip before throwing it. If the sign was for a fastball, he'd never peer into the glove and would simply continue with his motion and throw the pitch. It was such a basic mistake, something that a high school pitcher would do, that it's comical that none of us noticed it and warned Gooden.

Of course, even with the advance notice, batters had to try and hit Gooden's nasty curve and his incredible fastball, which was a daunting assignment. But Gooden gave them a better chance by sprinkling information about what to expect.

Paranoia follows pitchers in a relentless way, like the drip, drip, drip of an unfixable faucet. It's always there. Pitchers are paranoid about so many things, and the possibility of tipping their pitches might create more paranoia than anything else. Masahiro Tanaka was a dominant pitcher in Japan, so successful that the Yankees invested $175 million to sign him to a contract. He is tough, talented, and confident.

But, as skilled as Tanaka is, he is as paranoid as any other pitcher who wondered why that batter just looked so comfortable against his last slider. After Tanaka acknowledged that coaches in Japan told him that some of his movements might have been tipping his pitches, he steadfastly declined to specify what those movements were.

"I really don't want to discuss this right now because I might be doing it and I don't want any hitters over here to know anything about it," he said.

Let's review Tanaka's explanation. He might have tipped his pitches several years ago while pitching in a different country with a different team and against different hitters, but even though he wasn't even certain that he ever did tip, he still didn't want to discuss it with any specificity. I understand and respect Tanaka's desire to protect what he's doing on the mound, even if, as Yogi Berra might have said, he's not doing it anymore.

A dangling index finger was troublesome for Joe Nathan long before he ascended to a career in which he saved 377 games, the eighth-highest total in major league history. As Nathan was trying to become a full-time major leaguer, he split the 1999 season between Triple A and the San Francisco Giants, mostly as a starter. Some of his ineffective outings could have been related to a finger that tipped off batters.

Because Nathan was a former shortstop, he preferred to have his index finger poking outside of his glove because that's the way he had held a glove as an infielder. But, after one of Nathan's demotions to the minor leagues, a friend from the Diamondbacks organization told Nathan that his stray finger was acting like a marquee sign of information to hitters.

Unbeknownst to Nathan, he would flare his finger and position it away from the glove every time he threw a fastball. A batter sees a pitcher's glove before he sees the baseball so Nathan's flared finger was a signal to expect a fastball. When Nathan was getting ready to throw an off-speed pitch, his finger remained pressed against the glove, and again, the batter saw that relaxed finger and knew what to expect. Since Nathan was mostly a fastball-curveball pitcher at the time and threw only the occasional changeup, the batters who detected his mistake were in enviable positions. Nathan's solution was to have a finger guard placed on his glove so that his finger could still be outside of the glove, but it was hidden by a strip of leather. He pitched in the majors for sixteen seasons with that type of glove, the finger guard protecting him and the identity of his pitches.

As annoyed as pitchers become when they discover they have been disclosing pitches to batters, they can reconcile it by remembering that every tipped or telegraphed pitch isn't going to be crushed for a hit. Batters see a succession of softly thrown fastballs during batting practice and they still hit pop-ups and weak grounders. Even when batters have early insight about a pitch, they still have to make contact and do damage, and, obviously, that doesn't always occur.

Whether I tipped my pitches for a few months or a few years, I rationalized it by telling myself that I had trustworthy pitches, and tipped pitches didn't always result in guaranteed hits. For instance, if a batter knew I was throwing a fastball: What kind of fastball was it? Was it in on their hands? Was it up in the zone to get them to chase it? What if a fastball missed its location and they swung anyway? I did the same rationalizing about inadvertently telling batters that I was throwing a splitter or a slider. Those are two different pitches, pitches that I could throw from different arm angles and to different locations. Even when batters knew they were about to face one of those pitches, my release point and my target were still unknowns. But, in addition to being rationalists, pitchers need to be realists. Tipping pitches is a potential nightmare, an issue that Pettitte glumly admits could cost a World Series game.

About a quarter of a century after Herr alerted me to how I had tipped my pitches, I was amused by a tweet from Mike LaValliere, a former catcher with the Cardinals and the Pirates. When a fan asked LaValliere about the toughest pitcher he ever faced, he said it was me.

"He tipped his pitches," LaValliere said. "Still couldn't hit him."

Chapter 11

SETTING UP HITTERS

No MATTER HOW MUCH PREPARATION, scouting, or visualizing I did before a start, I didn't know the exact way I would attack a lineup until I started warming up. Once I began throwing in the bullpen, my arm loosening and my sweaty skin sticking to my undershirt, I gained a feel for the movement and explosiveness of my pitches, and my plans could fully crystallize. Pitchers, at least the pitchers I respected, are always ready and willing to make adjustments, some subtle and some stark.

Because of my desire for an up-to-the-second feel about my pitches, I was consumed with the way the ball felt as it left my hand, that precise moment when the leather flew off my finger-tips, and that dictated how much confidence I had in my pitches. I needed to know the tightness of my grip on the seams of the ball, if I had generated enough snap in my wrist when I released it, and if my arm felt relaxed. The journey to being effective revolves around having a feel for your pitches, which can change from inning to inning. That's why the most obsessive pitchers, like me, asked themselves endless questions as the game unfolded.

Was I getting enough spin on my trusty slider? Could I throw it for strikes and pinpoint it just out of the strike zone, too? Was my fastball moving from side to side? If so, could I control the movement? Was my split-finger fastball giving the illusion of being a knee-high strike before dropping out of the zone? And if the answers weren't what I needed them to be, could I make alterations to those pitches and change the outcomes?

Whether the insight comes from coaches, from teammates, or from the way batters are reacting to pitches, every pitcher should seek as much information as possible from as many sources as possible because that's essential to developing and executing a game plan. As a pitcher who was a sponge for information, I wanted detailed answers in our advanced scouting meetings, too. But, since videotaped replays of games weren't commonly used until the end of my career, those meetings usually left me unfulfilled.

With a dozen or so pitchers and catchers sitting in chairs in a meeting room, all of us holding scouting reports in our hands, a coach would lead a discussion on the hitters we were about to oppose in the upcoming series. The meetings had a familiar theme, an appraisal of how a hitter had performed recently and some of the strategies we should employ against him. For instance, we might be told that a batter had "slider swing bat speed" and he had collected several hits off sliders recently, so we should be cautious about using that pitch.

One voice in the room, my voice, would bellow, "Whose sliders did he hit?"

It was a serious question, one that was rarely answered in a sufficient way. I wanted to know if the batter had notched the hits against Randy Johnson's slider or against a journeyman pitcher's slider because there was a significant difference between Johnson's historically nasty pitch and a pitcher who was hanging on and hanging sliders.

And even if I knew the location, the count, and the game situation for each slider that batters laced for hits, my slider had a different shape to it and I could throw it at different speeds and from different angles, so the advice we got in the meetings was disappointing. By repeatedly warning us about what the hitters had achieved and sometimes depicting every hitter as an All-Star, coaches nudged pitchers toward being passive, I think, a trait I despised. If a coach told me to avoid throwing a slider to a batter, I ignored the advice and determined for myself if the batter could hit my slider. The way the hitters reacted told me a lot more about my slider than what I heard at a scouting meeting. After Ryne Sandberg, a Hall of Fame second baseman, retired, he acknowledged how tricky it was to decipher my slider.

"Cone threw his slider at different speeds and it had different breaks," Sandberg said. "He threw one for a strike. He threw one that looked like the same pitch and was at a different speed and was out of the zone. So he mixed his speed on his breaking pitch which, for me, if you change speeds on your breaking pitch, that's three different pitches. It's got different breaks and it's very hard to gauge. It's really hard to zone in on it."

Sandberg was coy because he didn't take helpless swings against the slider, so I never sensed he was so uncomfortable against it.

"I always thought Cone was a smart pitcher," Sandberg added. "The hitters were smart back then, too, so it was cat and mouse and that's what was so great about it. And that was without all of this video and scouting. We did our own scouting. The pitchers scouted and remembered things and we did the same."

In the competitive, evolving batter-versus-pitcher world, pitchers should be adamant about focusing on their strengths, not a batter's weaknesses. While it's important to know which pitches and which locations batters might be susceptible to, it's more pivotal for pitchers to know how their pitches are behaving and how they can best utilize them. I would much rather emphasize what I did well, not what the batter did well, which is what confident pitchers do.

I like stubborn pitchers because they fight for themselves, and I like confident pitchers because they believe in themselves. Greg Maddux was a confident pitcher, a smart and competitive sort who relied on fastball command and changing speeds to subdue hitters. Maddux's plan was born more from what he could do to the batters, not what the batters could do to him. And Maddux annihilated hitters a lot more than they ever damaged him.

From sixty feet and six inches away, Maddux didn't think that batters could determine the difference between an 89-mile-per-hour fastball and an 83-mile-per-hour changeup, so he was diligent about throwing every pitch from the same release point.

Batters are often taught to picture an imaginary box around the area where the pitcher will release the ball because that will make it easier for them to begin spotting the ball. As the pitcher gets ready to throw the ball, the batter remains focused on that box and will wait until he sees the ball enter that area. Once the batter sees the ball inside the box, he has recognized the pitch and can begin deciding whether or not to swing at it.

Every time Maddux threw a pitch, he wanted the batter to see another white blur in that box, another mysterious pitch that he couldn't decipher because it looked like the identical twin of every other pitch. Since Maddux threw all three of his pitches from the same spot in that box, he believed that he could extend the mystery about his pitches from the mound to about thirty feet from the hitter. When the pitch was thirty feet away from the plate, Maddux said, some batters still couldn't recognize what type of pitch he had thrown. If Maddux executed properly, his pitches could remain a mystery for a longer period. Each of the three pitches he used would move in a different direction and end up in a different place, further confusing the batter.

"The concept is simple," Maddux said. "Being able to have three pitches with movement that actually do that, I think that's the secret."

It's a secret that turned Maddux into a 355-game winner and a Hall of Famer. Unfortunately, I watched Maddux use this formula to perfection against us in Game 2 of the 1996 World Series. The Braves had shellacked the Yankees, 12–1, in the series opener, and we desperately needed to feel better about ourselves by producing some offense and showing the Braves we weren't just spectators in this series. But Maddux stifled our batters because, in his own subtle way, he was as intimidating as a pitcher armed with a 100-mile-per-hour fastball.

Studying Maddux from my seat in the first base dugout at Yankee Stadium, I noticed how he dissected our lineup with his relentless approach. Maddux was using his two-seam fastball to get ahead in the count, so our hitters became aggressive and started to swing early in the count. None of our batters wanted to get into a two-strike situation against Maddux because he could bury them with three different pitches, those three mysterious pitches that all looked the same.

We were trailing by four runs in the sixth inning when Derek Jeter and Tim Raines smacked back-to-back singles to ignite the crowd at the Stadium, a crowd that had been aching to cheer for two straight days. Finally, we had some life. Finally, we had two base runners on in the same inning. Maybe, just maybe, we could solve Maddux and rebound to win this game.

Looking as unflappable as always, Maddux threw his two-seamer to get the normally patient Wade Boggs to ground into a double play on an 0-1 pitch. The Stadium grew quieter as Jeter stood on third, our fans hoping he could travel another ninety feet. In a seven-pitch at bat against Bernie Williams, Maddux threw two-seamers, cutters, and changeups, and Bernie never looked comfortable. That's because Maddux was disguising his pitches and, as I said, making them all look exactly the same. Eventually, Maddux threw a 3-2 changeup that faded to the outside corner; Williams was out in front of it and he tapped it to second.

We never threatened against Maddux again as he pitched eight scoreless innings in a 4–0 victory. How impeccable was Maddux? Of his 82 pitches, 62 were strikes. He also induced 18 ground balls that produced 19 outs, and he recorded 8 one-pitch outs. It was total domination because he was a total mystery. Fortunately, our batters had better at bats when we faced Maddux five days later and nicked him for three runs to win Game 6 and clinch that series. It was the Yankees' first World Series title since 1978, but I wouldn't have predicted it after the way Maddux had tamed us in Game 2. In fact, I always felt we stole that series from the Braves.

One or two innings into a game, I could usually detect the pitchers who had a plan and the pitchers who were a bit clueless. The pitchers with plans always looked a little sturdier on the mound, while the clueless pitchers always looked more wobbly. Bob Ojeda was a pitcher who almost always had a concrete plan.

To watch Ojeda, looking feisty and standing taller than his seventy-three inches, all while armed with a changeup that hovered around 80 miles per hour, was to watch another pitcher focusing on his strengths. Ojeda was clever about using his changeup to challenge batters, throwing it with the same confidence that Roger Clemens had in his fastball.

Before I was traded to the Mets, I was just another TV viewer watching Ojeda and Clemens pitch in Game 6 of the 1986 World Series, a do-or-die game for the Mets and a game that is best remembered for the Mookie Wilson grounder that slithered between Bill Buckner's legs and helped produce the winning run.

Still, at the start of Game 6, I was studying Ojeda, despite the fact that my style was much more Clemens's power approach. As I said, Ojeda threw his changeup at different velocities, including one that he called a "dead fish" changeup, and his pitches were a juxtaposition to the overpowering fastballs that Clemens was throwing. Ojeda was masterful at throwing his fastball enough so that batters were confused when he used the same arm speed to throw a much slower changeup.

While Ojeda didn't have his best changeup in this game and allowed a few hits on the pitch, I was mesmerized by how he used it and how he remained loyal to it. Dave Henderson was an aggressive hitter, and Ojeda took advantage of that by throwing him a mixture of fastballs and changeups. After Ojeda threw a changeup to Henderson in the sixth inning of a 2–2 game, he shook off Gary Carter's signs because he wanted to throw a second straight changeup. Carter acquiesced and Ojeda threw a gorgeous change, a slick and clever pitch that resulted in a groundout to shortstop.

"Like a soap bubble, he got that thing up there," marveled Vin Scully, the play-by-play announcer.

Joe Garagiola, the analyst, added, "It just floated up there."

Five months later, I became Ojeda's teammate for the 1987 season and I had a front row seat to observe him baffle batters. It was amusing to watch Ojeda's tactics because batters knew the changeup was coming, but he was so shrewd about how he used it that they often looked unprepared. Typically, Ojeda would throw a change and would notice if the batter was off balance or swung too early. Then he would throw the next changeup even slower and a few inches outside of the strike zone. Then when the batter thought he had a complete understanding of the ways Ojeda could utilize his changeup, Ojeda would throw the next one even softer, the fading action increasing and making it a devastating pitch.

By continuing to throw the changeup and varying its speeds and locations, Ojeda turned an already solid pitch into something even more daunting. As Ojeda tormented batters, we would sit in the dugout and predict when he was going to go from slow to slower to slowest with his versatile pitch. There was a precision in what Ojeda did and, just as important, there was a commitment to doing what worked best for him, not what worked worst for the batter. That's a smart pitcher, a pitcher with a plan.

Pitchers know whether an aching elbow will prevent them from throwing their best curveballs or whether a fatigued shoulder is going to subtract some velocity off their fastball or whether their command is erratic because the front side of their body isn't aligned with the plate as they power forward. We know everything about ourselves. But pitchers aren't mind readers, and they will never come close to knowing all of those intimate details about what batters are thinking and feeling. In deciding what pitches to use, pitchers should depend on what they know about themselves and not what they can speculate about the enemies at the plate. That doesn't mean a pitcher should ignore everything about the batters. When I evaluated each batter's tendencies, I was more interested in their strengths than their weaknesses because there is an intelligent strategy for exploiting a batter's strengths.

Skinny as a foul pole and serious as a Marine, Bruce Kison was a pitching expert who, as I've mentioned, taught me a style of pitching called X-Games, which was the notion of crisscrossing pitches on both sides of the plate to form Xs and befuddle batters. X-Games worked like this: I would throw a splitter that broke from left to right against left-handed batters and a backdoor slider that broke from right to left, the path of the two pitches forming an X. Kison, who was my pitching coach when I won the Cy Young Award with the Royals in 1994, was also the first coach to advise me to tempt batters with pitches that resembled what they most preferred, but were actually trap pitches. It was an ingenious way to exploit a batter.

Against the batter who hunted for inside fastballs, Kison instructed me to throw a pitch so far inside that the batter, who would initially be excited about the prospect of seeing an inside pitch, would actually put himself in an awkward position. I would pump a fastball or a cut fastball at the batter's belt buckle, the type of pitches that were moving inside to such an extreme that a batter usually couldn't connect, or if he did, he couldn't hit the ball so that it stayed fair. Based on how many batters swung at these shabby pitches, I could see how uncertain they were, and how and why I needed to keep using this strategy of pitching poorly to a strength.

Intelligent batters recognize their strengths and know when pitchers are trying to avoid challenging them with certain pitches in certain areas. If a batter who devoured inside fastballs saw that type of pitch from me, he was liable to jump on it because he wasn't sure when I would throw inside again. The batter's swing is geared to hit a pitch that is on the inside corner, not a pitch that's six inches more inside, so the more inside the pitch, the more complicated it can get for some hitters. I would uncork fastballs that were designed to get batters to move their feet, pitches that literally would have hit them in the stomach if they didn't move, and they still swung.

Kison's advice about teasing the hitter with suspect pitches was astute because it allowed me to outwit hitters by setting traps for them. I was using their own routines against them, using the way they usually made solid contact to stop them with pitches that they shouldn't have even dreamed of trying to hit. There are very few hitters who have the wrist speed to cut off a pitch or forcefully hit a pitch that is headed for their navel.

I set numerous traps against batters by getting them to swing at poorly located pitches. Once I saw a left-handed hitter like Brad Fullmer standing close to the plate, almost hunched over it and poised for an inside fastball, I would set the trap. Fullmer's stance and his history as a fastball hitter were the pieces of evidence I needed to throw cut fastballs way inside, and if he didn't move or swing, they would hit him. I threw one cutter that grazed Fullmer's uniform after he had swung and he complained to the umpire, but it was a futile argument because it was obvious he had swung. Fullmer took the bait and swung at a pitch that wasn't decent, but it seemed appealing to him because it was near a spot that was typically productive for him. When I retired a batter on one of those trap pitches, I had a sly smile because I had outwitted another hitter.

Talking, mumbling, and even shouting on the mound, Andy Pettitte was a constant critic, assessing himself from pitch to pitch. While exploiting a batter by pitching to his strengths was an effective option, once again, my first priority was always pitching to my strengths. Pettitte adhered to that philosophy, too, and he gradually advanced to a point in his career where he was comfortable using several different sequences to get outs, highlighting his strengths. Ornery and demanding, Pettitte relied on those sequences because they made him comfortable and gave him an outline of how he needed to pitch, regardless of what the batter was doing.

Depending on the specific hitter and the specific situation, Pettitte would adjust his sequence. But one of his favorite sequences was to start right-handed batters with a first-pitch curveball; it was a softer pitch that he didn't use too often, so they wouldn't be expecting it. After the curve dropped in for a called strike, Pettitte would throw a cut fastball, his trademark pitch and a pitch that barreled inside on a batter's hands, in the hopes that the batter would pull it foul.

If the batter displayed bat speed and pulled the cutter foul for the second strike, Pettitte would follow that up by tempting him with another cutter. But this time, he would take advantage of the batter's eagerness and throw it so far inside that it handcuffed the batter and he swung and missed. Sometimes, in that 0-2 situation, Pettitte would also throw a four-seam fastball that was up and in because, again, he wanted to exploit the batter's aggressiveness with a pitch that was out of the strike zone.

In a two-strike situation against batters who were wary of Pettitte's cutter on the inside corner, he was in an enviable position because he had several options to secure the outs. He could throw a changeup, a sinker, or a backdoor cutter on the outside corner, theorizing that antsy hitters who were focused on the inside wouldn't be able to extend for those pitches. Having so many two-strike options enabled Pettitte to avoid being predictable. With a series of pitch sequences that he trusted, Pettitte actually felt that the game slowed down for him and pitching became less burdensome.

Pettitte's first goal in being able to set up hitters was to have command of his fastball, meaning he could throw it where he wanted to throw it, something that is a given and a priority for any pitcher. When pitchers have difficulty in the early innings, it's usually because they can't locate their fastball properly, and they are throwing hittable pitches in dangerous spots. In games where

Pettitte struggled with his command, he'd pivot and try to throw breaking pitches to wriggle through an inning and buy some time to refine his fastball.

But, if Pettitte had exceptional command of his fastball, he would try to deceive hitters by starting them with a first-pitch changeup in their third or fourth at bat because they would usually be expecting a fastball. Pettitte's change looked like a two-seamer or a four-seamer that he was trying to throw on the outside corner so batters would bite. When they did, they would be off balance because his changeup was an average of about nine miles per hour slower than his fastball. Another dependable sequence was to throw a first-pitch breaking ball and then throw the changeup because, again, batters weren't anticipating those softer pitches earlier in the count. For Pettitte, it was an easy way to collect some one-pitch and two-pitch outs, which is the equivalent of finding a hundred-dollar bill buried under a pile of socks.

One more win for a championship. One more win to enjoy baseball nirvana. One more win to celebrate. That's what the Yankees were pondering before Game 6 against the Phillies in the 2009 World Series. That's what Pettitte was pondering, too, as the Yankees decided to start him on three days' rest in one of the most important games of his career. It was a sound choice, since Pettitte had already won the clinching games in the Division Series and the American League Championship Series.

On that night, the best player in the series and maybe the best player on the planet was Chase Utley, a left-handed batter with a quick and powerful stroke and a batter who could be especially dangerous at Yankee Stadium. Utley clubbed five homers in the first five games to tie Reggie Jackson's World Series record—and, yes, Mr. October was watching before Game 6.

"If he hits a couple of homers and we win it, it doesn't bother me," said Jackson, who is a Yankees advisor. "If he doesn't hit any more homers and we don't win, that would bother me."

Naturally, Pettitte's mission was to squelch Utley, the humble, old-school second baseman. In the first inning, Pettitte pushed the count to 1-1 before throwing a fastball under Utley's hands. Utley probably thought he could drive the pitch, but he didn't get to it quickly enough and grounded into a double play. Four innings later, in a similar situation, Pettitte advanced to a two-strike count against Jimmy Rollins. Since Rollins was batting right-handed, Pettitte threw a cutter and Rollins bounced into another double play.

I'm sure Pettitte would admit that he didn't have his best stuff that night as he walked five and whiffed three in 5⅔ innings, but Pettitte had enough reliable pitches, just enough of them, to figure out a way to stymie the Phillies. He had a plan, he knew what his pitches were doing, and when he really needed a vital pitch, he made it. And he helped guide the Yankees to a 7–3 victory and their twenty-seventh championship in franchise history. That happened because Pettitte was so savvy.

"It was really nothing special, but he made one great pitch every at bat, it seemed like, and when you get that one pitch, he was able to make it, get some double plays and really shorten the inning for a team," said Rollins. "That's what Andy does. He keeps his team in the game, and you walk away shaking your head like, 'How didn't we get to him?' Obviously, he's pretty good."

Great hitters with great plate coverage can destroy any pitcher's confidence because they can disrupt quality pitch after quality pitch and make pitchers feel helpless. When a pitcher repeatedly throws stellar pitches and the batter doesn't swing at the close pitches or fouls them off, a pitcher can grow edgy. *What do I throw now?*

I have explained why the at bat versus Doug Strange in the 1995 AL Division Series haunted me, haunted me because I lost a lead to the Mariners in the decisive fifth game on a fateful splitter. It ended our season, ended the Yankees careers of Don Mattingly and Buck Showalter, and ended an era in franchise history. Anyway, I'm also unnerved by Edgar Martinez, who had such a short stroke that it was immensely challenging to get pitches past him, especially on the inside corner.

Martinez frightened every Yankee pitcher in that series, causing all of us to become tenser every time we opposed him. We burst to a 5–0 lead in Game 4 and were optimistic that we might subdue the Mariners and advance to the ALCS. Unfortunately, Edgar became Superman. I can still see Scott Kamieniecki firing an inside fastball to Martinez in the third inning, the kind of fastball I had thrown hundreds of times and the kind of fastball that most batters would have taken for a ball or missed or hit foul. But, because of Martinez's quick wrists, he whipped his bat into position, got the barrel of the bat to the ball before it soared too far inside, and belted a crucial three-run homer to left field. When I see replays of that homer, I'm amazed at how Martinez pulled his hands in close to his body and turned on the pitch and destroyed it. If Martinez hadn't swung, the ball might have nicked his back elbow. The lesson in the at bat is that some superb batters are too strong, too quick, and too smart, regardless of where the pitch is thrown. By the way, Martinez also hammered a grand slam in the game as Seattle prevailed, 11–8. Yes, Edgar haunted us.

With excellent hitters like Martinez or Paul Molitor, trying to beat them with inside pitches that were designed to trap them was complicated because they were so good at clearing pitches out. By that I mean that they were adept at getting their bat to that inside pitch before it could buzz in on their hands and handcuff them. They were quick and didn't surrender an inch on the inside corner, so a pitcher had to be careful about venturing inside against them. But for every tremendous hitter like Martinez or Molitor, there are dozens of hitters who won't ever reach those pitches.

The supremely talented and difficult-to-retire Molitor reinforced something that I already knew: Pitchers are too defensive. When I was teammates with Molitor on the Blue Jays in 1995, he complimented me for having some deceptive pitches, but he told me I didn't need to be as much of a trickster. Molitor recommended that I be more aggressive because I could negate a lot of batters with my fastball, my slider, and my splitter, and I didn't have to worry about changing arm angles or throwing the perfect pitch.

Pitchers can be a skittish bunch, worrying about the next pitch and the next batter and, sometimes, elevating every batter to the level of Mike Schmidt or Tony Gwynn. But every batter isn't a Hall of Famer, and they will make mistakes and get themselves out. Even before Molitor's advice, I knew batters were liable to make mistakes, which was why I relished the idea of pitching poorly to their strengths.

Whether it was a fastball, a slider, or a curveball, there were always options for pitching to a batter's strengths in a way that could turn that strength into a weakness. If a batter was exceptional at hitting breaking balls, I would throw a shabby breaking pitch that bounced in front of the plate. If he saw the ball spinning out of my hand and thought it was attractive, he might be so eager that he ended up swinging at a pitch that was in the dirt. Even the greatest breaking ball hitters have difficulty connecting with those types of pitches. Against fastball-seeking hitters, it's also possible to move the ball up and down to change their eye levels and create confusion. If a batter was waiting for a fastball, I would throw him a fastball that was up around his eyes, realizing that there was a minimal chance for him to make powerful contact.

As much as Mariano Rivera's fabulous career was predicated on throwing cut fastballs, sharp-breaking pitches that barreled in on left-handed batters and destroyed an untold number of bats, he added a wrinkle to his approach by sometimes elevating pitches in two-strike counts. If Rivera was ahead in the count and he knew batters were bracing for that cutter, bracing for it the way a boxer braces to receive that next jab, he would go "up the ladder," meaning he'd fire a fastball up in the zone to trick a hitter. To remind Rivera to elevate the pitch, catchers would even rise a bit from their crouch and hold their targets about as high as the batter's shoulders.

Because Rivera was so smooth and so reliable, I could pick dozens of games in which he surprised a batter with a high fastball. On the day in which Rivera became the first reliever to appear in one thousand games for the same team, he collected two outs against the Blue Jays in the ninth inning and had two strikes on J. P. Arencibia. All catcher Russell Martin did next was give a sign and position his glove in front of his mask to remind Rivera to throw a fastball up in the zone. Rivera fired a shoulder-high fastball, and Arencibia took a feeble swing, almost a half swing that he tried to check, and became another victim of Rivera's high heat. A smiling Martin jogged to the mound and deposited the baseball in Rivera's glove. I'm sure that Rivera inscribed "1,000th game" on it. He could have also written, "Arencibia killed by high fastball."

While Kison preached the philosophy of attacking a batter's strengths in a different and interesting way, there weren't many pitchers that followed his advice as passionately as I did. I thought that strategy was astute because I was throwing pitches that were tempting to batters, and I was throwing them in a way that shouldn't have let me get hurt by them. Since I could toss a fastball toward a left-handed batter's back leg and still get consistent strikes because he was so keyed in on hitting an inside pitch, I did it over and over.

Every time I faced a major league hitter, a voice in my head lectured me about trying to get ahead in the count to put myself in the best position to get outs. Every pitcher hears that same voice because it's much easier to set up batters when you are ahead of them, even if it's 0-1. But one of the most challenging parts of pitching is staying in attack mode even after you've fallen behind in the count. As demanding as those situations are, there are still ways to set up batters and pitch like you're in control of the at bat.

As pivotal as it is to get ahead, I hated when coaches expressed that notion with a suggestion of finality, as if we were doomed once we tossed a first-pitch ball. Pitchers know the importance of getting ahead in the count, but we also know that it's not always going to unfold so seamlessly. In 2018 major leaguers threw a first-pitch strike an average of 60.6 percent of the time, so that means a pitcher is behind in the count in four out of every ten at bats. Pitchers will fall behind. Every pitcher.

Understanding that inevitability, the litmus test for pitchers is how they respond when that happens. What kind of pitches does a pitcher have at his disposal when the advantage is with the batter? The ability to escape from those spots is what separates the mediocre pitchers from the superb pitchers. Any pitcher can perform effectively when their pitches are producing and they keep getting ahead 0-1 and 0-2. But that doesn't happen as often as pitchers want it to, and they need to acknowledge that and be prepared to react to those adversarial counts.

In an always challenging job, here's the challenge a pitcher must overcome: There are runners on first and second and it's a 2-0 count to a potent hitter like Manny Ramirez or J. D. Martinez. Can he throw something besides a fastball for a strike? It takes confidence and fortitude to be able to thread the needle and throw a quality pitch. Some young pitchers measure the situation, know they can't throw a third straight ball, and throw a fastball right down the middle. Suddenly, they have allowed a three-run homer. The great pitchers are the ones who know how to throw to the corners and make a pitch that can't hurt them in those 2-0 and 3-1 counts.

As soon as a pitcher falls behind in the count, one of the keys is knowing which hitters will guess a fastball is coming and will try to launch it four hundred feet. In those situations, I knew I had to throw off-speed pitches for strikes to prove to those hitters that I would and could throw something besides my fastball to stay competitive in the at bat. The approach of throwing off-speed pitches in fastball counts, like 2-0 or 3-1, is called pitching backward because you're straying from throwing what seems like the obvious pitch.

It's easier for pitchers to throw off-speed pitches when they are ahead in the count because they aren't as worried if the pitches are precise and they can simply locate them near the strike zone. But as I've said, the more difficult test is throwing those pitches for strikes when pitchers are behind in the count. Sometimes, the quality of the off-speed pitch diminishes in those situations because pitchers don't snap their wrists as hard and they're almost trying to place the ball in the zone.

Pitching backward can also involve using the fastball. Once I had fallen behind in the count and used my slider or my curve to get the count back to 2-2 or 3-2, I would go back to the fastball to pursue that final strike. Since I had thrown off-speed pitches for strikes, the batter would sense that I would continue using that pitch and I could surprise them with a fastball.

I had my fastball and a lot of other things on my mind before Game 2 of the 1999 ALCS. There's no baseball rivalry with as much intensity and as much drama as the Yankees and the Red Sox, and as a starting pitcher, I tried to ignore all of the hype and all of the attention and just pitch. One day after Bernie Williams's walk-off homer gave us a win in Game 1, I was hoping to give us a 2-0 lead in the series. One of the smartest things I did in that game was use my fastball as a finishing pitch to help get me through difficult situations, especially against Troy O'Leary. I had mostly retired O'Leary with splitters in my career, and he had managed only two hits in twenty at bats off me. But, with runners on second and third and two outs in the third inning, O'Leary inched forward to cover the outside part of the plate and protect himself against my slider and splitter. Based on how aggressive O'Leary was, I determined that he didn't think I had enough power on my fastball to throw that pitch past him.

O'Leary's approach was sensible because the end of the 1999 season had been a slog for me. Even though I had pitched a perfect game in July, I had struggled after that magical day and lost some power on my fastball. I only pitched once a week in the last month of the season to conserve my arm, so Boston's scouting reports must have surmised that my velocity had dipped a couple of miles on the radar gun and that I didn't trust my fastball. With two strikes on O'Leary, a left-handed hitter, I unleashed an inside fastball that started at him and then veered sharply to the right so that it touched the inside corner for a called third strike. I peeked at O'Leary's face, and he had an expression that said, *Where did that come from?*

That pitch came from knowing my strengths at that point and knowing that I always had the option to try and bury a hitter with a fastball. That was a crucial out in a game we won, 3–2, especially since O'Leary collected hits in his next two at bats against me. We defeated the Red Sox in five games and also swept the Braves in four games to win the World Series.

If I hadn't slipped a fastball by him in the third, I'm not sure if we would have prevailed. The decision to throw that pitch, which was more educated than it was a hunch, was made a few seconds before I fired it because of how I felt right then and there. The pitcher's plan has to evolve because the smartest and boldest decisions are made during the game, not in the scouting meeting before it.

Chapter 12

THE PITCHING LESSONS NEVER END

I WAS A CURIOUS AND ENERGETIC kid, perpetually questioning how things worked and why things were done in a specific way. My mind was fairly active in most classes, but it moved into overdrive when I left school and the subject shifted to pitching. I wanted to know every detail about pitching, no matter how infinitesimal, so I analyzed everything about the ways to manipulate a baseball. Even in retirement, I remain a voracious student regarding the art of pitching.

Imagine being twenty years old and playing catch with a man who possessed a pitching secret you craved. He was balding with sloped shoulders and a protruding belly, so he didn't look like the Hollywood version of a major leaguer, but he was a great and clever pitcher. I studied all the things he did with a baseball, from how he hid it to how he gripped it to how he spun it. I studied Gaylord Perry because I wanted to learn how to throw a spitball.

When I was a minor leaguer and was recovering from a knee injury, the organization assigned me to rehab with the 1983 Royals. Perry was signed by the Royals in July of that season, and I was instantly obsessed with his mysterious pitch, a pitch that squirted out of his hand like a flying ice cube. The baseball would be lathered with some lubrication, usually Vaseline, and it would slide off

Perry's fingers, make some funky moves, and confound the batter. I didn't always know when Perry was preparing to throw it, but I could spot it as soon as he did.

What made the spitter devastating was the way it darted so sharply, starting about waist high before shooting out of the strike zone. The spitter had no spin but it had late lateral movement, making it a pitching cousin to the knuckleball, except with a lot more velocity. Perry called it his super sinker and proudly described it as being as slippery as a watermelon seed.

Solving Perry was a chore because he wanted batters to think about the spitter, even when he wasn't throwing it. Before throwing a pitch, Perry would adjust the brim of his cap, rub his fingers across his eyebrows or his forehead, touch his neck, or stroke the hair near his ears, a stream of gestures that helped him moisten his fingers or at least made batters think he was moistening his fingers in order to do something sinister to the baseball.

Sometimes, Perry's fingers were still moist from the previous pitch so he didn't need to go through his gyrations to load up the ball, which tricked the confused batter when the spitter arrived. Other times, Perry went through his gesticulations and bypassed the spitter to throw a changeup, another way to exasperate the opposition. Not only did Perry gain an advantage because of how the spitter danced, he also played and won a lot of psychological games because of the simple possibility that he might use the pitch.

Watching the batter's suspicious reactions could be comical. After Perry threw a vicious spitter, the batter would usually look at him, as shocked as someone who just lost a reserved seat on an oversold flight. Then the batter would stare at the umpire or complain, hoping that Perry wasn't daring enough to load up another pitch with whatever substance he was hiding. Perry, who often dabbed Vaseline on his face or his neck, sometimes looked at the batter with a wry smile, an expression that indicated the cagey Perry knew exactly what he was doing and would do it again.

In the unending search for an edge, any edge, some pitchers will doctor the baseball because a nicked, scuffed, or greased ball is going to have more movement than the pitcher can create with an unblemished baseball. It's illegal to use a foreign substance on the ball or deface the ball, but it happened more than a century ago and it's still happening today.

I've seen pitchers spit into their gloves and jam the ball into the mitt so the saliva settles on the baseball and I've seen pitchers apply suntan lotion on their arms and use that as the lubricant. When a spitter is thrown properly, the pitcher's fingers slide off the ball smoothly and the lubrication reduces the friction on the ball as it travels toward the plate. This results in the ball not spinning, and that flusters hitters who are trying to identify what type of pitch it is from the rotation of the seams.

Just like Perry, I wanted to master that magical pitch and learn how to make it dance enough to collect strike after strike and stare after stare. The man playing catch with me was the man who could teach me, a spitball muse who knew how to hide the substance, apply the substance, and make the moisture on the ball work to his advantage. Perry was even bold enough to write a book entitled *Me and the Spitter* in 1974 (while he was still an active major leaguer) so I hoped this swashbuckler would give me a course in the art of throwing the illegal pitch.

As the team assembled in the outfield grass to warm up one afternoon, I worked up the courage to ask Perry for an invitation into the exclusive club of spitball pitchers. Perry barely made eye contact with me before spewing a one-word answer: "No." We played catch in silence that day, one of us pouting, the other one (I'm guessing) irritated that the 176th pitcher in a row had asked him to reveal the secrets that helped make him special.

Undaunted and committed to having that sneaky pitch as part of my arsenal, I made several more attempts to convince Perry to teach it to me. But he declined. Because Perry was friendly and welcoming on all topics that weren't spitter related, I was persistent and kept pestering him for the secrets of his pitch. I must have worn him out because a fatigued Perry eventually showed me the grip he used. But he wouldn't tell me how he loaded a substance on the ball, stressing he would never teach a kid who was two years out of high school how to throw a spitter.

In some respects, using a spitter—an illegal pitch—was akin to going through the back door to succeed as a major league pitcher. If that spitter was the only quality pitch a pitcher depended on, and he got caught throwing it or he lost the ability to throw it, his career could be destroyed. I had an above-average slider and a fastball that reached the low 90s so Perry was indirectly telling me I could walk through the front door to launch my career. The spitter had been essential to Perry's career, but he didn't want to stunt my growth by putting me on a minefield of a path toward the spitball.

I was disappointed. Who wouldn't be? I viewed Perry as a genius, a savvy pitcher who had first doctored a baseball in 1964 and who continued to do it without getting caught until the twenty-first season of his major league career. On that fateful August day in 1982, Perry was pitching for the Mariners as they trailed the Red Sox, 1–0, in the seventh inning. After Jerry Remy's fly out, Rick Miller was batting when the Red Sox demanded that the umpires check the ball for a foreign substance. The umpires uncovered a baseball stained with Vaseline and ejected Perry. And, finally, the spitball artist had been unmasked for the first and what proved to be the only time. He didn't argue with the umps and served a ten-game suspension.

A year later, Perry was a Royal when he faced the Red Sox in August 1983. I was eager to watch this rematch, and I wondered if

Perry would be daring and throw the spitter against the team that had outed him. I think the Red Sox were expecting Perry to throw a spitter every time, but he's the only person who knows how many he did or didn't throw. What I do know is that the forty-four-year-old Perry, his career trickling to its final few starts, baffled the Red Sox across seven scoreless innings.

As the tell-it-like-it-is broadcaster for the Red Sox for more than three decades, Remy is a popular personality in New England. Remy was a small, skinny kid from Massachusetts who eventually became the second baseman for the Red Sox, and he also appeared in both of these games against Perry in 1982 and 1983. While discussing Perry on NESN, Remy sounded like every frustrated hitter who had ever been fooled by a spitter.

"I've heard all of the rumors about him," Remy said during one game. "And he didn't throw anything straight at all. Nothing."

Although Perry didn't usher me inside the spitball world and advise me about how and where to hide Vaseline, he opened up the rest of his pitching world by lecturing me about valuable aspects of his craft. With a ball in his hand and his body as a teaching device, Perry counseled me about keeping my balance, about landing properly after throwing a pitch, about protecting my arm, and about deceiving hitters.

Regardless of whether I was long-tossing a ball 150 feet or just flipping a ball thirty feet, Perry said that it was imperative to step into every throw with conviction and to turn my shoulder smoothly as I released the ball. "Don't ever take your arm for granted," Perry said, words that resonated. Still, like a lot of pitchers, I did end up ignoring some pain and pitching through it because I thought it was the right thing to do. If Perry saw a pitcher standing flat-footed while throwing a ball, even if it was a playful toss, Perry would call that man a foolish pitcher.

The connection between Perry and the spitter is undeniable, but he won 314 games because he combined that pitch and the threat of it with other stellar pitches and because he mastered the fundamentals a pitcher must master to be successful. Perry preached about how critical it was to deceive the hitter, whether it was by hiding the ball, by varying my windup, or by doing whatever was necessary to make my pitches as much of a mystery as possible.

In analyzing a pitcher's motion, there's a circular aspect to it in which his hands move over his head, then behind the back, and then forward to throw a pitch. Perry emphasized that when a pitcher completes that circle, it's important to make sure that his nonpitching shoulder is still closed, which means that his body stays sideways longer. When a pitcher keeps that shoulder close to his body, the hitters don't actually see the ball or his release point until the last millisecond, so they won't have any early information about the pitch. But when a pitcher's shoulder drifts away from his body and flies open, it's like opening a door early and disclosing a surprise. The batter gets a clearer view of the pitcher's throwing arm and can see the grip sooner; and, for instance, he could also see the pitcher's wrist turning over to throw a curveball.

Perry's creativity impacted me and impressed me because he was willing to lower his arm angle and throw a sidearm fastball or a sidearm slider, the same kind of pitches I had always thrown in my backyard Wiffle ball games. As I said, minor league coaches lectured me about not dropping down to throw some pitches because that was an inconsistent approach and it might result in an injury. But Perry was the first influential pitching guru who encouraged me to do that because it added deception. I only spent a few months around Perry, but his devotion to being deceptive left a serious imprint on the way I pitched.

After all those catches with Perry where I was in search of the recipe for an elusive pitch, I never learned how to throw a spitter, and as it turned out, I didn't mind. Perry was bold and was more of a pitching genius than a pitching trickster. "Don't be afraid to be daring," he told me. And I think he was right. I didn't need the spitter to flourish, but I definitely needed the input of a smart, clever pitcher like him.

Even without Perry's spitter, I still searched for edges in handling the baseball, just like every pitcher. Before the beginning of an inning, I would occasionally bounce my last warm-up pitch so that it touched the dirt and had a little smudge on it. I never tried to intentionally scuff the ball with a belt buckle or sandpaper or anything else, but if I had a baseball with an imperfection, I knew how to exploit it. If the baseball had a mark on the right side, it would move to the left when I threw it because the left side wasn't soiled and didn't have as much resistance.

But I found out how dangerous a smudged baseball can be while pitching for the Blue Jays in July 1995. After I got my hands on a baseball that was scuffed from hitting the dirt or being fouled off, I positioned it in my hand so the blemish was on the left side and I threw a two-seam fastball to Oakland's Mark McGwire. The ball blasted out of my hand like no fastball I had ever thrown and hit McGwire in the helmet.

When the ball plunked McGwire, it was a nauseating sound and he took a few steps backward before collapsing to his knees. McGwire left the game with a mild concussion and had to pull out of the All-Star Game the next day. Over and over, I stressed to reporters that I wasn't throwing at McGwire and that I felt terrible about hitting him. I tried to apologize to McGwire after the game, but the A's wouldn't let me in their clubhouse. After that frightening incident, I was so rattled that I never tried to use a scuffed baseball to my advantage ever again.

Like me, Mariano Rivera said he never purposely defaced a baseball, but he was aware that pitchers "can do something" with a smudged baseball "if you know how to do it." And Rivera acknowledged that he knew how to do it. Rivera did not consider it cheating if a baseball ended up getting blemished during the game and it remained in play. In a succinct and sensible way, Rivera explained that it was acceptable to manipulate that baseball because the umpires had left it in the game.

With the endless stream of baseballs that umpires remove from games these days, it's tougher for pitchers to find one that might remain in action long enough to have a bruise on it. If Rivera noticed a ball had been scuffed from contact with a bat or from bouncing in the dirt, he would throw it normally, and, as I noted, it would move in the opposite direction of where the scuff was located. So imagine that scenario. Rivera, who already possessed a cutter that moved several inches from right to left, sometimes scooped up a smudged baseball and picked up some additional movement, and, of course, that surely became a batter's nightmare.

After my failed attempts to copy Perry's spitter, I later encountered pitchers who threw another type of spitter, a pitch we called a dry spitter. For a typical two-seam fastball, a pitcher positions his index finger and his middle finger along the narrow seams of the baseball. For a dry spitter, a pitcher still has a two-seam grip, but he places his fingers about two inches lower on the ball so that they are touching the leather, not the seams. When the pitcher throws a dry spitter, the fingers aren't separating from the seams so the pitch will drop more.

The dry spitter is legal and is a pitch I saw Roger McDowell use successfully when we were teammates on the Mets. Once McDowell put his two fingers on the leather part of the ball, he would throw the pitch as hard as he could and get superb sinking action. It's very difficult to throw a ball without any friction between the fingers and the seams because that contact is what helps guide the pitch. The simple act of playing catch with McDowell was challenging because a ball that was headed toward your chest might descend and hit you in the shins. Because it could have such sensational movement, some pitchers would save it and use it as a two-strike pitch.

To get a better grip on the dry spitter, there are pitchers who would rub their forehead or the back of their neck to get some moisture on their fingertips. If a pitcher was adept at moistening his fingers with sweat and helping the ball move even more, I considered that a legal pitch. But there were also pitchers who used a bar of soap to coat the piping of their uniform pants and then rubbed their fingers along the pants. Or they might hide some Vaseline on their body. When a pitcher used a foreign substance like soap or Vaseline, I thought that veered into being illegal. We all perspire, so I have no problem with a pitcher using his own sweat to get a stronger grip. But, when a pitcher sneaked a foreign substance onto the mound, I considered that cheating.

Whether it was Perry's spitter or McDowell's dry spitter, both pitches are actually held and thrown the same way. Even if a pitcher was using Vaseline, he wanted to keep his fingers off the seams of the ball because the Vaseline added more weight to one side of the ball, so it would move unpredictably when it collided with the wind. If the pitcher's fingers made contact with the seams, that friction would lessen the impact of the Vaseline in getting the ball to dive.

Since I had a competent split-finger fastball, I never spent any time trying to develop a dry spitter. I preferred the splitter because my fingers were split near the seams, so I had more control over that pitch than someone has with a dry spitter.

While I didn't throw a dry spitter, there's a constant reminder of what it's like to throw the pitch on a wall in my father's home, an inside joke of sorts among the pitching fraternity. On the plaque Cy Young Award winners receive, there is a three-dimensional hand holding a baseball.

The grip that the hand has on the baseball includes the middle and index fingers between the two seams and resting on the leather, the grip that is used to throw a dry spitter.

———

Orlando Hernández was an artist and a magician, a pitcher who could torment batters because he threw appealing pitches, because he threw them from different arm angles and at varying speeds, and because he never acquiesced. He did it his way, always his way. Slowly, surely, and successfully.

Perfectly and blissfully stubborn, the pitcher nicknamed El Duque treated every pitch seriously and delicately, like a surgeon planning his next incision in the operating room. Actually, all pitchers should be as devoted as Hernández was to every pitch because one pitch can ruin an outing. That was why Hernández wasn't content with merely subduing batters. He wanted to dissect them, confusing them and irritating them as he forced them to play at his pace and play by his rules.

That motion. That physique. That dominance. Who is this mysterious man from Cuba? That was what I asked during El Duque's first season with the Yankees in 1998, a season in which the Yankees won an unprecedented 125 games (including eleven in the postseason) and won a World Series title. It was a season in which Hernández made his debut in the rotation in June after Veronica, my mother's four-month-old Jack Russell terrier, bit me on my right index finger and I was forced to miss a start. It was your typical "dog bites man, mystery pitcher gets a start" baseball story.

I was amazed by Hernández's athleticism, by his competitiveness, and by his funky motion in which he elevated his left knee so high that it almost touched his left ear before he released the ball. And, of course, I was also intrigued by his collection of pitches and how he utilized them, including the cunning way he used his curve-ball.

Ever the clever tactician, Hernández had a sneaky strategy in which he would float a first-pitch curveball to left-handed batters and repeatedly get strikes called. El Duque wasn't throwing his sharpest curve, a quick-breaking and knee-buckling pitch that was meant to get batters to chase it. This other curve was a looping pitch that looked like it belonged in a slow-pitch softball game, hanging in the air so tantalizingly. It seemed like it should have been crushed, but batters weren't expecting it so they hardly ever swung. Strike one.

Against an unpredictable pitcher like Hernández, batters wanted to get comfortable, so they searched for a pitch they could hit robustly, which was his fastball. Most batters are eager, and that eagerness intensifies against a pitcher they can't decipher, so expecting a fastball is a natural approach. Once the batters recognized the ball spinning out of Hernández's right hand was a breaking ball, they usually abandoned any notion of swinging.

It was a simple yet crafty approach by El Duque because the softer curve is a slick pitch to throw for a strike, and it provided an easy way to get ahead in the count. To reduce the speed of the curve, a pitcher buries the ball deeper into his palm because that tighter grip "chokes" the ball and helps decrease how fast it will travel.

If Hernández didn't throw a strike with the first curve, he would sometimes throw it again because batters were just as unlikely to swing at it on a 1-0 count. Batters swing at pitches they recognize, not pitches they rarely see.

At first, I was mesmerized by Hernández's silky curve because he consistently notched strikes with that pitch. The ball would leave his fingertips, travel about 70 miles per hour to the plate, and then drop into the strike zone. Soon, very soon, I switched from being mesmerized to being perturbed because I wished I had thought of this strategy with my curveball.

Every time I studied which batters I was facing that day, I counted how many right-handed batters were in the starting lineup because my slider, which broke from right to left, gave me an advantage against them. I would throw a slider directly at a right-handed batter and cause him to flinch as the pitch broke late and eased over the plate, or I would expand the zone by getting him to chase the slider that seemed like it was down the middle and then veered outside.

If I had unfurled a Hernández-like looping curve earlier in my career, I could have had a breaking pitch that would have been effective against left-handed batters, too. Not only did that curve help pitchers get early strikes, it also disrupted a batter's eye level and had a residual effect. When the batter saw the pitch, he was forced to peek up at a curve that seemed to be about shoulder high. When a pitcher followed up with a knee-high fastball, he forced the batter to adjust to different locations, which can disrupt a batter's timing.

As easy and effective as it is to throw a first-pitch curve for a strike to the opposite-side batter, it's not a tactic that is used as frequently as it should be. Strikes are precious and there are strikes, very attainable strikes, to be seized by honing that pitch. One reason pitchers don't do it is because they're worried about having the finesse to throw the pitch for a strike, but that's achievable with the right amount of wrist control and repetition, lots of repetition.

What's just as challenging as controlling the pitch is having enough trust in yourself to actually throw a pitch that's fifteen to twenty miles slower than a fastball. For the pitcher who is about to lob a spinning baseball to a batter, there's an automatic concern that the batter will drill it four hundred feet. Obviously that can happen, and it happened to me in a postseason game.

As a 114-win team during the 1998 regular season, the Yankees were supposed to win it all, or else we would be considered epic failures. I knew that. Everyone on our team knew that. In the second game of the ALCS against the Indians, I threw a first-pitch curve to David Justice that fluttered in for a strike, seeming to baffle him. I had notched a quick strike so my strategy had worked, but I got greedy. Based on the way Justice reacted, I thought I could deceive him with another curve. I had seen El Duque do it, so I wanted to do the same thing. When I did, Justice blasted it for a homer as the Indians tied the game and eventually beat us. Justice 1, Slow curve 0. Still, despite Justice's adjustment, I think it was worth a risk to throw a second straight curve because, as I said, it's rare to see batters even try to swing at it.

Sometimes I see young pitchers who begin an at bat by snapping off their best curve and throwing it for a ball. As they review the pitch, they may think the curve had a terrific break and they are content with their performance. That's a shoddy assessment. Not only are they behind in the count, but they gave the batter a glimpse of their sharpest curve, stripping away some of the identity of one of their pitches. The solution for them is to use a softer curve on the first pitch and save their sharp-breaking curve for later in the count. As I said, most batters are more confused than aggressive against a first-pitch slow curve.

Of the hundreds of curveballs I've seen, the most hellacious was the one thrown by Bert Blyleven. What made Blyleven's curve so devastating is that it seemed to stop in midair, right at its apex, before it dropped precipitously, like a sled barreling down a steep hill. Blyleven's pitch was the curve from heaven unless you were a hitter. Then it was the curve from hell. He used a different grip from most pitchers and generated an incredible spin on the ball, which caused it to look like a fastball before it broke.

To throw a curve, the pitcher typically puts his middle finger and his index finger on the seams of the horseshoe part of the baseball and positions the thumb underneath the ball. With this grip, he mostly uses the middle finger to create spin. Using the face of a clock as a canvas, that grip should produce a curve that has a twelve o'clock to six o'clock break.

Some pitchers don't even involve the index finger and have it pointed upward when they release their curves. Mike Mussina threw knuckle curves in which his index finger wasn't touching the baseball when he released it, emphasizing how inconsequential that finger was in throwing the pitch.

Blyleven differed from these typical grips. He used a cross-seam grip in which he placed his middle finger and index finger across the seams and kept his thumb beneath the baseball. By using the cross-seam grip, Blyleven had two fingers on the seams and used both fingers to create more friction and a tighter spin.

Since I have stressed how much of a proponent I was of borrowing from other pitchers, I was thrilled to meet with Blyleven at a hotel bar in Kansas City in 1983, a sit-down that was arranged by Steve Fehr, our mutual agent. For all the wasted nights I spent in hotel bars doing nothing to help my career, this was a productive night as Blyleven educated me about dancing curves.

But even after Blyleven's tutelage and my numerous attempts to refine the pitch in the bullpen, I couldn't mimic his curve. Who could? I put my middle and index finger exactly where Blyleven did, twisted my wrist like he did, and hoped my curve would plummet the way his curve did. Right-handed batters thought Blyleven's curve was about to hit them in the head and then it plunged and landed in the strike zone. But Blyleven's grip never felt comfortable for me. I was accustomed to the grip I'd been using since I was twelve, and no matter how much I tried a cross-seam grip, I never felt confident enough to even try Blyleven's version in a game.

When a pitcher is throwing a curve, he has to simultaneously snap his wrist when the ball rips off his fingertips. The pitcher has to extend his arm forward and really trust the grip he has on the pitch, something I couldn't do with the cross-seam grip. I would cut myself off and not extend as far as I should have, because the grip felt uncomfortable. If a pitcher doesn't have confidence in the grip and doesn't get that extension, he's never going to get the kind of tight spin on the curve that someone like Blyleven had.

After I studied Hernández and imitated him by throwing some first-pitch curves, I also reminded myself that I could throw them later in the count, too. Even with a 2-0 count and runners in scoring position, I would eschew my fastball and throw a curve to a power hitter like Jim Thome. Unless I was confident about throwing a perfect fastball that was down and away from Thome, he would likely pummel my fastball. I could throw a splitter, but it's a swing-and-miss pitch, and if he didn't swing, the count could be 3-0. Often the best option was to surprise the batter with a curve in the zone.

There are desperate situations where a pitcher absolutely has to throw a strike, so he can't rely on a chase pitch, because the batter might not swing. In those spots, the pitcher can throw a soft curve because he should be able to throw that pitch for a strike and not worry about the batter attacking it. Being able to throw that kind of pitch for a strike allowed me to climb back into some counts, but more importantly, it gave me a way to get ahead in the count.

Whether it's a curve that drifts over the plate or a fastball that catches the corner, there is an art to stealing a strike with the first pitch of an at bat. Since I nibbled at the edges of the plate later in my career, a lot of batters would take pitches and try to get into deep counts. If I sensed that, I would be much more apt to attack with the first pitch, but it was a softer attack because I used my curve a lot.

I loved jolting a batter with a first-pitch curve because it was a smart and reliable pitch. If I had only met El Duque, the master of the slow curve, sooner, I could have incorporated it into my repertoire even earlier in my career.

I learned some of the secrets of the split-finger fastball in a strange place (Dodger Stadium) and at a strange time (shortly after the Dodgers won the 1988 World Series title). Let me explain why this was strange. As I mentioned, I made reckless remarks about the Dodgers in a ghostwritten newspaper column, and that led to me pitching nervously as the Mets lost to Los Angeles in the second game of the NLCS. We lost that series in seven games, and I felt responsible.

I was depressed and in search of a distraction, so it seemed reasonable to travel seven thousand miles to play in an exhibition series between major leaguers and Japanese players in Japan. But before we embarked on the trip, we had a workout at Dodger Stadium, the place where I had just been humiliated a couple of weeks earlier. *Great*, I thought. *This is exactly where I want to be.* As I would soon learn, it really was exactly where I wanted to be.

Traveling with our team was a baseball savant, a coach named Roger Craig and a man who spoke the language of the splitter as adeptly as anyone. After the sleepy-eyed Craig watched Bruce Sutter paralyze hitters with a forkball, a pitch with sensational downward movement, he instructed his pitchers to position their fingers a bit differently in a variation of the pitch.

When a pitcher throws a forkball, he spreads his middle and index fingers as wide as possible on the outside of the horseshoe seam of the baseball and stuffs it into the webbing of his fingers. With a forkball, the gap between the fingers creates the rotation on the pitch, causing it to tumble quickly. If a normal person tried to hold a baseball the way Sutter did, their fingers would actually hurt; his fingers were spread about four inches apart. The person would also have trouble merely holding the ball, never mind throwing it, because their fingers would be spread like a V, with one leg of the V stretched to the left and the other stretched to the right.

The wide grip inhibits a pitcher from throwing a forkball as hard as a fastball, but that's not crucial because it's the insane movement, not the speed, that makes it a sensational pitch. When they weren't pitching, some splitter-throwing pitchers wedged softballs between their fingers to help create a bigger spread between them. After they switched back to a baseball, it would be easier to grasp and the unusual grip would feel more comfortable.

To throw a splitter, a pitcher splits his two fingers about two inches apart (think of a wishbone from a turkey) because he wants to be able to throw that pitch harder, just like a fastball. When I was dabbling with a splitter, my misconception was that I had to split my middle and index fingers as wide as I could, but Craig—who was the manager of the San Francisco Giants at that time—taught me differently. Not only was Craig the godfather of the splitter, he was also a very willing teacher. So, while I was warming up at Dodger Stadium, Craig said, "OK. Show me your splitter."

I had been introduced to the splitter by Diego Segui, a former major league pitcher, while I was playing winter ball in Puerto Rico a few years earlier, but it was far from a polished pitch. There were times where my splitter zoomed at a batter and looked like a fastball for about fifty-seven feet and then dived under his knees, a perfect splitter. But sometimes it didn't dive enough, stayed in the middle of the zone, and was susceptible to being crushed. I was worried that Craig, who had seen so many quality splitters, was going to giggle when he saw mine.

After Craig watched me throw several splitters, he gave me this powerful advice: "Don't split your fingers too wide. Just think of it like a two-seam fastball. Just get your fingers off the seams. And throw it as hard as you can." That was it. And he was right, so right.

Unlike the forkball, the splitter is held higher on the fingertips, and the thumb is used to manipulate the pitch. I would put the pads of my fingers on the leather, not the seams, because that's the friction point for the pitch. Basically, a splitter is a hard sinker that has a little more velocity and a little less movement than a forkball.

As pitchers tinker with off-speed pitches like splitters, there is an inclination to think that they must be thrown softer, too, because by design, the pitch doesn't have as much velocity as a fastball. If a pitcher is throwing 90-mile-per-hour fastballs, he might think that his splitter needs to be about 80 miles per hour to really accentuate the difference in the two pitches.

But again, with the splitter, the difference in velocity from the fastball isn't what makes the pitch successful. If I simply threw the splitter like a fastball, I would get the late tumbling action that made the pitch a special pitch. With the assured confidence of a man who had landed the airplane on the same runway a thousand times, Craig stressed that I should be pursuing movement with my splitter and not any specific separation in velocity with my fastball.

Knowing that I was supposed to throw my splitter like a fastball was a relief because I didn't have to train my arm to throw the ball with less power, which would have required slowing my arm down to refine that one pitch. Once I became proficient at thinking fastball and trusting my grip on the splitter, I had my improved weapon and a pitch I could throw as hard as I wanted to throw it. I didn't have to split my fingers wider to try and make it tumble. The splitter had been something that felt completely different from all my other pitches, but after following Craig's advice, I just threw it like a fastball; it felt more comfortable and it started diving.

To start the 1989 season, I had a new toy in the splitter and I was eager to use it. Because I became more comfortable throwing it and had immediate success with it, I never hesitated to use it in games. Being able to use the pitch so confidently was a blessing, but I've seen some pitchers who worked for weeks on a pitch and still lacked the confidence to test it in a game. While the new pitch might not be instantly effective, the only way to cultivate it is by using it, a mental hurdle that pitchers must scale.

Fortunately, I scaled those hurdles with my splitter and my slow curve. Just as fortunately, I never bothered trying to throw a spitter. I was blessed to have some awesome teachers throughout my career, and as I've said, pitchers can learn so much from studying other pitchers and quizzing other pitchers. I never stopped asking questions about pitching. Even as a retired pitcher, I still ask questions about pitching, my mind always willing to add more knowledge about a vocation that has always been my obsession.

Chapter 13

THE YANKEES UNIVERSE:
1995–1997

My RIGHT ARM WAS PLOPPED on the airplane armrest and I couldn't move it, an arm so tired that it felt as if it were glued in that position. This was how worn out I felt on the flight from Seattle to New York after my 147-pitch outing in Game 5 of the 1995 American League Division Series, which I've already described as one of the worst nights in my career. The deadness in my arm should have petrified me, but my whole body was numb and my brain was scrambled, so the arm pain didn't alarm me as much as it should have. I was a major league pitcher and I couldn't even raise my arm, but I was oblivious to it. That's how deflated and defeated I was after this season-ending loss.

In that game against the Mariners, my failure to communicate was remarkable and remarkably reckless. I didn't even look at Manager Buck Showalter in the dugout, refusing to acknowledge the possibility that I might be removed after 130, 135, or 140 pitches. That outing epitomized my blind faith and my refusal to acknowledge anything else that was happening, especially the condition of my sagging arm. I always had the mentality that I could make the baseball move a little more and throw one more clutch pitch to help me get through a tricky situation. While it's a commendable attitude, a pitcher needs to be truthful with himself, too, and he must understand that it's sometimes better for his health and for the team's chances if he gives up the baseball. How does he know that? It comes from experience, instincts, intelligence, and, most of all, honesty.

But I was the pitcher who never wanted to stop pitching. I took that loss in the ALDS extremely hard because I knew how monumental it was in the present and in the future. I knew the 1995 Yankees would probably undergo a makeover after that loss. It pained me to see Showalter sitting in his office with moist eyes, crying the tears of a manager who just watched his season end and who would soon see his nineteen years with the organization end. It was oddly refreshing to see how content Don Mattingly was after hitting .417 in his first postseason appearance, a sign that the great Yankees captain might be ending his career. During the flight home, I made sure to tell catcher Mike Stanley that we shouldn't second-guess our decision to throw a split-finger fastball to Doug Strange. I still think it was the right pitch and it took guts to throw it. I just didn't execute it.

As brave as I tried to sound and seem, I was so drained from that loss that I didn't leave my apartment in Manhattan for about three weeks. It was me, the couch, some takeout food, a small TV, and not much else, my mind wandering back to Seattle and dissecting all 147 pitches. My bases-loaded walk to Strange tied the score in the eighth and we lost to the Mariners, 6–5, in eleven innings.

When Andrew Levy, my friend and business associate, finally persuaded me to get off my couch and walk around Greenwich Village, I was a zombie until I spotted a homeless man who was shouting profanities and causing people to scatter. It seemed like something out of a horror movie with people treating the man like his name was Jason and he was wearing a goalie mask. In my somber mood, I was interested in someone who seemed even more dejected than me. I approached him, he grew silent, and we sat down together on the stairs of a church and each smoked a cigarette. As much as I had tortured myself over a game that ended our season, that encounter reminded me that losing a game isn't as traumatic as what millions of other people endure each day. I could still find some positives about pitching and began thinking about a new season.

With my three-week sulk session over, I needed to figure out where I would be playing in 1996. I was interested in returning to the Yankees, but the Baltimore Orioles and Peter Angelos, their owner, made a very compelling offer of three years and $17.7 million. I respected Angelos for his refusal to field a team of replacement players during the 1995 work stoppage and started to picture myself pitching for the Orioles. As I pondered the Orioles' offer and wondered about the Yankees, the Mets made a late attempt to sign me. Joe McIlvaine, their general manager, visited my apartment at 8 a.m. and offered me three years for about $15 million. It was flattering, but Yankees owner George Steinbrenner, who had recently undergone eye surgery, clinched the deal when he called me from a pay phone outside a hospital in Tampa and offered me a three-year, $19.5 million deal with a no-trade clause. You haven't negotiated a contract until you're listening to Steinbrenner lay out the parameters from a pay phone, with cars beeping and people talking and Steinbrenner's voice outdoing all of those other noises. Steinbrenner was convincing and complimentary and told me how instrumental I could be in helping the Yankees win their first World Series in almost twenty years. I was all in.

After my stint with the Yankees in 1995, Steinbrenner had called me "Mr. Yankee," a lofty title for someone who had made a mere fifteen starts for the organization and a compliment that I didn't take lightly. I enjoyed negotiating with Steinbrenner and I enjoyed playing for Steinbrenner because he was an owner who wanted to win and did whatever he could to put his team in position to win. Was he demanding and blustery? Absolutely. But I enjoyed the pressures of playing for Steinbrenner and playing in New York. I liked being in the Bronx Zoo. To thrive in the Bronx Zoo, I needed to compete my ass off, pitch well, and please Steinbrenner and the fans. I was cool with those expectations.

George wanted to be involved with every aspect of the Yankees, even if that meant he had to take over someone else's job. During the 1997 season, I was in the clubhouse when a Yankees official said, "George is parking cars." I thought it was a joke and I ignored it, but I later found out it was true. Because George's car had been delayed leaving the Stadium parking lot by a major traffic jam the previous night, the owner showed up this day to solve the problem. For almost two hours, Steinbrenner stood at the entrance to the one-hundred-spot parking lot holding a clipboard and matched each approaching car with the reserved spots on his list. It was a stunning sight, but in a small and humorous way, it showed how exacting George could be about his team.

Having lived through those Mets years where I thought we had underachieved, I had no issue with Steinbrenner being so strong-willed. I was demanding, too, and, at the age of thirty-three, I just wanted to get back to the postseason and try to win another ring. With the Yankees' talent and with Steinbrenner's financial might, I thought the Yankees gave me the best chance to do that.

Steinbrenner hired Joe Torre to replace Showalter and, from the first moment I ever interacted with Torre, it was calming. The way that Torre talked to me as an equal and a partner, and the way he treated everyone with respect, showed that he had nothing left to prove and that he was comfortable in his own skin. Torre was very confident without being arrogant, a personality trait that can't be taught. He was a former Most Valuable Player and had an outstanding career, but he didn't disrespect anyone, whether you were the best player on the team or the twenty-fifth man on the roster. Because of the way Torre treated us with respect, he commanded respect. Torre's actions and mannerisms told me he never forgot how difficult it was to play the game, and players appreciated that understanding.

Oh, I was wrong when I said Torre had nothing left to prove. When Joe took over as the Yankees' manager, he had played or managed for thirty-one years and had never been to a World Series, so, yes, he had something to prove. In one of our first spring training meetings in Tampa, Florida, Torre stood in the center of the room and spoke very directly and very confidently about how he viewed our team's future.

"When I look at this team," Torre said, "I see the World Series."

Looking around and spying Paul O'Neill, Bernie Williams, Andy Pettitte, and Jimmy Key, I agreed with him. I was angry about what had happened in 1995, and Torre's words were motivational and realistic. Torre was right and we all knew it. We were all thinking about being champs from the first day of spring training.

Because the Yankees' had reviewed my medical records when they acquired me from the Blue Jays in 1995, they never gave me a physical for the 1996 season. Since Steinbrenner knew I was close to agreeing to a deal with the Orioles, I think the organization wanted to get me signed, sealed, and delivered, and the physical was never scheduled. These days, it would be shocking for a team to sign a player without performing a physical.

As I worked my way through that spring training, something weird happened because my fingers kept falling asleep. I trudged along and never had a great feel for the ball because of the tingling in my fingers. In our season opener against the Cleveland Indians, I pitched seven innings in thirty-eight-degree weather to get the win, but I still couldn't feel my fingers. I was concerned, naturally, but I still wanted to pitch. After being examined by doctors, I ended every conversation by saying, "Can I keep pitching?"

If I had signed with the Orioles, a new team, I'm sure they would have given me a physical. But I'm not sure if the aneurysm would have been discovered, because it would have taken an angiogram to detect it. An angiogram is an X-ray procedure in which dye is injected into the body to make the blood vessels and arteries more visible. Even if the Yankees had given me a physical, there wasn't anything structurally wrong with me, so an MRI wouldn't have found the aneurysm. Unless I had complained about a lack of circulation in my hands, which, at that point, I wasn't, I don't think a routine physical would have uncovered an aneurysm.

Before my second start of the season, my fingernails turned blue, another obvious sign something was wrong. For most of April, my hands were cold and clammy and my fingers were discolored. After two straight sluggish starts in which I had trouble gripping the ball, I agreed to have an angiogram on April 26 and missed my first start in nine seasons. But the test didn't discover the aneurysm. The Yankees put me on heparin, an anti-clotting blood thinner, because they were treating my issue as a local problem in my hand and not as a circulatory problem. I didn't use the blood thinner on the day I pitched. As it turned out, putting me on heparin was a questionable choice, because when I was on blood thinners, that compromised the aneurysm. I literally could have been the pitcher who threw until my arm fell off.

I came back and pitched on May 2 and used a looser grip on my split-finger fastball. That proved beneficial as I threw 127 pitches in beating the Chicago White Sox, 5–1. Interestingly enough, it was my best start of the season. Despite the statistics, my fingers were still numb.

At the insistence of Dr. George Todd, the head of vascular

surgery at Columbia Presbyterian, and Dr. Stuart Hershon, the Yankees' physician, I underwent a second angiogram on May 7. Hershon actually told me he would quit if I didn't get a second angiogram. Todd said I hadn't suffered any trauma in my hand that would cause the tingling and discoloration, so the problem had to stem from somewhere else in the body. On the second angiogram, they discovered the aneurysm underneath my right armpit. Even at that point, even as I learned that I had an aneurysm that could be career threatening, my focus was on whether I could keep pitching. It's only a flesh wound, right? As I noted earlier, the aneurysm stemmed from the stress I endured while throwing pressure-filled pitches year after taxing year.

I was so scared about the unknown, but in a bizarre reaction, I was more angry than relieved that they had found the aneurysm. I wasn't thinking clearly about how this could impact my life and was just pushing forward as the tough-guy pitcher. During this time, Dr. Lawrence Altman, the chief medical correspondent for the *New York Times*, did some thorough reporting in which he asked why the Yankees allowed me to pitch in my condition on May 2. He quoted an unnamed doctor involved in my case who said it was a risky decision to let me pitch and that I could have lost one or more fingers from blood clotting and gangrene by pitching against the White Sox. I didn't want to get into a pissing match with Steinbrenner or the Yankees about what did or didn't happen with my treatment. I was desperate to defend the Yankees because I wanted to pitch.

Did I realize my arm felt irritated in the ALDS game? Sure, I did. But I didn't know how problematic it might have been and it didn't matter anyway. I wanted to keep pitching. In less than seven months, I went from a 147-pitch game that deadened my arm to signing a contract and never receiving a physical to circulation issues to having surgery to remove an aneurysm. Even as my world spun and twisted in some chilling directions, I wanted to continue throwing more pitches. One hundred and forty-eight, one hundred and forty-nine, one hundred and fifty.

On May 10, I had a three-hour surgery to remove the aneurysm and insert a one-inch vein graft from my left leg. As I convalesced at Columbia Presbyterian, I had the New York newspapers scattered across my bed. I was antsy and tense, and I spent hours reading the accounts of my surgery, the potential time line for my return, and what the Yankees were planning to do in my absence. It was depressing, incredibly depressing, to be a pitcher who couldn't pitch anymore. The doctors reassured me and insisted I would pitch again, but this wasn't a sore shoulder or an achy elbow, so I always had lingering doubts about my future.

Four days after my surgery, I lay in bed and listened on the radio as Dwight Gooden, my old pal from the Mets who had replaced me in the rotation, pitched a no-hitter. It was a memorable and emotional night for Gooden, the pitcher who had no-hit stuff with the Mets many a night, but never actually pitched a no-hitter. In his seventh start with the Yankees, Gooden, who missed almost two years because of substance abuse problems, did pitch a no-no. With Gooden's father, Dan, awaiting heart surgery the next day in Florida, Gooden suppressed a Mariners lineup that included Ken Griffey Jr., Edgar Martinez, and Alex Rodriguez. I didn't actually see Doc's pitches that night, but, as the descriptions from announcers John Sterling and Michael Kay emanated from the radio, I imagined the overpowering fastball, the curveball that dropped from a batter's shoulders to his knees, and the more abbreviated delivery that enabled him to release the ball sooner. Gooden silenced many of the same batters who I couldn't defeat while throwing 147 pitches in the previous October.

Through my window on 168th Street, I felt like I could see the blazing lights of Yankee Stadium across the Harlem River. That was how close I was to baseball history. But, man, I was so far away. I had such a conflict of emotions when I listened to Doc's no-hitter. I was so happy for Gooden because of how many potholes he had endured in his life and how he had revived his career. But I was depressed about my situation, and I wondered if I would ever make it back to the mound and ever have the chance to do what Gooden just did. I was an emotional wreck.

The next day, I was back at the Stadium to hold a press conference, and it turned into another emotional experience in which I almost cried a handful of times while trying to guess when I might pitch again. The surgery had sapped me of some mental and physical strength, and it was uncomfortable to not know exactly what the future held. I waited six weeks for the vein graft to heal, but then I picked up a baseball and started my journey back to the majors. Less than four months after the surgery, it felt surreal to be starting against the Athletics in Oakland. I wanted to kiss the mound and kiss the baseball because I wasn't sure this would ever happen again. Not only did it happen, I was rejuvenated and strong, and I tossed seven no-hit innings on an unforgettable and blissful day. It was Labor Day and I was beyond thrilled to be back to work.

Standing on a mound all over again and throwing my pitches all over again was nerve-wracking and exhilarating, which made that the most emotional game I've ever pitched. By far. That return game was more emotional than the perfect game I would pitch in 1999 and more emotional than any World Series game. Why? I think the answer is self-explanatory. That game gave me my pitching life back. Come on, let's be honest. That game gave me my life back. If I hadn't been able to return after the aneurysm, I would have been the most miserable thirty-three-year-old man in New York. And, a year later, I would have been the most miserable thirty-four-year-old, and on and on.

To help erase my doubts, Dr. Todd had told me the vein graft would mesh with the artery and become the artery so I didn't have to worry about causing any damage when I unleashed the baseball. Instead of the vein graft being the equivalent of a patch on a bike tire, it had now become part of the tire. In the back of my mind, I had wondered if I threw a fastball and really let it loose, would anything happen? But Dr. Todd's analogy was sensible; I trusted all my doctors, and I trusted the way I felt. The baseball was zooming out of my hand because my arm was rested and refreshed, so I was cautiously confident I could be successful again. Before going on the disabled list, I had led the American League with a 2.02 earned run average.

Under the heading of "Ominous Beginnings," the first five pitches I threw were balls, and I walked two batters in the first inning. But, after that, I was almost pitching on autopilot because I had so much adrenaline and all four of my pitches were no longer in hibernation. My fastball was lively, my splitter and my slider were both darting, and my curveball was dancing. That caused Mark McGwire to say, "It doesn't take a rocket scientist to figure out how he was throwing. The guy threw great. Period."

Perched behind the first base dugout during that game was a familiar and friendly face: my father. He wanted to surprise me by flying from Kansas City to Oakland to witness my return start, but I found out about his plans the night before the game. My first pitching coach wanted to see how I would perform after a trying layoff. I was so stunned and so thankful that I could experience a day like that again, and I was so thrilled that my father witnessed it. It might sound corny, but I had never made eye contact with my dad during a major league game because the family seats weren't typically in my line of sight and because I was so obsessed with what I was doing. But, on this tense day, I looked for my dad often, and it was relaxing to see him. Every time I finished an inning,

I looked behind the dugout and thought, *Oh, yeah, there's my old man sitting behind the dugout*, as if it were a Little League game in Kansas City.

As the innings piled up and I didn't allow any hits, I knew that Torre would be faced with a formidable decision. No sane manager would tax a pitcher who had just undergone surgery to remove an aneurysm, even if that pitcher was tossing a no-hitter. I tried to make it easy on Torre and told him my preference would be to stay in the game, but he had to make the choice that was best for me and best for the team. Having pitched three one-hitters at that point in my career, I knew how the stress mounted during the final outs of a no-hit bid, and I didn't know if my arm was ready for that challenge. Torre removed me after I had thrown eighty-five pitches in seven innings, and I didn't argue. I was happy, so damn happy. I remember asking myself, *Did I just do that?* I wasn't sad about losing the chance for a no-hitter. However, I was delirious about returning to the majors and being part of that drama, even if that drama faded to black six outs shy of a no-hitter.

"If they had left the decision up to David," my dad said, "they would have needed a tractor to get him out of there."

Of course, my father was right. Mariano Rivera gave up a one-out single to José Herrera in the ninth, so we combined on a one-hitter. Afterward, Girardi told me he was impressed with how I didn't fight to stay in the game. It wasn't about the individual. It was about the team.

"One game that sticks out to me the most was when he came back from his aneurysm and realized the prize was in October, not the no-hitter that day," Girardi later said. "That is David to a tee. David was about winning championships, not individual achievements."

Do you know who else was all about winning championships? A

player named Derek Jeter. By September, it was clear that Steinbrenner was right when he said in spring training that Jeter was going to be "a special one." Believe it or not, Jeter was one of the unknowns heading into the 1996 season, and the Yankees almost made a trade for a veteran shortstop. But there were enough powerful voices, like Torre and team executive Gene Michael, imploring the team to stick with Jeter and let him blossom. He was twenty-one and there were bound to be some growing pains, but those growing pains didn't last too long.

I've already detailed how Jeter blasted a homer off Dennis Martinez and made a sweet over-the-shoulder catch in our 1996 season opener in chilly Cleveland, a little flash and a little style in one of his first big moments on the baseball stage. I won the game, but I wanted to talk about the new kid with the fade haircut, the extra energy in his step, and the quiet confidence. With Steinbrenner as an unrelenting owner, I actually think it was important for Jeter to have a superb debut like that. Listen, I know it was one game out of a 162-game season, but it was still meaningful, and honestly, Jeter showed us that day the type of player he would be for his entire career. He showed up with a moxie and a relentless nature that rookies rarely have, and he remained that way for two decades.

I never thought Jeter looked overmatched. His confidence was overflowing. If Jeter was 0 for 19 against Randy Johnson, he would still perform his quirky habit of kicking the bat with both feet as he walked briskly to plate and then he would settle in against one of the greatest pitchers of our generation and truly believe he was going to get a hit in the twentieth at bat.

Before games, Jeter had a routine in which he would play long-toss with a teammate on the field. Jeter would stand in foul territory near home plate while the teammate would position himself in shallow right field, about 180 feet away. As Jeter flung the ball, he would always scream some fake scream and act as if his body was creaking and cracking. But, beyond the histrionics, I watched Jeter talk to reporters, team officials, and opponents, and never stray from his routine of tossing and catching and tossing some more. If I had a video of Jeter doing this, it would be impossible to tell if we were about to play a meaningless game in May or a postseason game in October. That was how comfortable Jeter always looked. That's an amazing approach and is probably why Jeter's regular season and postseason numbers were so similar. Big games didn't faze him. About a month into the 1996 season, I had seen enough of Jeter to believe he would be a perennial All-Star and, if he stayed healthy, even better than that. Jeter stayed healthy and he will go to the Hall of Fame.

As someone who had enough off-the-field issues in New York to teach a college course about them, I was impressed with the way Jeter avoided the temptations and distractions that exist in New York. The friends who knew the young Jeter have said he matured early and was acting like a twenty-one-year-old by the time he was fifteen. Anytime a pro athlete was involved in an embarrassing incident, Dr. Charles Jeter would call his son, and they would speak about what had happened and how it could have been avoided. It was the father's way of reminding the son that every action has consequences. That helps explain why Derek was never big on partying and was savvy enough to stay out of the limelight and avoid trouble. If I saw Derek with a drink, it was usually something like a Malibu-type drink with a pineapple in it, and it was the only one he had all night. As wildly popular as Derek was, it was almost as if the matinee idol looks and the superstardom really didn't suit his modest personality. He really didn't like that look-at-me part of being an elite player, and he hated talking about himself. Derek was clearly driven to succeed on the field and wasn't like the party animals we had on the late 1980s Mets. In fact, he was the opposite of that.

On the field, Jeter was the best player I've ever seen at being able to turn the page on what happened today, good or bad, and focus on tomorrow. A lot of players talk about doing that, but the poor performances and the losses consume them. Jeter didn't just say he was looking ahead. He really lived his life that way. Whether Jeter went 0 for 5 or had four hits, I typically saw him strolling out of the clubhouse with the same exact look on his face while chirping at a teammate like Jorge Posada or Tino Martinez and eating an ice cream bar.

In a sloppy first inning, Jeter bounced a throw home to allow the first run to score as the Angels blitzed us for seven runs in the frame on the way to a 12–4 win in August 1997. It was one game in August, one anonymous loss. But Jeter's error had opened the door to a huge inning. I had just been placed on the disabled list with shoulder tendinitis, so I didn't think much about the error. No one did because errors happen. Jeter spoke about the error and quickly forgot about the mistake and then he made sure everyone else did, too. He smacked eight hits and helped us win the next three games, turning the page on that throwing error as swiftly as he could.

On a much bigger stage, Jeter struck out against Armando Benitez with a runner on base in the ninth inning of Game 3 of the 2000 World Series, and we lost to the Mets, 4–2. If Jeter had managed to get on base in that at bat, maybe we would have rallied and won that game. Who knows? Again, I didn't overanalyze the situation. Neither did Jeter. He just turned the page by homering on the first pitch from Bobby Jones in the next game, an emphatic shot that carried over the left field fence. The Mets would have tied the best-of-seven series if they had won Game 4 at Shea Stadium, but Jeter ruined whatever momentum they had one pitch into the game. Forget about today and focus on tomorrow. That was Jeter's mantra. We won that game and we prevailed in Game 5 to win the title in the Subway Series.

The man who became the Yankees' captain in 2003 had leadership skills, too, skills that I initially overlooked. When I walked Strange and was replaced in Game 5 of the 1995 ALDS, the first person who emerged from the dugout to shake my hand was Jeter. He wasn't officially on the roster, but he traveled with us for that postseason. He was twenty-one years old and he had the presence of mind to try and console me after that devastating pitch. The dugouts at the Kingdome were even with the playing surface, so I was looking down because I didn't have to walk down any steps. I blew Jeter off and bolted past him, not even knowing it was him until much later. With the benefit of hindsight, I now see it was a sign of who he was to become.

Jeter had a mischievous side to his personality that usually came out when he was chilling out with close friends like Posada, Gerald Williams, and Tim Raines. Raines and Jeter had lockers next to each other, and their comical banter could have made them sitcom stars. Since Raines was fifteen years older than Jeter, he acted like the older brother, and he would teasingly scold Jeter for silly things.

"Get all that fan mail away from my locker," Raines would say. "That's too close to my locker."

Jeter would respond by saying, "Leave my mail alone and stop taking stuff out of my locker."

Inevitably and often, Raines would laugh, and he had a high-pitched cackle that would fill the clubhouse. No matter what I was doing, I always looked over at the two of them when Raines started to cackle. Raines loved to tease Jeter about everything. Listen, I'm no fashion expert, but there was one period where Jeter was wearing some boxy, ill-fitting suits and Raines would playfully evaluate every suit he wore.

"You're going to wear that on the plane?" Raines would say.

After I left the Yankees, I was victimized by Jeter's playful side.

In my second start with the Red Sox in 2001, I faced the Yankees at the Stadium. As Jeter strolled to the plate, I kept my head down because I didn't even want to look at him. We were friends and I didn't want to make eye contact. But Jeter wouldn't step into the batter's box until I looked at him. When I finally did, Jeter made a goofy expression that a ten-year-old might make as he's trying to tease his five-year-old brother. I tried not to laugh, but it distracted me and I lost my game face. I threw a fastball up and in, and Jeter used that inside-out swing of his to rap a double to right field. He had three hits off me that day and went 5 for 5.

The next time I faced the Yankees at Fenway Park, I was plotting my revenge against Jeter. This ended up being the game where Mike Mussina came within one strike of a perfect game before losing it on Carl Everett's single. Still, the score was tied 0–0 when Jeter batted with a man on base in the eighth. I whiffed him on three pitches as he took a wild swing at my Frisbee-like slider for strike three. Jeter glanced at me after the strikeout, and I made that same goofy face that he had made to me a few months earlier.

So much of 1996 was about Torre and Jeter because it was their first year together and they were the catalysts for what we did that season. It was the soothing manager and the rookie shortstop, two total professionals, who guided us that season and became the linchpins of a dynastic run that would include four championships in a five-year span.

To me, the most emotional part of that 1996 season for Torre was simply getting to the World Series, a hallowed place that he had never participated in during more than 4,200 games as a player and a manager. Torre's brother, Rocco, had passed away during the season and Frank, his other brother, needed a heart transplant as we pursued a championship in October.

After we clinched the ALCS in Baltimore, I remember Torre's face was a blend of relief, excitement, and bewilderment because he was going to a series that he had only heard others discuss. I ambled up to Joe in the visitors' clubhouse at Camden Yards, gave him a hug, and shouted, "You made it. You made it." Torre buried his head in my shoulder, his body shaking. Joe was the type who would cry in emotional moments, but these were different tears. These were powerful tears, the kind that rushed forward after more than thirty years without a date for the greatest event in October. Torre said he never watched teams celebrate winning a championship because "it was like watching someone else eating a hot fudge sundae." Now Joe finally had his own sundae, and we made sure it was a tasty experience by winning the last four games of the series to defeat the Atlanta Braves in six games.

I actually remember that exchange with Torre as much as I remember our 1996 celebration at the Stadium. Of course, I remember everything about winning it all. I remember Charlie Hayes catching Mark Lemke's pop out in foul territory. I remember Paul O'Neill dashing in from right field and diving into a pile of players on the mound. I remember Wade Boggs jumping on the back of a mounted horse and allowing a police officer to trot him around the Stadium. I remember Steinbrenner getting sprayed with champagne. I remember Torre leading a victory lap around the field. But Torre was so emotional about just getting here that the scene in Baltimore is as vivid for me as the winning celebration in the Bronx.

One of the main reasons we all celebrated was because of Bernie Williams, one of my favorite teammates and a player who doesn't get enough credit for his achievements in Yankees history. "The Core Four" is a catchy nickname, and it's a clever way to honor what Jeter, Rivera, Posada, and Pettitte did during their careers, but the nickname annoys me because it excludes Bernie.

We should hit the delete button on that nickname and switch to "Fab Five" or something like that. Williams preceded all those players and paved the way for them by enduring some difficult experiences.

Because Bernie looked like a wobbly giraffe when he started and later developed into an All-Star center fielder and a batting champion, I think the Yankees were more patient with the players who followed him. He debuted with the Yankees when they were one of the worst teams in baseball in 1991, and he had to deal with malcontents like Mel Hall hazing him and calling him "Bambi" because he was quiet, kept to himself, and wore gold-framed glasses like an accountant. (That treatment wasn't as prevalent by the time Jeter was a starter in 1996, and that was why he had it easier than Bernie ever did. Like I said, we didn't want to bully talented players like Jeter. We wanted them to help us win.)

As a switch-hitter who had power and who had a strong command of the strike zone, Williams was a nightmare for teams to match up against in the late innings. In typical under-the-radar fashion, one of Williams's earliest classic moments came in a game that is most remembered for what an overzealous twelve-year-old kid did to help us. Jeffrey Maier reached over the right field fence to interfere with Jeter's fly ball in the eighth inning of Game 1 of the 1996 ALCS. Baltimore's Tony Tarasco was camped under the ball, but Maier helped scoop it into the stands and it was ruled a game-tying homer.

Three innings later, Williams faced Randy Myers, a left-handed closer with an explosive fastball and a hard-breaking slider. Williams was a better right-handed hitter, but Manager Davey Johnson decided to stay with the lefty. I'm sure Johnson didn't love that matchup. A few seconds later, he definitely hated it as Williams crushed a 1-1 slider for a game-winning homer in the eleventh inning. I can still picture Bernie looking back at us and gliding, almost dancing, as he moved around the bases. Afterward Williams, whose heroics were dwarfed by the attention Maier received, said he was "like a surfer" who was just "riding the wave." Bernie surfed through the ALCS and was named the MVP.

Bernie was an intelligent player who received unfair criticism during his career for being aloof and being an airhead. That was false. Bernie was a deep thinker, and he also understood that a blank slate worked better for him than overanalyzing each situation. Williams was the type of hitter who believed in recognizing the spin on the baseball and then hitting the ball, not spending a lot of time studying scouting reports. I thought there was some genius in that approach because it worked for Williams.

Some old-school baseball personnel criticized Williams because they didn't see him as a gym rat or a baseball nerd or someone who thought about baseball 24/7. Bernie was the opposite of that and played baseball and the guitar to his own beat, but that beat worked for him because he was so unflappable and so consistent in his daily routines.

In a game against the A's in 1999, Bernie did something I had never seen a player do, maybe something only Bernie could do. With the bases loaded, Mike Oquist threw him a pitch that tailed out of the strike zone, and Bernie promptly started to go to first base because he thought he had walked. There was one slight problem: That was only the third ball of the at bat. Bernie retreated back to the plate, and we all laughed at Bernie's gaffe and thought it was a typical Bernie moment. Well, guess what else was a typical Bernie moment? He hammered the 3-2 pitch for a grand slam and we won, 12–8. Like I said, Williams never got unsettled at the plate, even after he thought the at bat was over. He just turned around, stayed in his zone of Zen, and bashed a homer.

When Bernie's career is evaluated, it's a borderline Hall of Fame career, but there are still people who want to say he was detached and "out there." Even Torre used to playfully say that about Bernie, but I thought it was an unfair assessment. Bernie was all there, not out there. He was simply true to his style, and that was a simple style.

I once asked Bernie what he thought of when he walked to the plate and he said, "Nothing." It was a perfect answer. It was the same way that I wanted to be in the final hour before a start. I wanted my mind to be uncluttered. As accomplished as Bernie is as a guitarist (he's been nominated for a Latin Grammy Award), he sometimes preferred to have no walk-up music. Bernie, who once played his guitar in the clubhouse as Paul Simon smiled and bobbed his head, preferred the sounds of silence.

During my time with the Yankees, one of the most dubious moves they ever considered was essentially replacing Bernie with Albert Belle. Bernie was a free agent after the 1998 season, and he was negotiating with the Yankees and the Red Sox. At one point, it looked as if the Red Sox were going to sign Williams to a $90 million contract while the Yankees, who had offered considerably less, were going to pivot and pursue Belle.

When Torre mentioned the flirtation with Belle to me, I gave him a dumbfounded look. Before I could speak, he said, "You don't like it, do you?" I hated it. Torre thought the strong chemistry among the players in our clubhouse would have helped us absorb Belle, a cranky character who was also a great hitter. I wasn't sure about that. I despised the idea of losing Bernie, an elegant player who had succeeded in New York, for Belle, a surly player who detested the news media and who would have been a target in New York. It would have been a colossal mistake to lose Williams, and I'm glad the Yankees didn't let it happen. Steinbrenner intervened and signed the player who had been a Yankee since he was a teenager to a seven-year, $87.5 million deal.

I will write much more about my famous nose-to-nose meeting

with Torre during the sixth inning of Game 3 of the 1996 World Series in a subsequent chapter. But that was a game where Torre wondered if I had enough ammunition left in my arm to retire Fred McGriff, and I absolutely refused to let him replace me. I hadn't felt any pain since the aneurysm surgery earlier that year, so it was just a matter of how far I could extend myself in a game. Even after an injury that could have ended my career, I still had that "go until you blow" mentality. I didn't want to be labeled as a "five and fly" pitcher, meaning a pitcher who would pitch the fewest innings to qualify for a win and then disappear. I never wanted to wear that scarlet letter, even for one game. What was I supposed to say to Torre—"You'd better get Graeme Lloyd in here"? I couldn't allow those words to come trickling out of my mouth. The way I had been trained as a pitcher was to believe I could get McGriff out, telling myself, *Of course I can do this.* My mind was formulating a plan of attack as opposed to telling Torre, "I'm a little tired. I don't think I can do this." I retired McGriff and made it through the inning with a one-run lead. We won that game, and I think it really tilted the series in our direction.

"I trust him," Torre said about me after the game. "Whatever the result, I trust him. I know he's going to go out there and not be afraid of the challenge."

Anyone who watched the Yankees during that 1996 season saw a stoic Torre in the dugout and also saw a Popeye look-alike named Don Zimmer pinned by his side. Zimmer was a baseball lifer with more than four decades of experience when he was hired as Torre's bench coach, and the two of them formed a successful brain trust. Zimmer was a riverboat gambler, a man who compelled Torre to take some extra risks and try some daring strategies.

Zimmer loved to take chances and bend the game in a different direction. When he was managing the Cubs and I was pitching for the Mets in 1988, Zimmer actually called for a hit-and-run with the bases loaded and Ryne Sandberg batting. Yes, with the bases loaded. Sandberg fouled off four straight pitches during the at bat and the nervous base runner on third had to peel off toward the dugout because he was worried about being drilled with a line drive. I don't recall if the hit-and-run was on for every foul ball Sandberg hit, but Sandberg eventually grounded out. Years later I asked Zimmer about this rare and risky strategy, and he said he was trying to apply some pressure on me by putting the runners in motion.

"Did you feel pressure?" he asked.

I told Zimmer, "Yes, I did. You were right. I did feel pressure. It made me nervous out there. It was definitely a distraction."

While Zimmer was Torre's confidant and was serious about every pitch and every decision, he was a joy to be around. Zimmer was thirty-two years older than me, but that gap didn't matter because he was such a funny and engaging guy. I started a routine with Zimmer in which I would ask him how he thought I should pitch to a particular team. Zimmer would stare at me as if I had just asked him to paint my house and tell me he didn't want to discuss strategies. "I don't care how you get them out," he would say. "Just get them out." Then I would continue to pester Zimmer by showing him the grip on my slider and asking him what he thought about my pitch selection. Feigning aggravation with me, Zimmer would say, "I don't care how you hold the damn ball. Just get them out." That was our running joke, but it led to a resilient attitude. Basically, Zimmer was telling me to figure out what works and just do it. There wasn't one specific style that was always going to work, and whether Zimmer meant to do it or not, he was reminding me of that.

As someone who appreciated baseball history, I quizzed Zimmer about his career and what it was like to be Jackie Robinson's teammate. I loved hearing about those old Brooklyn Dodgers teams and what New York was like at that time. When the movie 42 came out in 2013, depicting how poorly Robinson had been treated after he broke the color barrier in 1947, I asked Zimmer how accurate it was. Zimmer, who became Robinson's teammate seven years later, bowed his head, then looked up at me and said, "It was worse. It was a lot worse for Jackie than what the movie showed." More than half a century later, there was still some sadness in Zimmer's voice.

With a World Series trophy secured in 1996, we all thought we could repeat as champions again in 1997. Since John Wetteland left as a free agent, Rivera, the superb setup man, became our closer. I never doubted that Rivera would thrive, even after he blew two of his first four save chances and seemed distraught. After I pitched seven scoreless innings against Oakland in April, McGwire bashed a 464-foot homer off Rivera to tie the score, 1–1, in the ninth. In the postgame session with reporters, a sullen Rivera said he was going to act as if the ninth inning was the sixth or seventh because that would help relax him. That was an example of Rivera tricking his mind, the mind game I had adopted from Jack Morris. I told Rivera to take a deep breath and added, "I want you in my games." And I always did.

Soon after those early mishaps, Rivera evolved into a very relaxed closer and, I think, the greatest of all time. Rivera had an unbelievable calmness about his persona, both on and off the mound, and that one instance with McGwire in 1996 was the only time I ever saw him rattled. He was diligent about his routine, and no one ever tried to disrupt it. He would hang out in the clubhouse and likely get a massage for the first few innings, then retreat to the bullpen by the fifth or sixth inning, and then he would come into the game and dominate batters with his cutter. He was a machine.

I know only one pitcher who didn't need to search for a second pitch for most of his career and, of course, that was Mariano. I know there are other pitchers who made great discoveries with pitches, but the most incredible discovery of a new pitch might have occurred during a throwing session between Rivera and Ramiro Mendoza in June 1997. Both sons of Panama, the dignified Rivera and the silent Mendoza played catch before games, the baseballs soaring across the freshly trimmed grass.

Mendoza was so reserved that he sometimes slept in his locker stall, with clothes dangling from hangers to shield him from the light. But, on this day, Mendoza was perturbed because Rivera's throws were darting so much that it was difficult for Mendoza to catch them. Mendoza thought Rivera was toying with him and was purposely trying to make every pitch an adventure, so he yelled for Rivera to stop doing it.

But a just-as-puzzled Rivera insisted that he was trying to throw his four-seam fastball straight and the ball was zigging and zagging, a late and severe movement that handcuffed Mendoza. Initially, Rivera tried to regain his regular four-seamer and eliminate the cutting action on his new pitch, but after a few attempts, he and pitching coach Mel Stottlemyre agreed that he should keep throwing the ball in the exact same way. It was the savviest decision either of them ever made.

For the cutter, Rivera placed his middle and index finger on the horseshoe seams of the baseball and kept his thumb underneath it, almost identical to his four-seam fastball grip. Some pitchers put their thumb on the side of the ball when throwing a cutter because that gives them more movement.

Because Rivera used his four-seam grip and threw the cutter so naturally, he was able to throw the pitch as hard as his fastball and still get the pitch to move considerably. There are a lot of pitchers who have very good cutters, but they can't throw them with the same velocity as their fastballs. Pitch after pitch, Rivera's cutter had imposing velocity and magnificent movement, which was what made it so devastating.

From the randomness of one game of catch with Mendoza in 1997, Rivera inadvertently altered his career and, really, impacted dozens of careers and an organization's path as he and his miraculous cutter helped guide the Yankees to four more World Series titles. Without the discovery of that cutter, Rivera would have still been an outstanding pitcher, but with the tremendous cutter, he seemed invincible.

As Rivera's teammate, I don't remember witnessing the specific day he actually discovered the cutter, but I watched the evolution of that mesmerizing pitch. At first, I was skeptical about how long Rivera could use the cutter in each outing before batters adjusted to it, speculating he could subsist with that pitch for one inning at a time. And then Rivera started to break bats with the cutter and infuriate batters with the cutter, and it became evident how dominant he could be, inning after inning.

Because Rivera's cutter moved from right to left and zoomed in on a left-handed batter's hands like a miniature chainsaw, I wondered what would happen if some batters backed up from the plate a few inches to try and counter the movement of the pitch. Could some batters do that and give themselves more room on the inside corner because they knew that cutter was coming?

But, everyone soon discovered, batters couldn't do that to Rivera because, as I said, Rivera threw his cutter like a fastball, an imposing fastball. Rivera was the first pitcher I ever saw who threw a 95-mile-per-hour cutter, preventing batters from inching away from the plate and trying to sneak-attack him. The cutter retained its velocity, and the movement occurred so late that lefties, even when they were poised for it, couldn't unleash their swings fast enough to get to the pitch and hit it with any authority. They weren't sure if it was a fastball or a cutter because the ball traveled so close to the plate, probably within a few feet, before moving dramatically.

Rivera had impeccable control with his cutter, a pitch that was born from a simple, repeatable delivery, and could pinpoint it on the inside corner, then throw it two inches more inside or four inches more inside, something that also stymied the batters who tried outwitting him by backing off the plate. Occasionally, a lefty batter might speed up his swing and drill Rivera's cutter down the right field line, but even doing that was a rarity because it was difficult for the hitter to keep the ball fair. Rivera's cutter dominated the corners, keeping the ball away from the middle of the plate, the most dangerous place to pitch. He was the coolest customer and the most efficient pitcher I've ever seen.

To watch Mariano evolve as a pitcher was a thing of beauty. When he was a setup man in 1996, he threw a lot of high fastballs that jumped, and he also threw some sliders. But once he discovered that cutter and worked both sides of the plate with it, it was remarkable to see what he could do with one pitch. Batters knew what was coming and they still couldn't come close to hitting it. And Mariano was defiant. I mentioned to Rivera that he had a good changeup and could implement that into his repertoire, and I don't think he even heard me. He had a cutter, and that cutter guided him to the first unanimous election to the Hall of Fame. His defiance about using that pitch was impressive.

Unfortunately, my 1997 was impacted by an injury. Again. I had a problematic shoulder late in the season, but I wanted to keep pitching. What a shock, right? I was pitching against the Texas Rangers at the Stadium in the middle of August and my arm was in agonizing pain. But again, I was conditioned to say, "I'm OK," and keep pitching. I retreated to the clubhouse and used a resistance band to stretch out my shoulder and try to eliminate the tightness. I always remembered those veteran pitchers who told me I should keep pitching unless I couldn't throw the ball over the plate. And that actually happened in that game. I walked out to the mound for the second inning and I literally couldn't throw my warm-up pitches to the plate. Everything was bouncing in front of the plate. It took that much for me to finally say *"no mas,"* leave the game, and go on the disabled list.

I returned and pitched decently in September, and Torre asked me if I was OK to pitch Games 1 and 5 against the Indians in the American League Division Series. I had my doubts about whether I would be strong enough to do it, but I told Joe I would be ready. I was torched for six runs and didn't last four innings in the opening game of the series. During a bullpen session between starts, I heard a *pop, pop, pop* in my shoulder while warming up and knew my season was probably over. I couldn't lift my arm at that point, so I was done for the series. Once again, I had that mentality to keep pitching until I heard a *pop, pop, pop*. In retrospect, I believe there has to be a better balance. I still think pitchers need to push themselves to find out how deep they can extend themselves. In some ways, I think today's pitchers are too coddled. But I also know my bullish way and my mentality were detrimental to my career at times. I had shoulder surgery after the season, my second surgery in a year and a half.

We were four outs away from beating the Indians in the ALDS when Sandy Alomar Jr. hit a shocking homer off Rivera's 2-0 fastball to tie Game 4 in the eighth inning. Even then, it was startling to see the mighty Rivera surrender such a critical hit. The Indians scored another run in the ninth to win the game and beat us by one run in Game 5. O'Neill doubled with two outs in the ninth inning in the decisive game, barely making it to second with a lunging and sprawling slide to the outside part of the base. I think that awkward slide helped him earn Steinbrenner's nickname of "the Warrior." Anyway, we couldn't deliver the tying run and lost the series.

That loss to the Indians was numbing. We were the defending champions and I thought we were just as good as the 1996 team, if not better, but our season ended so abruptly and so harshly. The clubhouse was like a morgue. It was so silent, eerily silent. Even after the worst of losses, I've seen weary, angry players grab a plate of food and begin to eat, so you at least hear the utensils clinking against the plates. But no one ate. We were all too startled. In less than twelve months, we went from delirious champions to a first-round exit.

Shortly after the game, Torre left the visiting manager's office at Jacobs Field and made the short walk into the adjacent clubhouse. Joe's eyes moved from locker to locker, seemingly making sure we were all there. When Joe realized everyone was at their lockers, he took a chair, placed it in the middle of the room, and sat down. I was waiting for Torre to say something, anything, about what had just happened. He didn't speak. One minute passed, then two, then five, then ten, and then fifteen. Those fifteen minutes felt like an hour to me as we all looked at Joe and waited. Joe didn't say a word. He just sat there and stared at us.

Eventually, Joe stood up and went to every player and hugged him and whispered a thank-you. That was Joe's team meeting after a devastating loss, and it was one of the most powerful team meetings I've ever witnessed. I just sat there and thought, *Wow*. That display, a silent display, reiterated to me how special Torre was as a manager and as a leader.

As we sat there together, our brains probably all focused on the last inning or the last nine innings or maybe the last five games, I thought Torre's actions were the equivalent of a funeral in which we were all saying good-bye to the 1997 season. Joe didn't say anything, but he didn't have to say anything. We were all smart enough to figure out what Joe was telling us, which was something like this: *You know what? We won it all in 1996 and that was tremendous. We just lost a heart-wrenching game and our season is over. But I want you to know I'm thankful for the season we had and I'm thankful for each and every one of you.*

More than two decades later, I can still see Joe sitting there, the pain on his weary and weathered face as overpowering as the silence in the room. I knew why he sat there in silence with us. We all knew why he did it. It was Torre's way to eulogize the season, and it was one of the classiest managerial moves I've ever seen.

Chapter 14

LIFE IN YANKEELAND: 1998–2000

I WAS SO EAGER AND SO excited about getting back on the mound again in 1998, but I wasn't even sure I would start the season in the rotation because I was still rehabilitating from the shoulder surgery I had in October. When Manager Joe Torre hinted he wasn't expecting me to pitch until about May, I knew that he was just trying to reduce the pressure on me. But of course, I'm a maniacal pitcher, so Torre's comments actually increased the pressure and motivated me to make the Opening Day roster. And I did. I was hoping this would be a special season for the Yankees, and I wanted to relish every inning of it.

It didn't start out too special. We were bitter about the way our 1997 season ended, and there was a recurring theme, sometimes spoken and sometimes unspoken, about how we needed to erase those annoying feelings with a daily commitment to excellence. We had a powerful lineup featuring Jeter, Bernie, O'Neill, and Tino, a stacked rotation with me, Pettitte, Wells, and, by June, a mystery man named El Duque, and a strong bullpen headlined by the invincible Mariano. So I was confident we would be serious contenders for another title. And then we started the season 1-4 and suddenly everything seemed to be in disarray.

Five games is 3 percent of a 162-game season, but in a Yankees universe where owner George Steinbrenner hated to lose spring training games to the Mets or the Red Sox, it was a fiasco of a start. Obviously, that season climaxed with an unprecedented 125 wins and a World Series championship, so to some, it may seem ludicrous to suggest that we had much adversity, but we did. We had adversity in the first week of the season, with Torre's job security even being questioned by some reporters. Would Steinbrenner really fire him if we continued to sputter? I wasn't the only player who was uneasy about hearing that question.

As we were plodding through this season-opening West Coast trip, Torre was concerned enough to have a team meeting before our sixth game of the season. I'm glad we had it. With everyone congregated in the clubhouse at the Kingdome in Seattle, I was searching for a way to motivate us, so I stole a quotation from Dave Parker, a former MVP and an all-around bad dude. I had heard Parker say that players should find something they hate about their opponents because that will make them perform better. I think that's especially true when a team is struggling because some anger can be helpful in getting a team ready to, well, kick someone's ass. We were overdue to kick someone's ass.

"Did you guys see Edgar Martinez swing from his heels at a 3-0 pitch last night?" I barked. "I didn't like that. None of us should like that. Let's make sure we let him know we weren't happy with that. If we have to knock guys down to get the message across, let's do it. We need to have some dirt dog in us."

With each explosive word I spewed, Darryl Strawberry nodded his head in agreement. Strawberry was a bouncer on every team he ever played on, so it wasn't shocking that he was aligned with what I was saying. He probably wanted to immediately confront Martinez over the fact that he fouled off a 3-0 pitch with a 4–0 lead in the fifth inning. Was that a major baseball transgression? No, but

I wanted our players to be angry and I wanted to create some hate and adrenaline.

In that same game, the soft-tossing Jamie Moyer drilled Paul O'Neill with a high-and-tight pitch that glanced off his wrist and could have hit him in the face. Moyer quickly apologized, but we were annoyed because Lou Piniella, the Mariners' manager and O'Neill's former manager with the Cincinnati Reds, had previously targeted O'Neill with inside pitches. During my spiel, I noticed that Andy Pettitte had a deer-in-the-headlights look because he hadn't retaliated for O'Neill being plunked. Pettitte did ask O'Neill during the game if he thought Moyer had intentionally hit him and O'Neill said no, so my words weren't directed at Pettitte. They were directed at all of us. I wanted to give our entire roster a collective smack in the face.

I'm not naïve enough to think that a team meeting is ever going to magically lead to a win, but I believe in chemistry and emotion and how they can contribute to a team's success. As much as I embrace sabermetrics and the analytical side of the game, I also know there are human beings, not robots, who are throwing the baseballs and swinging at the pitches. Some players have told me they performed better when they were mad. When I was pitching, I didn't necessarily despise batters because I was trying to maintain a level of emotional stability and stay focused. Still, for that moment, I thought it was wise to instruct our players to hate Edgar. It couldn't hurt, could it?

Chuck Knoblauch opened the game with a homer that night, and we steadied ourselves and then we soared. We beat the Mariners in the next 2 games, we won 8 straight, then 22 of our next 24, and an astounding 64 of our next 80 games, as it became increasingly evident that something special was brewing with our team. We were a team of destiny, and I was elated to be a part of it.

For a passing moment or two, I almost wasn't part of it. After two lousy starts to start the season and the distressing news that my mother had a tumor in her lungs, I briefly wondered if I should retire. But that foolish notion vanished after my mother had successful surgery to remove the tumor and I regrouped and pitched much better. Suddenly, I was in a better mental place. And who would have wanted to retire from this deep and well-rounded team? We were potent; we knew it, and opponents knew it. I was a student at analyzing the body language of players, and there were numerous games in which I saw pitchers panic after we scored some early runs because they didn't think they could rebound and defeat the mighty Yankees. We were gentlemanly bullies, if there is such a thing, and we wanted to annihilate teams that season.

Every time I think about our 1-4 start and the silly speculation about Torre's job, I also think about how we were almost involved in a serious bus accident before we ever played one inning. Prior to our season opener against the Angels in Anaheim, we made a pit stop in Tijuana, Mexico, for an exhibition game against San Diego State. We were using a European plane that wasn't permitted to make two consecutive stops in American cities. Since the 747 had picked us up in Tampa, it couldn't fly directly to San Diego. The plan was to land in Tijuana and take a bus to San Diego.

As our bus departed from the airport, the United States–Mexico border was about two hundred yards in front of us. There were cement barriers lining the exit and our bus driver made a faulty turn and ended up driving on top of the two-foot barrier. All of a sudden, two wheels of the bus were on top of the barrier and two wheels were on the street and it felt as if our bus was a few seconds away from toppling over and landing on the passenger side, the side where I was sitting. Jeff Nelson was bracing for David Wells to come tumbling across the aisle and land on him. I was sitting next to Hideki Irabu and he panicked as the bus teetered and seemed to be about halfway toward crashing into the pavement. It was a harrowing experience, and I thought the Yankees, the team with a $63 million payroll, were a few seconds away from having some well-compensated arms, legs, and bodies incurring some serious injuries.

Somehow, the driver made a quick recovery and the bus landed with a thud, but it also landed on four wheels and didn't tip over. As soon as the driver righted the bus, everyone was screaming at him and questioning how he could make such a mistake. He was so rattled that he stopped the bus in the middle of the street. The poor guy looked like he had seen a ghost. Within a few seconds, every player and every coach barged off the bus. We all retrieved our luggage from underneath the bus and walked the rest of the way to the border. Just about every face was sweating. Just about every mouth was cursing.

By the time everyone cleared customs, we had a chance to exhale and regain some of our composure. We all boarded the same bus and we were driven to the team hotel, without any further incidents. I've been on hundreds of buses, trains, and planes in my career, but that experience, though brief, was one of the scariest.

And that was the beginning of the season. And that happened before we started 1-4. I thought we were cursed. But it turned out we were blessed.

On a team oozing with talent and confidence, I was a starting pitcher, and I was also a pitcher's keeper because I spent a lot of time hanging out with Wells. From Wells playing Metallica too loud beside Torre's office to Wells feeling that Torre didn't respect him to Torre criticizing Wells's conditioning, the two had a frosty relationship. I considered Wells the rebellious son and Torre the strict father, although Torre wasn't that strict. They never meshed. As ornery as their relationship was, Torre and Wells never actually had a fistfight. But me and Boomer, my close friend, did have a fight in Miami during the 1997 season.

In this corner, weighing in at 185 pounds, the Kansas City Kid...David Cone. And, in this corner, weighing in at 235 pounds, the San Diego Slugger...David Wells. While Wells had the sizable weight advantage for our scuffle, I had more speed—and I also threw the first punch, even if it was an accidental punch.

Pitching against the Marlins on a sticky night, Wells stumbled through a five-run first inning that featured a grand slam by Gary Sheffield and included Wells griping about some of Umpire Greg Bonin's calls. When Wells wandered to the plate to bat in the second inning of the interleague game at Pro Player Stadium, he offered a blunt appraisal of Bonin's strike zone and was instantly ejected. It was a selfish act by Wells, a temper tantrum that meant Torre would have to exhaust several pitchers to work through the next eight innings. We had lost 2–1 in twelve innings the night before, a game where I had pitched nine innings, so Wells's behavior was inexcusable.

Everyone in our dugout glared at Wells and watched him collect his glove and shuffle back to the clubhouse. I followed him. I wasn't going to let his actions go unchallenged. When we reached the clubhouse, he spotted me and I used an R-rated version of the question, "Dude, what the heck was that?" He dropped some F bombs, complained about the umpire, and was taking no owner-ship of his actions. So I cut him off and said, "You just hung us out to dry. Now we have to clear out our whole bullpen to cover for you. You just quit on us." Wells spit out a few more profani-ties and moved toward me. As I tried to avoid him, I also stuck out my right fist and ended up punching him in the mouth. It wasn't a punishing punch or anything like that, but I did connect. It could have escalated, but, thankfully, it didn't. At that point, though, I would have fought with my teammate because I was incensed. I told him, "If you want to fight, let's go. This wouldn't be the first time I've gotten my ass kicked. If you want to fight, we'll fight, but, remember, you quit on us tonight."

My final words resonated. Once Boomer heard me accuse him of quitting on us for a second time, he got a sheepish look on his face. It took a few minutes, a lot of expletives, and one soft punch, but I think he realized how selfish he had been and how difficult a position he had put Torre in. We shook hands, spoke civilly in the clubhouse, and agreed to go out after the game and continue discussing it. Incidentally, the game was stopped by rain shortly after Wells's tirade. Still, the rainout didn't absolve Wells because we had to play a doubleheader the next day. Torre started Kenny Rogers, who lasted only three innings, in the first game, and Dwight Gooden, who hadn't pitched in more than two months, in the second game. We needed six pitchers to win Game 1 and used four pitchers while losing Game 2.

Over a few beers in a Miami bar on our fateful fight night, I told Wells how important he was to the Yankees and to what we were trying to accomplish. Wells was the type of pitcher who responded better to a pat on the back than to a kick in the behind, which was why I told him, "You can't let something like that happen. You're better than that. We need you to be a leader out there, not someone who acts like that and puts the team in a bind." Between sips, Wells kept nodding and he seemed to agree with me. Boomer can be a stubborn dude, but he thanked me for looking out for him. We didn't dwell too much on the fight because it was a tussle, not a real fistfight. And by the end of the following season, I was thanking Wells, too. He won all four of his postseason starts, and we wouldn't have won the 1998 World Series title without him.

Even though me and Boomer reached an understanding quickly and had no ill feelings toward each other, that incident really damaged his already fragile relationship with Torre. Torre called Wells's behavior unprofessional and gave Wells the silent treatment for a couple of days after the pitcher was ejected in Miami. I know that bothered Wells, who acknowledged that he had made a mistake and wanted to close the book on his forgettable night.

"I was wrong, 110 percent wrong," Wells told reporters. He admitted that he was frustrated with the umpire's calls, but added, "I don't think anybody should do it, especially as a starting pitcher."

Powering through the 1998 season and winning at an amazing pace, we started to feel more and more confident about our chances of doing something historic. But even great teams have spats, and Wells and Torre had one in May. After we jumped out to a 9–0 lead against the Rangers on a steamy night in Arlington, Texas, Wells was bruised for seven runs, didn't look like he was trying too hard, and didn't make it past the third inning. We hung on to win, 15–13. But Torre assessed Wells's outing by saying his weight was "a big deal" if it contributed to his problems in the warm weather. It was a shot at Wells's beefy physique, a sensitive topic for Wells and something that trailed him for most of his career, and it infuriated Wells. I was actually surprised Joe said that about Wells. Whenever we had spring training meetings, Joe told us, "I will always have your back. I will never rip you to the media." But Torre broke his own rule with Wells, and it might have been because he was simply tired of dealing with Wells's antics. An irate Wells told me he was going to destroy Torre in the media, which I begged him not to do. I suggested that he request a meeting with Torre and ask that Mel Stottlemyre, our pitching coach, also attend as a mediator. This time Wells listened to me, and they had a noisy meeting in which the rebellious son and the strict father both explained their positions. No matter how loud it got behind those four walls, it was better than having a spitting match through the media.

Eleven days after Wells's meltdown in Texas caused Torre to criticize him, Wells cruised to the mound at Yankee Stadium while nursing a hangover and pitched a perfect game against the Minnesota Twins. Yes, the pitcher who had been far from perfect in Torre's eyes was superb and stylish in pitching the fifteenth perfect game in baseball history. While it's considered bad luck to speak to a teammate when he is throwing a perfect game or a no-hitter, I sensed that the chatty and jittery Wells was aching to say something. So, in the seventh inning, I said, "I think it's time to break out the knuckleball." He laughed and exhaled, which is exactly what I was hoping he would do. I think Wells's meeting with Torre gave him some peace of mind, because he was one of the best pitchers in the American League for the rest of the season.

Despite the joy that existed after Wells's perfect game, I knew he and Torre weren't ever going to be close, so I repeated to Joe that he should just let me handle Wells and I would "keep him out of jail." Torre trusted me and he didn't want to deal with Wells's nonsense anymore, so he was fine with me playing babysitter to a player who had been a headache for him.

Part of making Wells feel comfortable was getting him away from everyone else and allowing him to have a little more freedom. For most of 1998, I hatched a plan to help Wells as we stayed in different hotels from the team on road trips, something that I knew would appeal to his rebellious side. Wells's mother was nicknamed Attitude Annie and she dated a chapter president of the Hells Angels motorcycle club in San Diego, so Wells was comfortable with being a nonconformist. By staying on our own in hotels in Boston, Chicago, Toronto, and other cities, we were in charge of our schedules and we felt some power in defying authority. We didn't have to worry about anyone monitoring our routines at the hotel, and we didn't have to be concerned about getting into trouble in the hotel bar. Typically, I would book us a suite that had a common area and two adjoining bedrooms on either side, and then we would invite our friends and some of our teammates to hang out with us. After games, there would be musicians, actors, and roadies chilling in our club for two. We were a couple of well-compensated major leaguers, so it was a worthwhile expense to have so much freedom on the road, and it was a freedom that Wells absolutely cherished.

As our road show developed and I could see how comfortable Wells was, I realized it wasn't about partying or debauchery. It was about bonding. We laughed, we had fun, and we relaxed. I'm not going to lie about the fact that we had some late nights in those suites because, after all, we were starters who had to pitch once every five days. But this really was a way for both of us to decompress during the grind of the season. Although many of our teammates knew what we were doing, we never divulged it to upper management because they definitely would have made us stay in the team hotel. And, since we invited any interested teammates to join us, no teammates ever criticized us for simply trying to avoid the spotlight.

Wells thrived in that atmosphere and so did I. Pedro Martinez won the AL Cy Young Award that season, but Boomer and I did more than just host parties in our suite as he finished third and I finished fourth in the voting. I was 20-7 with a 3.55 earned run average, and 209 strikeouts and 59 walks in 207⅔ innings. Wells was 18-4 with a 3.49 ERA, and 163 strikeouts and 29 walks in 214⅓ innings. We were friends before we formed the club for two, but we became even closer that season. Listen, I understand that Boomer is boisterous and opinionated, and that can be annoying to some people, but I respect and understand him, and we have a strong friendship. I tell him the truth, and sometimes he even listens to me.

In my final start of the regular season, I pitched seven scoreless innings against Tampa Bay and I was in line to win my twentieth game. Watching the ninth inning from the players' lounge in the clubhouse, I smiled when Rivera secured the final out and finished the game. I wasn't ready for what happened next, as a few of my teammates screamed and celebrated as if they had just been handed the keys to a free BMW. I was speechless.

A few minutes later, Girardi handed me the game ball and hugged me, and my emotions erupted. Tears trickled down my cheeks. Girardi cried, too, and, like a true copilot of a catcher, he said, "I wanted that bad." Steinbrenner sent me a bottle of Korbel champagne with a note that said, "Congratulations from the Boss. Keep up the good work." After earning that win, I set a record for the longest gap between twenty-win seasons, having also won twenty with the Mets in 1988.

There was one coaching constant when I won my twentieth with the Yankees and when I won my twentieth with the Mets: Stottlemyre was my dedicated pitching coach both times. In more than a decade with Mel as my coach, he was the same exact coach in every season: a relentlessly positive person I don't ever recall seeing in a bad mood. Mel pitched in the 1964 World Series as a twenty-two-year-old, but he never appeared in another postseason game, as the Yankees experienced several lean seasons. He won 164 games in eleven years. I think Mel grasped how moody pitchers can be, and that was why he was always upbeat as a coach.

Anytime I was scheduled for a bullpen session with Stottlemyre, he would breeze past my locker with a catcher's mitt on his hand and say, "Let's get this going." Regardless of how I was feeling, it was uplifting to hear those words. I never wanted to let him down. It would have been like disappointing my father. With Mel, I always felt as if I had a coach who was ready to prop me up, not knock me down, and in a job that is so mentally challenging, that positivity was appreciated.

Once a game began, it was rare for Mel to speak with me.

I didn't like to have deep discussions with my manager or my coaches in the middle of games, and Stottlemyre agreed with that approach. Obviously, if Stottlemyre noticed something glaring, he would mention it to me, but mostly he would save his advice for the next day. He wasn't obsessed with mechanics and telling a pitcher his hands or his feet needed to be in a certain spot. Stottlemyre's forte was working a pitcher's mind and offering some different grips for sinkers, which was his best pitch.

However, Mel taught me one trick that involved starting my motion with the baseball a few inches outside of my glove. Sometimes pitchers are late in breaking their hands apart and starting the circular part of their motion, in which they bring their arm behind their back to get ready to throw. By already having the baseball out of my glove, I wouldn't be late to start that process. This was especially important with breaking pitches because I wanted to be able to get my hand on top of my splitter or my slider and really get in position to snap those pitches off when I released them. If I felt I was late, this adjustment always helped get me in sync.

Throughout that 1998 season, our greatest competition soon became ourselves. As the wins piled up, we were asked about how we might stack up against some of the best teams of all time. We were 61-20 at the halfway point and we won our hundredth game on September 4, with almost a month left in the regular season. We were energized by chasing history, but as the season unfolded, we all knew what those accomplishments meant. Our 114-48 record was amazing, but those 114 victories would feel hollow if we didn't win a championship.

We won the first two games of the American League Division Series against the Texas Rangers and I didn't think anything or anyone could stop us. Then, on the workout day before Game 3, something stopped us and sent a chill through our bodies: We learned that Strawberry had colon cancer. It was shocking news.

Cancer? As soon as the C word was mentioned, everyone in our clubhouse was gravely concerned and started to ask questions about Strawberry's prognosis. I was in a daze because Dan Quisenberry, the pitcher and mentor who lectured me about maturity in Kansas City, had passed away from brain cancer that same week. Our postseason workouts were usually noisy, with players teasing each other by the batting cage, but that was the quietest workout we had all season. We were a bunch of players with red-rimmed eyelids who understood that misplaced sliders and hit-and-runs weren't that important anymore. My father was at that workout, so I found him in the stands and chatted about Straw, hoping his words would provide some solace.

Still, with sadness smothering me and filling my world, I pitched 5⅔ scoreless innings the next day as we won the series. I had planned to honor Strawberry by scrawling his number 39 on the back of my cap, but the clubhouse staff responded quickly and embroidered it on the back of everyone's cap. When we returned to New York, I brought one of the "39" caps to Strawberry at Columbia Presbyterian and let him know how much we missed him. Strawberry told me how hungry he was and implored us to finish the job so he could attend another championship parade.

Throughout that postseason, Strawberry's health hovered over us and made us all aware how fragile our lives and our careers were. When I visited Strawberry, it was natural to flash back to lying in that same hospital after aneurysm surgery two years earlier and wondering about my future. We had Straw with us that whole postseason and even kept his locker intact, even though we knew he wouldn't be joining us.

We conquered the Indians in the ALCS in six games, but it was a tense series. In the twelfth inning of Game 2, Knoblauch, our second baseman, had a lapse in judgment that cost us. With the score tied, 1–1, and Enrique Wilson on first, Travis Fryman tried to advance the runner with a bunt. Tino Martinez's throw to first hit Fryman in the back and trickled behind Knoblauch, who was covering first. Rather than retrieve the ball, Knoblauch argued with the umpire that Fryman should have been called out for interference. As Knoblauch argued and even blew a bubble with his gum, Wilson scored the go-ahead run as the Indians prevailed, 4–1. Almost instantly, Knoblauch's brain cramp resulted in him being compared to Bill Buckner, who made the infamous error for the Red Sox in the 1986 World Series. The candid Wells said, "If this doesn't work out, he's going to be criticized for that for the rest of his Yankee career."

On our flight to Cleveland, Knoblauch was livid and was still complaining about how the umpire botched the call. Having once argued with an umpire and allowed two runs to score in a regular season game, not a postseason game, I felt qualified to give Knoblauch advice. I told Chuck it didn't matter anymore who was right or wrong about the call. The play was over and the game was over, and it would benefit him if he simply admitted that he should have gotten the ball. If Knoblauch did that, even if he disagreed with the umpire's call, I figured the story would fizzle out. The longer Knoblauch moaned about the call and remained in denial, the longer the story would persist and remain a distraction for him and for us.

One day later, Knoblauch told reporters, "I screwed up the play and I feel terrible about that. I should have went and gotten the ball, regardless of what the outcome of the umpire's call was." That was perfect and that was all Knoblauch needed to say. I had been in some delicate positions in my career and I learned it was smarter and easier to deal with controversies directly.

But regardless of anything Knoblauch said, the person who saved us in that series was Orlando "El Duque" Hernández. After we fell behind 2-1 in the best-of-seven series, we were tense, and

Steinbrenner said we would find out what we were made of now that we were in the most perilous spot of the season. Hernández was masterful in twirling seven gorgeous innings as we defeated old friend Dwight Gooden and the Indians, 4–0, in Game 4. I loved watching El Duque pitch because he was such an artist and because he refused to give in, an approach that I always tried to have.

After lecturing Knoblauch, I needed to lecture myself a few days later. I had said my start in Game 6 could be "a defining moment" in my career, since I had the chance to send us to the World Series. I had a five-run lead in the fifth inning so I should have been cruising, pitching with confidence and silencing the Indians. I should have been, but I wasn't. I was more fatigued than normal, but I persevered. Keep going, I told myself.

With the bases loaded and Jim Thome batting, I threw a back-door slider, a pitch that I wanted to start way off the plate before it broke from right to left to hit the outside corner. The ball pulled on me as it left my hand and I hung the pitch, basically giving Thome a gift-wrapped slider. After Thome smashed it into the upper deck, I felt numb. That cut our lead to 6–5. I was morose, so morose that first baseman Tino Martinez noticed my drooping shoulders and came over to me and shouted, "Hey, we're still winning." I understood that, sort of, but I was still processing that homer, still absorbing it.

For a few minutes, I was frantic about letting the Indians surge back into the game. The baseball sounded so loud off the bat, like a gong had been set up behind the mound. And you know what? I kept hearing that noise, that loud, horrendous sound of a bat crushing a pitch, my pitch. I heard it as Thome trotted around the bases, as he crossed the plate, and as Fryman settled into the batter's box. That gong was blasting my ears, the after effects of an already damaging grand slam.

We were still ahead and I still needed two outs to complete the fifth inning, but that homer harpooned my confidence. If Torre ever had the ability to read my mind, he would have replaced me, because, at that moment, I was the least confident pitcher in the ballpark. Somehow, I retired the next two batters and barely protected the lead. I didn't return for the sixth and watched the rest of the game pensively, a pitcher who would end up getting the win, but a pitcher whose confidence was in shards.

We won the game, 9–5, and won the ALCS, but I headed to the World Series as a less confident pitcher. When I had a bullpen session between starts, it was troubling because I felt considerable soreness in my right shoulder. With my most important start of the year looming, I walked into the trainers' room and said, "I need some help to get me through the next start." We learned that my shoulder was inflamed so I received a cortisone shot and the pain dissipated. I tossed six solid innings in my only start against the Padres in Game 3 as I rebounded from the Thome homer, regained my confidence, and we won the game. That's the complicated life of a pitcher. I was miserable after the ALCS win, but I got a shot in the shoulder, I felt much better, and soon after that, I was exhilarated by my strong World Series start. We swept the World Series in four games and I was proud to be part of the best roster I'd ever seen assembled.

In the celebratory clubhouse, reporters asked where our team should rank in baseball history. Were we the best team ever? Maybe. I know we felt pretty damn special, and I know no team had ever won more games than us. But were we better than Ruth and Gehrig and the 1927 Yankees? How about Mantle and Maris and the 1961 Yankees? I loved the fact that we were being compared to those historic teams. Steinbrenner was definitive about his thoughts.

Through tears that were caused by a lot of emotion and a little champagne, he said, "Right now, you would have to call them the greatest team ever. Based on the record, that's what they are."

Brian Cashman, who presided over this juggernaut in his first year as general manager, was similarly enthusiastic. Recalling how Don Zimmer, the veteran bench coach who started his professional career in 1949, had told Cashman that summer that he was never going to see another team like the 1998 Yankees, Cashman said, "He was right. If I live to be a hundred, I'll never see anything like this."

The champagne was spraying, the hugs and the high fives were endless, but we also stopped to do something very important. Wells shouted for everyone to gather in the corner of the crowded and soggy room, told us to raise our bottles of champagne, and yelled, "This is for the Straw Man." Perfect. Later, we learned Strawberry had beaten the cancer.

When you've played on a team that is considered one of the best, if not the best, of all time, you show up for the next spring training feeling like the marvelous journey hasn't yet ended. None of us wanted those intoxicating feelings to disappear. The weather felt a little warmer, the palm trees seemed a little more picturesque, and our team's outlook was very bright in the spring of 1999. Everyone was in a fabulous mood, and we believed we could repeat as champions. While we were all still excited about 1998, we had to remind ourselves to focus on the future, not the past. But, as pitchers and catchers were having their first workout in mid-February, we were forced to focus on the present when the Yankees traded Wells, Graeme Lloyd, and Homer Bush to the Blue Jays for the legendary Roger Clemens. Wow. Steinbrenner likened the acquisition of Clemens to adding Michael Jordan to a basketball team. Yes, it was a whopper of a trade, but it absolutely blindsided Wells.

Wells loved being a Yankee, loved it so much that he actually wore one of Babe Ruth's old baseball caps on the mound during a game in 1998. It didn't matter that he was traded for a dominant pitcher in Clemens, who had won his fifth Cy Young Award in the previous season. The Yankees could have traded Wells for Sandy Koufax and Satchel Paige and he still would have felt rejected. Pacing around his Palm Harbor, Florida, home after the deal was announced, Wells looked lost and devastated and kept saying to me, "Why?"

I asked the same question. I still do. Clemens was as talented and as intimidating as any pitcher in baseball, and of course, I understood why the Yankees wanted him. He was a game changer with an unbelievable work ethic. But I didn't love the trade, and I'm not just saying that because Wells was my buddy. With me, Clemens, and El Duque in the same rotation, I thought we featured three right-handed pitchers who were too similar. Pettitte was our only elite lefty. Losing Wells created a void because we didn't have the balance of two left-handed starters and two right-handed starters in the postseason. But maybe there's a reason I'm not a general manager. We won in 1999 and 2000, so it's difficult to question the trade.

With Clemens going from Yankee villain to Yankee pitcher and sliding into Wells's spot in the rotation, our focus shifted to the return of Strawberry. Less than a month before the 1999 season opener, there was a buzz in Tampa because Strawberry was ready to play in his first exhibition game since recovering from colon cancer. It was a March morning that was flooded with optimism, but those feelings were erased when we were told that Torre, our rock of a manager, had prostate cancer and would be leaving the team for treatment.

Just like with Strawberry's cancer diagnosis six months earlier, everyone in our clubhouse was concerned and devastated by the news about Torre. We had won two World Series titles in the previous three seasons and Torre's calm, soothing approach had been so important to keeping us prepared and motivated. In a matter of seconds, I stopped thinking about Strawberry, my buddy who had beaten cancer, and worried about Torre, my boss who was now trying to beat cancer.

That anxiety about Joe's health hovered over us until he visited the clubhouse a few days later to tell us about his upcoming surgery. In true Torre fashion, Joe was encouraging about his situation and explained how eager he was to have the cancer removed from his body. Zimmer, Torre's right-hand man, took over as manager. Since Zimmer and Derek Jeter often teased and bickered with each other, Torre ended his speech by standing in front of Jeter and saying, "Don't come to me and complain about Zim." It was a perfect way for Torre to end the serious meeting, with a joke that made everyone smile.

I thought Zimmer did an exemplary job filling in for Torre, but it would have been very hard for anyone to replace Torre. And it was very hard for any manager, even one as experienced as Zimmer, to appease Steinbrenner. Torre had a solid relationship with Steinbrenner, in part because he had a brilliant strategy of initiating conversations with Steinbrenner whenever times were tough. Most managers didn't want to talk to Steinbrenner when the team was struggling because they didn't want to hear his complaints, but Torre understood that was a shrewd time to contact George and let him vent. Instead of waiting for the phone to ring with potential bad news, Torre would call Steinbrenner and address that bad news.

During Zimmer's six weeks as Torre's replacement, I don't think he and Steinbrenner spoke with each other too much. I could see how the fun-loving Zimmer seemed much more stressed and anxious now that he was the man in charge of the Yankees. After I played a poorly timed practical joke on a teammate, Zimmer rightfully barked at us about being more mature. I quickly admitted it was my silly prank and apologized to Zimmer. Zimmer's change in personality was a reminder to me of how terrific Torre was at his job and, honestly, how simple he made it look. Still, behind Zimmer, we had a 21-15 record and sat in first place in the American League East.

Torre was strong enough to return to manage the Yankees on May 18 and his first game back was in enemy territory: against Pedro Martinez and the Red Sox at Fenway Park. Zimmer looked relieved to have Torre back in the manager's seat, while Torre didn't seem to mind how hot that seat could get. When Torre brought the lineup card to the plate before the game, the fans at Fenway gave him a standing ovation and cheered for about two minutes. I started that game for us and I actually had goose bumps as the Red Sox fans, the same people who hated the Yankees with a passion, welcomed Joe back. We all welcomed Joe back. We lost that night, but our team felt whole again because the beacon on our lighthouse was shining again.

I don't think Torre ever moved from his seat during one game in 1999, one magical game in which my slider helped me feel invincible, powerful, and, amazingly, even perfect. It was an uncomfortably warm Saturday at Yankee Stadium when my slider behaved more artistically than ever, almost stopping and making a left turn as it reached the plate. More than any other pitch, the slider is the reason I pitched a perfect game against the Montreal Expos on July 18.

Pick up a baseball and place your index finger and your middle finger across one of the U-shaped seams and place your thumb on the other side of the baseball. Most pitchers grip the slider in this fashion and use their middle finger, which is the strongest and the longest finger, to help generate spin on the baseball and create the late, dramatic movement.

In my eagerness to throw a slider as a teenager, I encountered a problem, a problem I couldn't solve. My hands were too small to allow me to use my middle finger as the only finger to spin the pitch out of my hand. Because of that, I placed my index and middle finger on the seams, like other pitchers, but I would use both fingers, especially my index finger, to generate the spin. The index finger was weaker and smaller, but I was comfortable with that approach because it gave me a little extra tug on the pitch, meaning I could guide it a little better. Most pitchers were shocked when I told them I used the index finger as the primary spin generator on my slider because it is usually the innocent bystander for most breaking pitches.

Besides the nasty slider I had against the Expos, none of their starters had ever faced me, which made me more of an unknown quantity to them and allowed me to use all of my strategies to try and stifle them. Obviously, I had been pitching in the major leagues for more than a decade at that point, but no matter what a batter studies on videotape or what he learns from teammates, he's only going to feel really familiar with the pitcher if he has faced the pitcher himself. That lack of familiarity was something I exploited all day, something I detail extensively in another chapter.

Naturally, I understand there's an incredible luck factor involved in pitching a perfect game and there's a crucial team factor, too. O'Neill made a sprawling catch in right field to rob the second batter of the game of an extra-base hit. Third baseman Scott Brosius scampered to his left to prevent a grounder from reaching the shortstop hole and likely becoming a hit in the seventh. Knoblauch ranged up the middle and made an outstanding play near second base in the eighth and fired a bullet to first base. Of course, Girardi was my shepherd for all nine innings.

While my perfect game was only one game, a one-in-a-million game, it's a microcosm of how our teams trusted each other and believed in each other. Yes, we had chemistry. It's so hard to quantify what chemistry is, but for me, it was just an overwhelming feeling that every player understood what was expected of him. Does that create a chemistry that helps a team? I think it does. I can't give you statistics to prove this, but I can describe the feelings I had in the dugout when Martinez held us to two hits through the first six innings in a game against the Red Sox in September 2000. I felt we were one or two base runners away from connecting against Martinez. I can't explain it, but it just felt that way. Then there was a walk, a single, and a two-out, three-run homer from Brosius in the seventh, and we had conquered Pedro.

I think the 1999 team is a good example of a team that was fueled by our comfort level with each other. The experience that many of us had accumulated by playing in the postseason together was crucial, and it allowed us to relax more. Can I say we collected some more hits and scored some more runs because of chemistry? Not necessarily, but sometimes that was the way I felt. Torre was fond of saying that players have heartbeats and they're not just about the statistics beside their name. As players, we were comfortable with each and we were comfortable playing in important games. That matters. I think that was why we won championships in 1999 and in 2000—especially in 2000, because we lost thirteen of our last fifteen games and seemed like a drowning team.

In those two seasons, the experience and chemistry paid off for us in the postseason. We had O'Neill's competitiveness, Jeter's determination, Tino's work ethic, Pettitte's passion, and Mariano's dominance. All of those talents and personalities blended together and created a calm atmosphere during a time when nothing is calm. We rarely felt bewildered by the anxiety that could have smothered us and we didn't utter "Uh-oh" when something sloppy or negative happened on the field. Maybe the Braves had anxious feelings if Mark Wohlers came into the game, and maybe some other teams had that "uh-oh" feeling with their relievers. I can't speak for them, but we didn't feel that way about our bullpen or the rest of our team. We respected each other, we all knew our roles, and we trusted each other to do them. Nobody ever panicked. To me, that helped immeasurably.

As serious and devoted as those Yankees teams were, our closeness was also based on some of the foolish and immature behavior that permeated our clubhouse. Yes, major leaguers will sometimes act like teenagers and play practical jokes on each other, which was a role I enjoyed with the Yankees. Mike Stanton and I used to spend most of spring training trying to outdo each other with practical jokes. I wish I could provide the play-by-play for these pranks, but many of them are too sophomoric to repeat. Put it this way: We both acted half our age and we used the bathroom as our pranks laboratory.

I was a starter, so I wasn't in the bullpen during games, but Jeff Nelson once told me about the messy way that they wished each other a happy birthday. If a reliever was celebrating his birthday, his peers would take a large plastic cup and fill it with the smelliest items they could find. Imagine a concoction of tuna fish, hot sauce, sour milk, Ben-Gay, and cream cheese, and then imagine that mixture being dumped on your head as the other relievers sang "Happy Birthday" to you. That's what happened in the Yankee bullpen.

For one of Stanton's birthdays, Ramiro Mendoza forgot to contribute to the "present," so he scooped up the rosin bag and shook some of the powdery substance into the cup. When Stanton made his appearance in the bullpen before the first inning, the relievers poured the sewage onto his head. None of the Yankees realized that rosin stiffens up when it gets wet, so Stanton's short, spiked hair looked like little slivers of plaster had sprouted from his head. It took Stanton so long to scrub the cement-like substance out of his hair that Nelson said he didn't make it back to the bullpen until the seventh inning.

To make sure that the relievers were watching the game, Nelson said there was a rule that required them to clap every time the Yankees notched a hit or scored a run. If a reliever forgot to clap, the other relievers were allowed to slap him in the head. During a road trip to Boston, Nelson visited a hardware store and bought goggles for the relief crew. Goggles? Since the relievers often passed the time by flicking sunflower seeds at each other's face, Nelson picked up the goggles to make sure no one would get hit in the eye. It would have been a bad look to go on the disabled list with "bruised eye from flicked sunflower seed."

Every time the calendar turned to October, Steinbrenner became a more visible presence around the team. We all know he was a hands-on owner. I always thought George, who had coached football at Ohio State, Northwestern, and Purdue, never stopped behaving like a coach because he loved to interact with the players. He wanted to sit in on the meetings, he wanted to be involved, and he wanted to give pep talks. When we were in the postseason, he often roamed around the clubhouse to offer encouragement and to challenge us, too.

Thankfully, I had a very positive and very playful relationship with George. When I have spoken with former Yankees about their relationships with Steinbrenner in the 1970s and 1980s, they have said it was almost impossible for a player to tease Steinbrenner. He was so serious and so demanding that the owner-player relationship was frequently adversarial. (See *Winfield, Dave.*) But I think the Steinbrenner of the 1990s was much mellower. While I enjoyed having a friendly banter with the Boss, I will never forget the one time I crossed him.

Following that aggravating loss to the Indians in the 1997

ALDS, I remembered how miserable I had felt after we lost to the Mariners in 1995. I didn't want anyone to mimic me and spend the next three weeks locked up in their houses or apartments, so after our plane landed, I invited some teammates to join me at a bar in the West Village to commiserate about the end of our season. A friend of mine owned the bar, so he kept it open. This was supposed to be a chance for us to have a few beers, reflect on the end of the season, and not be alone. I thought it was a great plan, but it turned out to be a disaster.

My friend, who is now a former friend, took some silly pictures of us guzzling a few drinks, and they ended up on the front page of the *New York Post* under the headline YANKEE PANKY. The subhead said, BOMBERS PARTY AWAY NIGHT AFTER LOSING TO THE TRIBE. It looked bad. We had just experienced a crushing defeat, and the pictures made it seem as if we didn't care and that we were a bunch of party animals. We were set up, but that didn't matter.

On the morning the story appeared in the *Post*, an irate Steinbrenner called me. I had never incurred the wrath of George, but I immediately understood what it felt like. George told me he was very upset with me and my teammates. He said we didn't act like Yankees, and he thought that the pictures made us look as if we were indifferent to the way the season ended. I told George he was correct and that I deserved the blame for what happened, no one else. I apologized. After I spoke, Steinbrenner was content. There was nothing more to say. He just concluded the call by saying, "That's it. I just wanted you to know how disappointed I was."

That call shook me. Steinbrenner was a powerful man, and I didn't want to anger the owner of the team and the man who was my boss. Fortunately, George never mentioned it to me again, and we moved forward with a cordial relationship. When my mother's Jack Russell terrier bit my right index finger and I missed a start in 1998, Steinbrenner was relentless in pestering me about it. Every time he saw me, he would say, "A dog bite huh? So what really happened?" The only saving grace for me was that El Duque replaced me, pitched well, and became an essential part of our rotation.

Steinbrenner's willingness to tease me about the dog bite opened the door for me to tease him right back, which is what I ended up doing. When we played the Mets in the 2000 World Series, there were thick broadcast cables running around the outside of our clubhouse. Pointing at the abundance of cables, I told George I had never seen anything like that around any major league clubhouses.

"Hey, George, did you see this?" I said. "I think the Mets are bugging us. I think they're using these wires and probably stealing our signs."

Steinbrenner took the bait and evaluated the bundle of cables and then, just as he was about to go complain to Major League Baseball officials, he stopped and looked at me and said, "Are you messing with me? You'd better not be messing with me." I smiled and told him I was. The cables were there in place so that television and radio stations could connect if they had to cover a clubhouse celebration.

That was the same World Series in which Steinbrenner was disturbed when he realized there wasn't any comfortable furniture for players to sit on in the visiting clubhouse at Shea Stadium, just a stool in front of every locker. George immediately turned into an interior decorator and ordered our clubhouse attendants to ship some blue couches from Yankee Stadium to Shea. When our couches arrived, Steinbrenner was the first person to sit on them, like a proud first-time homeowner. We saw George sitting on those couches a lot during the series because he was too nervous to watch the games from the stands at Shea. We were playing the crosstown Mets, our enemies from another borough, and I don't think George wanted to be bothered with other people while study-ing the action. He just wanted to watch the game and scream at the TV.

Steinbrenner was screaming at the ceiling, not the TV, when a pipe burst and it flooded our clubhouse at Shea. The carpet was soaked, and tiptoeing to our lockers was like walking through a marshland. George thought the Mets had purposely caused the flood, and he sloshed through the water and shouted, "These Mets will do anything to keep us from winning." But, once stadium per-sonnel and some New York City firefighters came to our clubhouse to address the problem, George turned into a gracious host. He thanked them, he made sure they all had water to drink, and he even stuffed hundred-dollar bills into the pockets of a few firemen.

That wasn't the only time I saw George express generosity to the folks who were working on behalf of his team. Anytime George arrived at the Stadium, the staff would whisper, "The Eagle has landed," on their walkie-talkies so everyone knew he was in the building. As I said, he loved chatting with the players and the coaches, so he usually visited us in the clubhouse. Many times, George would ask, "How many guys are working in the clubhouse today?" and he would then proceed to leave tips for each of them. Usually, the clubhouse attendants are high school or college kids who spend endless hours cleaning uniforms, digging the dirt out of cleats, folding towels, running errands for players, and doing whatever other tasks are required to help players get ready for the game. It's a tedious and thankless job, and George let the atten-dants know they were appreciated. While Steinbrenner made sure they knew he was the boss and he wanted things done in a certain way, he also made sure to thank them.

As Steinbrenner hung out in the clubhouse in 2000, I decided to have a little more fun. Like I said, I know how much Steinbrenner enjoyed being a coach and offering encouragement, so I told him that I didn't think the ultra-intense O'Neill seemed prepared for the approaching World Series game. It was a lie, but I was trying to be a prankster.

"Have you spoken to O'Neill?" I asked Steinbrenner. "He doesn't look ready to me."

Again, Steinbrenner was very willing to help and jumped out of his seat and was prepared to give O'Neill a pat on the back and a few words of support. But O'Neill was locked in and he didn't want to be bothered before the game by anyone, whether it was Steinbrenner or Torre or, of course, me. O'Neill stared at me for several seconds, his exasperation bubbling with each second, and he finally ordered me to get the bleep out of the clubhouse because I was creating a commotion. He was right. So I left and hung out in the bullpen.

During the 1999 postseason, I glanced inside our food room at the Stadium and saw Chris Chambliss, our batting coach, conducting a meeting with our hitters. Standing behind him was Steinbrenner, like a teacher watching over his students. Chambliss was speaking softly, as he always did, and the players were silent. The room was unusually quiet except for the buzzing of a defective soda machine. As Chambliss reviewed the information about the opposing pitcher, the noise continued. It sounded like a car alarm blaring a few blocks away. Eventually, Steinbrenner decided to mute the buzzing.

I watched with fascination as George rumbled over to the soda machine and tried to shimmy it away from the wall so he could unplug it. When George couldn't do it by himself, he enlisted the help of a few clubhouse attendants and they dragged the machine away from the wall. Steinbrenner, who was wearing his trademark blue blazer, knelt down, reached behind the machine, muttered a few words, and stretched and stretched and, finally, he pulled out the plug. The buzzing stopped. When Steinbrenner pulled his arm out from behind the machine, his sleeve was covered in dust and soot. He didn't care. He had stopped the buzzing.

The Yankees had a grooming policy that prohibited beards and long hair, so we all knew how passionate Steinbrenner was about the way the Yankees looked. He wanted us to be clean and neat, which, I'm sure, was a nod to his military background. But I was forced to do some fancy talking when Steinbrenner attempted to institute a dress code in which the players would have to wear a blue blazer with a Yankee emblem on road trips. I knew my teammates would be annoyed if we all had to dress like a bunch of prep school students. Knowing that some players probably had sponsorship deals for athletic wear, I told Steinbrenner that they would be violating their contracts if they didn't wear the clothing they had agreed to wear. I pulled that argument out of the sky, but George wasn't buying my spiel.

"I want us to look professional," Steinbrenner said. "We're representing the Yankees."

But I reiterated that the players would be put in an awkward spot if Steinbrenner insisted that we all wear blue blazers. Eventually, George relented and we never had to wear the blazers. New York Yankee Prep never played any games.

It was difficult for me to joke too much with Steinbrenner or anyone else once the 2000 season evolved and I was such a hapless pitcher. For the first time in my major league career, I had no control of my slider and I felt off balance on the mound. I have detailed how disconnected I felt with Jorge Posada as my catcher and how that season was a frustrating journey with a lot more questions than answers.

Naturally, I wasn't laughing when the organization ordered me to go to Tampa to work with Billy Connors, Steinbrenner's close friend and the Yankees' pitching guru, in July. I was so desperate to change my fortunes that I had hiked my pants up like El Duque and I started kicking my leg out a little bit like him, too. Those actions probably told the Yankees I was really searching and that I needed an intervention of sorts. I even wore a puka shell necklace for good luck that year, as if those shells were going to find my missing slider. Torre called me into his office and said, "You have to go do this with Billy in Tampa. You have to go." I told Joe they should release me, but he implored me to go work with Connors. At that point, I hadn't won a game in eleven straight starts.

Feeling alone and annoyed, I was angry about the banishment, but I couldn't argue with their decision because I had been so ineffective. I was a thirty-seven-year-old pitcher with a Cy Young Award on his résumé who was waking up at 7 a.m. to work on the minor league mounds with Connors. I hated being there because it made me feel like a failure. At first, I told Connors I should just take a couple of days off to free my mind, but he insisted that I needed to throw. So I threw and I threw and I threw. Billy pushed me through some intense workouts and tried to make some refinements in my delivery, but I wasn't too receptive.

On the third day, Connors instructed me to throw batting practice to some minor league hitters without using an L-shaped screen, which is placed in front of the mound and protects the pitcher. I didn't want to throw my middling fastballs in BP, but Torre's voice was in my head, so I agreed. I threw one pitch, one pedestrian pitch, and the kid hit a line drive that almost clipped my kneecap. That was enough for me. I threw my glove to the grass and I stalked off the field, cursing with every step. I headed toward the parking lot, and Billy, who weighed close to three hundred pounds, shuffled after me. But I was gone. After that incident, I called Torre and told him to tell the Yankees to release me. I was done.

"Don't torture me," I said. "You're embarrassing me at this point. If you don't want me around, fine. I will go quietly. If I'm done, I'm done."

As always, Torre calmed me down and told me I needed to keep working with Connors, whom I actually liked. I wasn't mad at what Billy was trying to do, but I was miffed that he had me throwing BP to a bunch of kids without a protective screen. Connors called me and we agreed that would be my last BP session, and we also agreed I should take a few days off. I returned and worked with Connors on some adjustments with the placement of my hands. I told Billy I really didn't want to quit pitching, but my pride and my temper forced me to lash out.

Paroled from Tampa, I actually pitched pretty well in August and went 3-1 with a 3.98 earned run average. Suddenly, I felt better about myself, especially on the mental side. But I dislocated my left shoulder while diving for a popped-up bunt against the Royals, and that was a taxing injury. I tried to pitch through the pain, but it was tough to stay balanced, and I was crushed in my last four starts. I didn't pitch in the ALDS, and I pitched one inning of relief in the ALCS.

Shockingly, Torre had enough faith in me that he was thinking about starting me over Denny Neagle in Game 4 of the World Series against the Mets. I spoke to Joe after Game 2 and told him that he should start Neagle because, at that point in a frustrating season, I felt more comfortable pitching in relief. I had been battling and doing the best I could, but I didn't know how many effective pitches I could give him as a starter. I had always been the pitcher who wanted to pitch, but in this spot, with my Yankees career probably nearing its end, I told Joe I couldn't do it. His face was a mixture of surprise and, I think, relief. He thanked me for being honest. Later, he told me to be prepared to face Mike Piazza in that game.

At some point, I thought Joe would bring me in to try and get Piazza out with sliders. But I didn't know it would be with two outs and nobody on base in the fifth inning. We had a 3–2 lead, and

Neagle was one out away from qualifying for the win, but Piazza had hit a two-run homer off Neagle in his last at bat, so Joe wanted me to oppose Piazza because I was a more unpredictable pitcher. If Neagle, a two-pitch pitcher, had allowed another homer to Piazza, Torre said, "I never would have been able to forgive myself" for failing to bring in Cone. It was a smart move by Torre because I'd been thinking about how I would attack him in an at bat. There's no way Piazza could have been thinking about me as intently because there's no way he could have thought that Joe would bring me in that early in the game and with the bases empty.

I'm sure there were lots of times in Piazza's career in which he swung at the first pitch, but he was definitely taking the first pitch way more often than he wasn't that season. Since I didn't think he was going to swing, I started him with a fastball. I tried to throw strike one and I missed with it. So now Jorge Posada called for a fastball again. I said, "OK, here you go. I have to get a strike." At that point, I didn't have a lot of velocity because of my injured left shoulder. Pitchers need their non-throwing arm to help them with balance and power, but I didn't have a stable left arm.

When I threw my second pitch to Piazza, it was another fastball and it was all based on hope. I was hoping he wouldn't destroy it. The pitch limped in at about 85 miles per hour and was over the middle of the plate, a perfect pitch for him to hit. He didn't swing and it was called a strike. I was relieved because that was the best pitch he had to hit in the whole sequence. Piazza must have thought I wasn't going to throw anything but sliders, especially after it started out 1-0.

But I had a very definitive game plan for Piazza, and it was all centered around getting ahead with fastballs early in the count. I was trying to get strike one with a fastball so, even after missing with the first one, I threw another one. Once he took that strike, it was 1-1, and now I had him. Now I could change arm angles and throw sliders, which is why Torre had summoned me. I threw one slider, and Piazza swung and missed. I threw another slider and he barely fouled it off. I was one strike away from getting out of this inning.

Momentum was with me, and I was trusting Posada, my copilot. After struggling all year with Posada, I told him I was sure Piazza would take a strike, so I planned to throw a first-pitch fastball. Other than that, I would throw whatever pitches Posada called. There would be no staring in at him and awaiting another sign and no shaking off his signals. Still, when Posada called a fastball on 1-2, I almost closed my eyes and said, "OK, here goes nothing." Posada wanted the fastball up and in, and I threw it inside just enough that Piazza was jammed and he popped it up to second base. I was so relieved, so damn relieved, when I left the mound. That was a huge out for the team, but it was a really big moment for me, too. That fastball to Piazza was the last pitch I ever threw for the Yankees. Two days later, we won another title.

Chapter 15

ANATOMY OF AN INNING

I PITCHED MORE THAN THREE THOUSAND innings in the regular season and the postseason during my major league career, and I imagined pitching at least another three thousand inside my mind. Every inning was a massive challenge until it wasn't. If the baseball felt comfortable flying off my fingertips and I completed an easy inning, I would exhale and amble back to the dugout. And start worrying about the next inning.

Of all the memorable innings I pitched, one inning that resonated as much as any was the sixth inning in Game 3 of the 1996 World Series. So much happened in the pursuit of those three outs that it felt as if I had packed an entire game into one inning, one stressful and demanding inning. Since it was influential to the Yankees eventually winning a title, I think it's appropriate to provide a pitch-by-pitch and thought-by-thought dissection of that inning.

I was submerged in my own unfriendly world in a corner of the third base dugout on October 22, 1996, a focused pitcher obsessed with throwing the baseball as efficiently as I could for as long as I could. Between innings, my thought process was always about how I would execute to get the next three outs. I didn't want to talk to my catcher, my pitching coach, or my manager because any conversations could mushroom into distractions.

On this night in Atlanta, I felt even more isolated because of our dire situation. After losing the first two games of the World Series by a combined score of 16–1, we needed to change the narrative that we were simply props to the mighty Braves. The clubhouse walls can be thin and some spies told us that the Braves were celebrating and talking about building a dynasty after they won Game 2 at Yankee Stadium. When I was told about this clubhouse scene, I saw an opening to use that as motivation for us.

"Hey, they're embarrassing us," I told my teammates. "Where's our pride? We are being taken advantage of. Let's stand up for ourselves."

Honestly, we were aggravated by the way we had played in the Bronx and the way the Braves treated us. While the Braves didn't do anything overt on the field or in the dugout to antagonize us, I could sense how confident they were. And, after winning their last five postseason games by a combined score of 48–2, the Braves had every right to feel confident. But you know what? I had every right not to like that. We hadn't advanced all the way to the World Series to be supporting actors. We had to change that dynamic. Immediately.

"I saw that look in his eyes that I hadn't seen in a while," said Manager Joe Torre about me. "We were down, 2–0. He knew how badly we needed this game. He gave it to us."

The Braves were the defending World Series champions and they were back home for Game 3. Of course, the Braves must have thought this series was close to being over. Chipper Jones has acknowledged that they were confident and were poised to apply the sleeper hold.

"That game was the most important game of the series," Jones said. "If we come out and take a three-to-nothing lead in the series, that series is pretty much over. I thought Coney pitched one heck of a game. He didn't give me much to go on at all. He never gave in."

I had navigated through five shutout innings, even though my arm and my body never felt quite comfortable. It was one of those games where I had to grind, not glide, through innings, my pitches fluctuating from good to decent to not so good. But those are the games where a pitcher needs to be creative and determined and, with the baseball still entrusted to me, I persevered and tried to hang on to our 2–0 lead.

Actually, I was grateful to even be pitching, grateful to be feeling that combination of excitement and fear after having an aneurysm removed from under my right armpit in May. I missed four months while recovering from the surgery, a stretch that included many hopeless nights in which I wondered if my career might be over.

Fortunately, I made it all the way back to pitch in the World Series. So, in Game 3, my mind was centered on the moment and on pitching carefully, even if that meant meandering through lengthy at bats to eventually throw the pitches I wanted to throw. I was maniacal about not throwing pitches over the middle of the plate, so I pelted the corners of the strike zone, repeatedly chasing calls on the edges.

Even when I fell behind in counts, I was stubborn and confident, believing I could make pitches on the edges for quality strikes. Not just strikes, but quality strikes. That's the important distinction between being a pitcher with command and a pitcher with control. A pitcher who has control can throw down-the-middle strikes, but a pitcher who has command can throw quality strikes, those pitcher's pitches that are as sharp as razor blades and can clip a sliver of the strike zone.

Throwing quality strikes against the Braves was paramount

because I had to adjust to Tim Welke, the plate umpire, who was seemingly calling more pitches off the plate for strikes than he was calling pitches that were on the plate. In the first few innings, I noticed that Welke was giving Tom Glavine, my counterpart, significant space off the outside corner to hunt for strikes. So I started to attack the outside corner more and secured some strike calls, too. If either of us delivered a pitch that was thigh-high and a few inches off the corner, there was a good chance Welke would call it a strike, so that became a smart and safe place to target. With his fastball-and-changeup combination, Glavine was a master at stretching the zone.

"To be perfectly honest, the pitchers who were really good at locating the ball made it hard for the umpires not to call it a strike," Glavine said. "Because if your catcher is setting up and he's a tick off the outside corner and then he's three inches off and then he's six inches off, if you keep hitting that mitt in the same spot, you make it hard for the umpire not to call it. Because he sees what you're doing. He sees that you're hitting your spots, not necessarily seeing that your pitches are six inches off the plate."

When Glavine, a superb athlete and a good-hitting pitcher, batted first in the sixth, my mission was to get ahead in the count and make him uncomfortable. "Get the first out," I told myself. I started him with a four-seam fastball and missed low in the zone. But as Glavine faked a bunt on my second pitch, I pumped a fastball past him for a strike. After Joe Girardi called for another fastball and slid his body a few inches toward the outside corner, I delivered a fastball that Welke called a strike to advance the count to 1-2.

So I had Glavine in a tenuous position, the equivalent of a mountain climber trying to move higher with one hand tied behind his back, because I was ahead and I had multiple options to get the out. I went for the strikeout and threw a splitter that tailed far outside and missed the strike zone by a lot. Suddenly, everything changed. That one pitch, one lousy splitter, frazzled me and made me antsy about a 2-2 count. I panicked and created a problem by believing that one pitch had more of an impact than it really did. Since my last splitter was ineffective, I decided to attack him with my fastball. Still, I was worried that the pitcher, who should have been my easiest challenge, might connect for a hit against one of my fastballs.

The pressure percolated inside of me, my stomach getting a little queasier and my arm feeling a little heavier. Sometimes one of the most difficult tasks for a pitcher is to throw a quality strike when he absolutely must do it because he overthinks the situation and lets his mind overtake his actions. I could feel myself guiding the ball instead of simply trusting the speed and positioning of my arm and throwing the ball. I uncorked a 2-2 fastball and it sailed high and away, the uneasiness increasing. On 3-2, I threw another fastball and it veered inside. Glavine thrust his backside toward the first base dugout to avoid the pitch. I was aiming down the middle, but the tension caused me to hang on to the baseball for too long and yank my arm across my body, as if I was snapping a whip, so that the ball tailed inside.

After the inconsistent path of my fastball, I opened my mouth in disbelief and mumbled something, probably a profanity, because I understood how reckless and ridiculous it was to walk the pitcher. My 1-2 splitter, which was the perfect pitch to unveil in that spot, ended up disrupting the rest of the at bat because I had grown restless after that pitch. I squeezed the ball tighter and lost the freedom and command of my fastball. Glavine never swung the bat, but it was a stellar at bat because he didn't chase my splitter and that forced me to throw strikes, which I didn't do. One batter into the most important inning of the season, I was a less confident pitcher.

Staring at me from the batter's box was Marquis Grissom, a free-swinging outfielder who was built like an NFL cornerback. A cornerback who was ready to barrel over me. I peered in for Girardi's sign and hoped that he would ask for a fastball because I needed to regain confidence in that pitch. He called for the fastball. I hit the outside corner for a strike, and with one pitch, I relaxed again. Anytime I was ahead in the count against right-handed batters, I always felt that my slider, which looked like a fastball before bending sharply to the left, was a pitch that could foil them. On 0-1, I threw a slider that bent several inches off the plate. Grissom took a weak swing and hit a foul ball into the seats down the right field line. Now I was feeling positive about this at bat, even as I noticed Mariano Rivera and Graeme Lloyd warming up in the bullpen down the left field line.

As I mentioned, Welke was giving the pitchers some extra space to mine for strikes on the outside corner, so I targeted that location with an 0-2 fastball. But I missed with it. Now at 1-2, I wanted to fool Grissom with a slider or a splitter, pitches with a lot of movement, to get the swing-and-miss. Girardi called for a splitter, which was actually a gutsy call because I had thrown only a few splitters to right-handed batters in the game. I never doubted Girardi's suggestion because I trusted his instincts and I wanted to stay in a rhythm.

I threw a decent splitter that was down and over the middle of the plate, and Grissom swung like a batter who was expecting a fastball because he was out in front of the pitch. Grissom hit it off the end of the bat and lined it softly to left field. Tim Raines moved to his right before finally coming forward and diving for the ball, but the ball landed about a foot in front of him.

While Raines initially misread the flight of the ball, he did a commendable job of smothering the ball on one bounce and not letting it trickle behind him. If that ball had eluded him, Glavine

almost certainly would have scored and Grissom would have probably scampered to third. So, as frustrated as I was because I thought
I should have had one out, I knew the situation could have been
worse.

With first and second, no outs, and trouble looming, I anticipated Mark Lemke, a slap hitter who stood far away from the plate,
would probably try and use a sacrifice bunt to advance the runners. I was praying that he would do that. Anytime a batter bunted
against me, I considered that approach a gift. Give me an out, any
type of out, and I would gladly accept it.

My plan against potential bunters was to throw four-seam
fastballs that were about shoulder high because that's the most
difficult pitch to deaden and bunt into the ground. After Lemke
squared around to bunt and let the first fastball go by, I think he
got anxious, because he reached across the plate for my next high
fastball and bunted it in the air. I hustled toward it and could
have made the play, but Cecil Fielder was chugging in from first,
all 275 pounds of him, and he corralled the pop-up. We came
close to colliding, but, instead, his right foot barely clipped my left
leg, and we had one of those precious outs. Again, Lemke's bunt
seemed inexplicable to me, especially since he handled the bat so
well and could have just as easily flicked a run-scoring single to
left.

With one out recorded, I felt a modest amount of relief, as much
relief as I had felt since I got ahead of Glavine with a 1-2 count.
Despite the fact that the lethal Jones was the next batter and despite the fact that he was the one Brave I didn't want to give
the opportunity to connect against me, I was finally able to calm
myself, at least briefly.

As soon as I gazed in at Chipper, the switch-hitter with the slightly
open stance from the left side, I knew what my strategy would be: I
wasn't throwing him any appealing fastballs. That sweet, level swing

of his wasn't going to have a chance to do any damage against a fastball. I started with a good slider that broke right to left and dipped out of the zone, and he began to swing and stopped. Ever reluctant to introduce a fastball, I followed with an excellent splitter and he swung over it. But I still wasn't confident, still wasn't ready to challenge him with anything over the middle of the plate. That was why I threw a fastball that was down and in. If I was going to miss the strike zone with a fastball against a powerful left-handed batter like Jones, my plan was to miss on the inside corner so Jones couldn't extend his arms and smash a shot into the left center-field gap. I was exhausted at this point and didn't feel incredibly sharp, especially as I kept pitching around the edges.

"With the Fred McGriffs of the world hitting behind me, I had been used to pitchers coming at me with fastballs," Jones said. "They were more likely to challenge me than to challenge the guys behind me. If I had a couple of more years of experience, I might have gone up there and sat off-speed against Coney. But looking for a fastball is the mind-set I had. Unfortunately for us, Coney used that mind-set to combat what we were trying to do."

Danger pitch. That was what I called the 2-1 offering to Jones because he was one swing away from clubbing a three-run homer. Again, this is what was on my mind: *Don't give in to him.* Just like me, Girardi realized that a fastball was a poor idea, so he signaled for a splitter. I threw a splitter, but it wasn't nearly as good as the previous one, and it drifted high and out of the zone. When I missed with that pitch, I could feel my body wilting, the at bat becoming a burden.

The 3-1 count was a supremely dangerous pitch, but I kept telling myself to be cautious. Either Jones was going to swing at my pitch, a pitch that wasn't near the strike zone, or I was going to walk him. Yes, I would rather walk Jones and load the bases before giving him a pitch that could alter the outcome of the game. So

315

I threw another splitter and it was one of my worst pitches of the night as I pushed it and it ended up outside and shoulder high. That was an example of a flustered pitcher making a nervous pitch to a very good hitter, and that pitcher was now in jeopardy of being removed from the game.

My careful approach would have infuriated a lot of pitching coaches because they would have preferred to see me throw a 3-1 fastball to Jones. Those coaches would have screamed, "Throw him your best fastball and trust that your defense will make the play." But that wasn't attractive to me. In such a monumental situation, I believed in maneuvering around the batters in a lineup, which includes knowing the value of a well-placed walk. My mentality was to bypass Jones and walk a future Hall of Fame player, even though I added to the messy situation by loading the bases for Fred McGriff, a borderline Hall of Fame player. I was compiling a different script in my head, a script that involved avoiding Jones and still getting through the inning unscathed.

Still trying to live in my own world and still trying to get those last two outs of the inning, I was interrupted when Manager Joe Torre jogged out to the mound. Torre's presence was unsettling because I hated mound visits; I thought they were unproductive and interfered with my rhythm. I almost always knew what I had to do as a pitcher. It was just a matter of doing it.

But in this precarious situation, I understood why Torre was standing a foot away from me. Torre asked if I could retire McGriff and I said, "Yeah, I can get this guy out." That wasn't convincing enough for Torre. He made me look him in the eyes, our noses almost touching, and begged for the truth, saying, "This is too important. I need to know if you're OK." I could see the concern stitched across his lined face, could almost see him debating about summoning Lloyd right there. I remained resolute, looked Torre directly in his eyes, made my voice sound as stern as possible, and repeated, "I can get him and I can get out of this inning." He retreated to the dugout.

Torre wanted me to convince him that I was OK and not stare at my shoes like a fifteen-year-old whose parents had caught him drinking a beer. There were many times where I would utter any words to get the manager or the pitching coach to leave me alone. That mound meeting was the only meeting I ever had where the manager wouldn't just take a rote, "I'm OK" type of answer. He wanted me to reassure him, and that was why he got close enough to study the distance between my eyebrows.

With my dirt hill back to being a home for one, I focused on Mc-Griff and employed a similar strategy to what I used against Jones. I was going to try staying away from fastballs and avoid throwing anything near the middle of the plate. I threw a backdoor slider that McGriff took for strike one, a pitch that was one of my nastiest of the game. I thought I should throw another slider, but Girardi called for a fastball because he thought it might surprise McGriff, who had just witnessed my approach with Jones. Girardi wanted the fastball to be high and tight, and that worked; the pitch tied up McGriff's arms, prevented him from getting the barrel of the bat to the baseball, and resulted in a pop out to shallow center field for the second out.

To me, that two-pitch sequence was a wise strategy by Girardi and was critical to squeezing through that inning. We went with a slider to get ahead in the count when it seemed like McGriff was anticipating a fastball. Then we followed that with a fastball, which seemed to catch him by surprise, too.

Still, I wasn't finished with the inning yet. My scouting report on Ryan Klesko, the next batter, was that he was susceptible to in-side fastballs and that he would swing at splitters that were diving down, probably guessing that they were fastballs, too. If I made ac-curate pitches and exploited his weaknesses, I felt I should be able to nullify him. But Klesko also had a lot of power, and if I made a mistake with a pitchout from the center of the plate to the outside part of the plate, he could blast it about four hundred feet.

Before I even threw a pitch, I descended the mound and walked toward Grissom at second base because I wondered if he was stealing our signs and tipping off Klesko. It was the typical paranoia of a pitcher in a delicate position, but in that moment, I wanted to make sure Grissom knew I was aware of his movements, even if he was doing absolutely nothing.

Back on the mound, I started Klesko off with a first-pitch splitter that was about chest high, and he was way out in front of it and waved at it. While it was a mediocre splitter, I slowed my arm down and reduced the velocity just enough to get the pitch to fade to the outside corner. Klesko's reaction was indicative of how much of a fastball hitter he was.

Encouraged by how off balance Klesko looked on the splitter, I threw another splitter on the next pitch. But I made too much of an adjustment and threw it too low, the ball bouncing in front of Girardi. With a 1-1 count, I thought I was still in good position to get an out.

As Girardi gave multiple signs to disguise our pitches, I overthrew a fastball and missed down and in. I rushed my delivery on that pitch, probably because of the tension I was feeling. With the bases loaded, pitchers are more prone to quicken their delivery because they're anxious. My heartbeat was accelerating because I knew our chances to win the game and maybe even the World Series were wavering. And now I was behind Klesko with a 2-1 count.

Even at that juncture, I still told myself, *Just make your pitches.* Girardi called for a slider and I tried to backdoor it to the outside corner, hoping the ball would spin perfectly from right to left. But I really got under the slider, didn't have a lot of conviction with the pitch, and missed badly with it, up and away. Still refraining from a fastball in a fastball count, I gambled with a splitter on 3-1. Klesko, the fastball hunter, was out in front of it again and grounded it foul. If he hadn't swung, it probably would have been ball four. Instead, the count was 3-2.

Earlier in the game, I had struck out Klesko with a fastball on the inside corner. I have always stressed how pitchers need to have inside fastballs as a weapon, especially pitchers who throw splitters and sliders. When a batter like Klesko was bracing for splitters and sliders because he saw only one fastball in the at bat, I thought I could get him out if I pinpointed a fastball on the inside corner.

Not surprisingly, Girardi had the same mind-set and he called for a fastball on the inside corner. "Make your pitch," I kept saying quietly, "and you will get him." And we made the pitch and it was inside, but it was a little high. Maybe two or three inches high. Welke called ball four, and I had walked in a run. Exasperation enveloping me, I lifted my arms up in protest before saying, "Come on, Tim." Those were much tamer words than the expletives being shouted from our dugout.

The pitch was on the plate, but Welke didn't call it because he thought it was above the strike zone. According to the way Welke was calling pitches, the pitch was a ball. He was consistent, I will give him that. He didn't call that pitch all night, but the magnitude of the situation made me react the way I did. In the end, I didn't make the pitch. It was really close, but I didn't make the pitch.

After that close call delivered Atlanta's first run and chopped our lead to 2–1, I didn't look toward the dugout at Torre because I had no interest in being replaced. This was still my game. Fortunately, my first pitch to Javy Lopez was a quality pitch, a slider that broke over the outside corner and caused him to swing and miss. Even if he hadn't swung, it might have been called a strike.

Based on that swing, I decided to force-feed sliders to Lopez.

Typically, when I went with back-to-back sliders, I threw the second one a little farther outside to see how aggressive the batter would be about chasing pitches. But this time I rushed the pitch, overthrew it, and left it up and in, the ball spinning right into a dangerous location. Sometimes when you a hang a slider, it's better to hang it up and in than to hang it out over the plate because the batter may initially see the pitch as a ball and may react more slowly. Lopez should have hammered it, but he didn't. I was lucky Lopez didn't extend his arms and simply popped up that pitch to Girardi in foul territory.

"David Cone is a money pitcher," said Girardi, "and he came up with the biggest start of the year for us."

I took quick steps back to the third base dugout, feeling like I needed to rush to get to a safe place after maneuvering around so many minefields. I felt fortunate that we still had a one-run lead because so many things happened in the sixth. I committed a cardinal sin by walking the pitcher. I allowed a single to Grissom that probably should have been caught. Lemke's pop out on a bunt was a gift. I refused to challenge Jones and walked him. I experienced the most memorable visit ever from a manager and convinced Torre I was OK. I outwitted McGriff on two pitches. I thought I had struck out Klesko, but I walked in a run. And, finally, I hung a slider to Lopez and was fortunate that he didn't destroy it. The inning ended with a mistake, the one thing I zealously tried to avoid.

I threw twenty-seven pitches in the sixth inning, twenty-seven grueling pitches, and I felt considerable pressure on every one. The postseason breeds those kinds of feelings. If there is a way for a pitcher to feel lucky and unlucky at the same time, that was how I felt throughout that inning.

After we won the game, I did postgame interviews in which I said I had lied to Torre about my readiness for facing McGriff. That exchange has been reported and repeated for the last two decades. Well, I'm here to correct the record and tell the truth. In all honesty, that was a situation in which I tried to be glib by saying I was a con artist who had convinced Torre that I was the perfect pitcher for that spot. But I actually didn't lie to Torre. For some reason, I decided to be goofy and joke with reporters about our tense encounter. Once a flake, always a flake. But, believe me, I thought I was ready for McGriff.

All professional pitchers are trained to believe that we are the best option and that we can still make a pitch. For me, it was believing I could throw a pitch to a precise location, like I did with McGriff. Some positive thoughts flooded my mind during the McGriff at bat, not the idea that I was fatigued or unequipped to face him. I never thought Torre should have removed me in the sixth, and I never thought I was done. I thought that was my game. And I proved it was. Four days later, we were World Series champions.

Chapter 16

THE DAY I WAS PERFECT

I<small>T WAS</small> Y<small>OGI</small> B<small>ERRA</small> D<small>AY</small> at Yankee Stadium—and like everyone else, I was thrilled to see Yogi and happy that he had ended his fourteen-year boycott and returned to his baseball home. Yogi had vowed that he would never again visit the Stadium after owner George Steinbrenner fired him sixteen games into the 1985 season, a decision that Steinbrenner long regretted. But now the Yankee legend and the Yankee boss were friendly again and now everyone was celebrating Yogi again, including me.

While warming up in the bullpen, I acted more like a fan than a pitcher because I was curious about the pregame festivities. I loved Yogi (who didn't?), so I paused throughout my warm-ups to watch Yogi's reactions and to listen for Yogi-isms in his speech. Since the temperature was also in the low nineties, I decided not to strain myself and had more of an effortless preparation. In retrospect, it was the most relaxing bullpen session I've ever had. It wasn't always easy for me to get relaxed so, even if I didn't think about it at that moment, the timing of Yogi's day benefited me.

Lumbering to the mound to throw out the first pitch was Don Larsen, who pitched the only perfect game in postseason history in the 1956 World Series, with Berra as the catcher. I asked

Larsen if he planned to jump into Berra's arms and repeat what they did more than four decades ago.

"You've got it wrong, kid," Larsen snapped. "He jumped into my arms."

Of course he did. The five-foot-seven-inch Berra ran to the mound and leaped into the six-foot-four-inch Larsen's arms after Larsen's perfecto against the Brooklyn Dodgers. I felt like such a fool for making that mistake. Larsen lofted the ball to Yogi; Yogi caught it with Joe Girardi's glove, then handed the glove back to Girardi. The handoff of the glove resonated with me, not because I thought Berra had blessed it with perfection or anything, but I thought it was cool that Yogi had worn the glove I would now be throwing to in this game. And, what the hell, maybe Berra did sprinkle a little pixie dust of perfection on it.

Twenty years ago, I followed Larsen, forever the perfect game pitcher, and pitched my own perfect game against the Montreal Expos on July 18, 1999. For the first time since that memorable day, I recently watched a videotape of the game to relive those eighty-eight pitches and to rewind to all the tense and euphoric moments. Fans constantly remind me of the perfect game by sharing their stories about how a New Jersey Little League team listened to the ninth inning huddled around a car radio and how a son watched it with his mother and how that was the last game they ever saw together. I appreciate those personal accounts, but, for the first time, I wanted to dissect my performance in search of the answer to this question: How did I manage to pitch a perfect game?

The older I got, the more I appreciated the warm weather because it allowed my arm to get loose and stay loose, so the sweltering conditions didn't bother me. The leadoff batter was Wilton Guerrero, and I struck him out on a 0-2 slider that pierced the outside corner. Well, on that day it did. The pitch was actually several inches off the plate, and I don't think it would have been called a strike in 2019. There is much more emphasis on having a uniform strike zone in today's game and umpires are graded, so there are fewer opportunities for pitchers to expand the strike zone. The batters were even conditioned for those pitches on the edges to be called strikes; Guerrero didn't argue the call and returned to the dugout. One batter into the game, I knew that Umpire Ted Barrett seemed willing to give me a few extra inches on the corners, and I planned to exploit that.

It's strange to watch a game in which I know the outcome and to still think Terry Jones, the second batter, had just lined a hit to right field. But, as a viewer, that was how I felt when Jones made contact with my two-strike fastball. On that day, I was beginning to head toward third to back up the base. But Paul O'Neill came in on the ball, then hustled to his right, lunged for it, and made a sprawling, one-handed catch about waist high. Trust me, at that moment I didn't feel perfect. I retired Rondell White on a deep fly out to left on one pitch to end the first inning, the first of five one-pitch at bats I had in the game. Those one-pitch outs were all bonuses, all examples of a team that wasn't interested in or capable of working the count.

The sight of the dangerous Vladimir Guerrero wiggling his bat and standing in the batter's box in the second inning was a reminder of how Girardi and I strategized about getting the Expos to chase pitches off the plate. None of the Expos had ever faced me. That helped me because they had never seen my slider and had never seen me change my arm angle to throw it. Obviously, Guerrero, a free swinger, was a candidate to chase. But Guerrero could also hurt me if I didn't throw pitches far enough outside; like Yogi, he was an excellent bad-ball hitter. After Guerrero missed an 0-1 slider a few inches off the outside corner, I threw another slider about two feet off the plate. It worked. Guerrero swung at a pitch that landed in the left-handed batter's box and missed it. Two groundouts helped me roll through the second.

Between innings, I made the brief walk from the first base dugout to the clubhouse and replaced an undershirt that was soaked with perspiration. I had worked only two innings, but I was comfortable with all my pitches (fastball, slider, and splitter) and I was also optimistic about Barrett's strike zone being loose on both sides. And, as we had anticipated, the Expos were chasing my pitches, so that meant my slider and my creativity could be their Kryptonite.

I don't think I've ever removed my cap to wipe away the sweat on my forehead as much as I did that day. Because of the scalding weather, I worked quickly and the Expos rarely stepped out of the batter's box to try and disrupt my rhythm. That's a simple way to bother a pitcher or at least slow him down, but the Expos were swinging away. With a 5–0 lead in the third and the skies turning gray, I induced Chris Widger to swing at a slider that was at least six inches off the plate for a strikeout. Shane Andrews had an equally futile at bat and waved at another two-strike slider, and I also whiffed Orlando Cabrera on another slider.

Something was brewing with my pitches. I could sense it. I'm not saying I was thinking about a perfect game, but even as I studied my body language from twenty years ago, I could see that I had some swagger after offering a clinic on sliders and striking out the side.

To say I threw a slider that day is misleading because I actually threw a variety of sliders, based on the different arm angles from where I released the pitch and the different ways the pitch broke. I had the perfect slider against the Expos because my pitches had some side-to-side movement and they also had some downward movement, meaning they behaved like my most attractive sliders since the Wiffle ball days in my backyard in Kansas City. And just like my brother, Chris, the Expos were flailing at my sliders.

What also helped make my slider especially effective is how I set the Expos up to be able to use it as my out pitch. The Expos didn't initially stroll to the plate and wave their bats futilely at slider after slider. But, because I never even had a three-ball count and was able to get ahead so often, I forced them to chase my swing-and-miss pitches. Once they did, I kept targeting my pitches off the corners.

Those threatening gray skies produced rain in the bottom of the third and the game was delayed. I was panicky about keeping my arm warm so I asked Luigi Castillo, one of our batboys, to play catch with me in the hallway outside our clubhouse. Imagine a narrow hallway that was about ten feet wide with ceilings that were about ten feet high, and you have the visual image of where I warmed up. It was me and Luigi tossing a ball and Charlie Zabransky, the kindly guard at the clubhouse door, watching us. My throws skimmed the ceiling a few times because it's not easy to throw pitches in such a confined area, but I didn't care if every throw caromed off the ceiling. I just wanted to stay loose. The delay lasted thirty-three minutes.

Relieved that the rain had passed, I soon realized that I felt stronger and that my fastball had more velocity. I hung a slider to Wilton Guerrero and he drilled it to the right field warning track, but then I whiffed Jones on a splitter and dispatched White on the first pitch in the fourth. Twelve up and twelve down. The fifth was pivotal because I had to face their fourth, fifth, and sixth hitters. I erased Vladimir Guerrero on one pitch, and I got Jose Vidro and Brad Fullmer on fly outs. After that, I finally allowed myself to think about a perfect game because I had retired their middle-of-the-order hitters twice and because I was more than halfway home. In the dugout, I sipped on a bottle of water to stay hydrated, and I wore a jacket over my right arm to keep warm, although I think it would have been impossible to feel cold on that day.

Changing out of sweaty undershirts multiple times in the club-house, I had heard radio announcers John Sterling and Michael Kay describing how I was pitching a perfect game. I know there is a baseball superstition that it's taboo to mention a perfect game or a no-hitter, but I've never thought that should extend to broadcasters. An announcer's job is to tell the story of the game, so it didn't impact me at all to hear John and Michael talking about my bid for perfection. Has there ever been a pitcher who didn't know he was pitching a no-hitter or a perfect game?

If I were pitching in fifty-degree weather, I'd still have veins bulging in my neck. But on a day where the heat index was surely over one hundred, those veins were even more pronounced and looked as thick as electrical cables. By the sixth, I noticed more fans standing and screaming and pushing me toward another spotless inning. I raced through a five-pitch sixth that ended with Cabrera popping up in foul territory and Girardi hustling to our on-deck circle and making a superb one-handed catch. When I tried to shake Joe's hand near the top step of our dugout, he wouldn't look at me. Yes, he was superstitious.

With nine outs to go, my crowded brain shifted into a form of hyperawareness about everything that was happening. I was so laser-focused on every sign Girardi put down, every grip I had on the baseball, and even every time the fans reacted to another out. Nine outs seemed attainable. Do you know many times I had retired nine straight? Dozens of times. That was all I needed to do to be perfect, but I also knew I was one misplaced pitch, one bloop single, or one well-placed grounder away from losing it all.

That almost happened to begin the seventh. The speedy Wilton Guerrero slapped a hard grounder to the left side, and third baseman Scott Brosius reacted quickly to snare it and throw him out. If Brosius hadn't cut the ball off and it had gotten to the shortstop hole, I think it would have been an infield hit. I struck out

James Mouton on a slider that landed about two feet outside and also whiffed White on another slider. As I left the mound in the seventh, I took a deep breath. I had six outs to go, six outs that I was envisioning in my head.

Pitchers strive to be efficient, throwing all of their pitches for strikes, keeping hitters off balance and notching as many quick outs as possible, and that was my most efficient game ever. Of my eighty-eight pitches, sixty-eight were strikes. When I threw my fastball, I almost always threw it on the edges and stayed away from the center of the plate. Because I was finishing some at bats on one or two pitches, I could see how the Expos were getting antsy, and that allowed me to expand the zone with my slider.

No one would talk to me in the dugout, except for one person. That person was Chili Davis in the bottom of the seventh inning. Earlier in the game, Girardi was delayed in getting back on the field so Davis caught my warm-ups. I threw very softly to Chili and that annoyed him. He sat beside me in the dugout and he said, "I caught in the minor leagues. Let it go. Don't baby it with me. I can catch your shit." In the midst of a perfect game, Chili thought I was disrespecting him by not throwing my best fastballs during warm-ups. That made me chuckle. Props to Chili for putting me in my place. He could catch my shit.

Stand up, walk around, sit down, and then do it all over again. That was my routine in the dugout as our bottom of the seventh seemingly stretched on forever. I was ready to return to the mound because Montreal's two best hitters (Vladimir Guerrero and Vidro) loomed in the eighth. After retiring Guerrero on one slider, I fell behind Vidro with a 2-0 count. I knew I had to give in and throw him a fastball in that situation. If I was pursuing a no-hitter, it wouldn't have mattered if I walked him. But with a perfect game, a walk would kill it. So I threw a fastball and Vidro smacked a hard grounder up the middle, a ball that smelled like a single

as it whizzed past me. But Chuck Knoblauch, our second baseman, glided to his right to field the grounder and fired it to first.
Knoblauch had experienced throwing yips in that emotional season and didn't always make reliable throws to first, but he threw
an absolute bullet on that saving play. And now I was starting to
think that might have been the break I needed to finish this thing.
I refused to throw Fullmer any fastballs because he was a dead-red
hitter, meaning he looked only for fastballs, and I whiffed him on a
slider, which, again, was a borderline call. That was fine with me.
Three outs to go.

All of these years later, it's interesting to see how I looked around
the Stadium after the eighth ended, my eyes seeming like they were
gazing all the way to the last row of the upper deck. I knew this
was my day now, and I was trying to soak up as much of the energy
from the fans as I could. I had come close to pitching a no-hitter
in the past, and I realized how draining every pitch could be. When
every pitch is the one that can end a masterpiece, a pitcher worries
every second. That was what I was doing, fretting on every pitch.
After I returned to the dugout, no one shook my hand or patted
me on the back and, obviously, no one said a word. I was off-limits,
even to Chili.

I retreated to the clubhouse in the bottom of the eighth inning,
changed my undershirt one last time, and didn't see a soul. Usually,
there would be some clubhouse attendants in the room or a player
dashing back to get batting gloves or use the bathroom. But no one
wanted to speak to me, so they scattered. It was a lonely existence,
but I was fine with being ignored because I never liked to talk when
I was pitching.

As soon as I popped my head out of the dugout for the ninth
inning, I heard the fans roar. Yes, they were pushing me and guiding me and helping me. *You can do this*, I told myself, a conclusion
I eventually reached after staring at myself in the mirror between

innings. I threw my final warm-up pitch from the stretch position because that was what I always did. But, in a way, it was a curious way to prepare for the ninth. The only way I would have needed to pitch from the stretch was if the Expos managed to get a base runner, and I was desperately trying to not let that happen.

Widger was the first batter, and his at bat typified everything I was trying to achieve that day and, really, everything I always tried to achieve with my slider. I threw the right-handed-hitting Widger a slider that looked like it was going to be a strike, but it dropped a few inches below his knees and he swung and missed. Then I threw a slower slider, which caused him to flinch, and the pitch clipped the outside corner for a called strike. Finally, I lowered my arm angle a bit and threw a harder slider, and he swung at and missed a pitch that ended up about a foot off the outside corner. Two outs to go.

In the span of three sliders, Widger swung at a ball, he stared at a strike, and he swung at another ball for the strikeout. When a pitcher can confuse a hitter in that manner, he can disrupt the hitter's approach and destroy the hitter's confidence. Even when a batter is looking for a slider, if a pitcher can consistently throw a slider for a strike or make it look like a strike, he can still befuddle the batter, as I did with Widger.

The next batter was Ryan McGuire, a left-handed pinch-hitter, and I threw a first-pitch fastball that grazed the outside corner for a strike. Girardi signaled for a cutter, but I shook him off for the first time to throw another fastball. I missed with a high fastball, then I rushed through my delivery and missed with a splitter. With a 2-1 count, McGuire called time-out and stepped out of the batter's box. That was smart. The Expos should have done more of that. I grimaced as I waited. I felt like I had to challenge him with a fastball. Joe called for a splitter, but I shook him off to get to a fastball and I threw it past the batter for strike two. We next decided to go with a slider, and it bent inside and caught a lot of the plate, and McGuire looped it to left field. And then the adventure started. It was a soft fly ball, but Ricky Ledee had been bothered by the shadows all day and he lost the ball as it descended from the bright sky. Somehow, he made a basket catch about chest high. It wasn't pretty, but I didn't care. I was one out away.

I was so exhausted for that final batter. I'm even a little exhausted now as I'm watching myself pitch, watching myself trying to finish this game. There was physical exhaustion, but the mental exhaustion was more taxing because, as I said, every pitch is precious. With Cabrera being such a free swinger, I knew I had to continue throwing sliders. On my third slider of the at bat, Cabrera swung under it and popped it up to third base. I pointed to the ball and placed my hands behind my head and waited and waited for the ball to come down. I knew I had done it. When Brosius caught it in foul territory for the final out, I dropped to my knees. I think I was trying to emulate a tennis player who I had once seen win Wimbledon or something like that. Girardi raced toward me, just like Berra had raced toward Larsen, and we hugged. Joe pulled me down on top of him to protect me, and my teammates piled on top of us. Underneath all of those pinstriped bodies, I'm not sure I uttered any words. I didn't know what to say.

To celebrate the sixteenth perfect game in baseball history, Girardi, Davis, and Knoblauch lifted me up and carried me off the field. Since I'd seen this happen to Dwight Gooden after his no-hitter and to David Wells after his perfect game, I had wondered what it would be like to be the king of the hill. Now I knew. I pumped my glove over and over to the fans, the same fans who helped will me through those twenty-seven outs. It started out as my most relaxing day and it ended as my most fulfilling day. Twenty years later, I discovered exactly how I did it. I won't wait another twenty years to watch it again.

Chapter 17

THE BASEBALL FIX

IT WAS FULFILLING TO WIN a World Series ring in 2000 and to get one out against Mike Piazza in Game 4, but the rest of the season was awful and my failure gnawed at me. I needed to cleanse myself of that year. A 4-14 record and a 6.91 earned run average? That wasn't me. That had never been me and I couldn't let that be the last stat line of my career and the last glimpse anyone would see of me in the major leagues.

The Yankees had some interest in signing me after I had struggled so severely, but they made it clear that I would have a reduced role at a modest salary. I didn't like the sound of that arrangement and I didn't want to beg for a roster spot, so I moved on, something that seemed to surprise them. I don't blame the Yankees for not guaranteeing much after the way I had pitched, but I also don't think they could blame me for deciding to seek a new baseball home.

The Kansas City Royals, the Montreal Expos, and the Texas Rangers contacted me about pitching for them. Alex Rodriguez, the $252 million man who had become the highest-paid player in baseball history, called twice to recruit me to the Rangers. I was flattered that A-Rod thought I could help the Rangers, but none of those situations felt right to me. I loved the crazy, passionate

East Coast baseball mentality, and I was trying to stay in the middle of it.

With the days before spring training dwindling, I basically tried out for the Red Sox in January by playing long-toss with Joe Kerrigan, their pitching coach, on a soccer field in Clearwater, Florida. The Red Sox were satisfied enough with what they saw in my delivery that they offered me a minor league contract. *That's all I need*, I thought. *I can make this team.* The Yankees and the Red Sox have the fiercest rivalry in baseball, and it felt strange to be switching sides, but I was beyond that emotion. I was now employed by the Red Sox, who wanted me and who offered me a chance to redeem myself.

Redemption came because I found my slider, my trusty slider, again, with help from Kerrigan. I barely studied any videotape in my career, but Kerrigan was excellent with video analysis and he was the first coach who ever did a split-screen comparison of me at different career points. He showed me video of my delivery from my dreadful 2000 season paired up against what I'd looked like a few years earlier. It was extremely useful to see those side-by-side comparisons and to be able to stop the tape during specific parts of my delivery to see what I had done differently.

While I sat in front of the screen with Kerrigan, he uncovered that I was collapsing on my back leg too soon and that caused my sliders to hang. And I hung a lot of sliders in 2000. Instead of standing upright for a longer period in my delivery and then driving my body downhill, I was bending my back leg too soon and lowering my body earlier. That positioning meant my slider had an up-and-over effect, and after I released it from a lower angle, it would hang in the zone. Kerrigan told me to quiet my body so I wasn't moving as forcefully toward the plate, sacrificing velocity for a better release point.

Regaining my slider allowed me to scale a mental hurdle and

333

allowed me to feel like a complete pitcher again. For so many years, the slider had been my lifeline, the pitch that could rescue me. But the slider deserted me in 2000 and, no matter how many grips I tried and how many arm angles I tried, I couldn't throw those sharp and biting sliders that I needed. What also confounded me was how I lost control of my body and felt unbalanced. When a pitcher can't make his body cooperate with what he's trying to do, he makes too many adjustments, and when they fail he becomes desperate, almost as if the mound is quicksand and he's stuck. Finally, I wasn't stuck anymore.

My troublesome right shoulder delayed my debut with the Red Sox until mid-May. But once I returned, I felt rejuvenated because my slider was a weapon again, and I felt balanced again. I opened the season with a 7–1 record and a 4.18 ERA. More importantly, we were battling the Yankees in the American League East. As late as July 21, the two teams were tied for first.

It was another season of hope growing in Boston, but we had as deflating a second half as a team could have. Pedro Martinez pitched only three times in the last three months and argued with the front office about the severity of his shoulder injury. Manny Ramirez, who was in the first year of a $160 million contract, was booed for not hustling, and there was talk about how he felt he had made a mistake in signing with Boston. Carl Everett and Manager Jimy Williams had a shouting match in Williams's office, their voices booming through the walls and into the clubhouse. Williams was fired and Kerrigan replaced him and Everett clashed with Kerrigan, too. The Red Sox tried to demote John Cumberland, the acting pitching coach, to the minor leagues. He refused to accept the demotion and was fired. After that development, Nomar Garciaparra was overheard saying, "That's why nobody wants to play here."

These scenes unfolded like a depressing soap opera as a once-promising season kept getting worse and worse. The Yankees beat us by thirteen games and won the division, increasing Boston's drought without a championship to eighty-three years.

Along the way, I did get an up-close view of one of the best pitchers I've ever seen in Martinez. One of the things I loved about Martinez was how he was true to his style as a pitcher, which was a different style than the one favored by old-school pitching coaches. Pedro was a power pitcher, but he threw the baseball from an angle in which he actually got underneath the ball. If you studied Martinez's release point on some pitches, his arm was almost directly sidearm when he let go of the baseball. He wanted to get under the ball like that so it would force the ball to rise up and sail out of the strike zone. Those old-school pitching coaches wanted a pitcher who had his arm up high and drove the ball downhill. Sometimes, Pedro looked like he was throwing the ball uphill.

I thought Pedro's style was interesting and invigorating because it reinforced the notion that there are a lot of different styles and a lot of different ways that pitchers can succeed. I've already mentioned how I argued with some pitching coaches because I didn't think there was a one-style-fits-all approach for pitchers and I rebelled against anyone who taught that. Every pitcher has a different style, based on his body type, and it's smart to pitch the way that feels most natural to you. That was what Pedro did. He was a five-foot-eleven-inch assassin.

Whenever we warmed up near each other, Pedro's arm would flash across his body, and he would throw his changeup so hard that I could hear the ball ripping off his fingertips. It sounded as if someone was ripping twenty-five-year-old wallpaper off a wall. I'd never heard that loud of a sound on a pitcher's changeup, and it was indicative of how incredible his arm speed was on the pitch, a pitch with amazing left-to-right movement that almost acted like a screwball.

Although Martinez was a wisp of a major leaguer at 170 pounds, he had insanely long and flexible fingers. Pedro could take his index finger and his middle finger and bend them back and touch his forearm. I've never seen that kind of flexibility and I'd never seen any pitcher do anything like that. It was almost like he was double-jointed. Those fingers enabled him to hang on to the baseball longer, and that helped him generate more spin on his pitches.

What also helped make Pedro extraordinary was his attention to detail. He was one of the first pitchers I ever saw who practiced throwing high fastballs in the bullpen. Most pitchers try to throw perfect strikes during their bullpen sessions, and if they hit the corners with enough pitches, they are content. But Pedro would practice throwing pitches that were considered bad pitches, which was what I liked to do, too. I saw Martinez throw ten straight high fastballs because he wanted to be sure that pitch was precise enough to entice batters to swing.

Martinez had tremendous stuff, but he loved his fastball, he loved to intimidate batters, and he didn't mind if a pitch strayed too far inside. During a game against the Yankees in 2003, Martinez hit Derek Jeter and Alfonso Soriano in his first eleven pitches of the game and both went to the hospital for X-rays. That mentality earned Martinez a reputation as a bit of a head hunter, something we really don't see anymore in today's game. The days of Nolan Ryan giving a batter a bow tie—which, of course, was a pitch under the neck—don't exist anymore. I consider that progress for the sport. I don't think pitchers need to throw close to someone's head to establish themselves on the inside corner.

Zero after zero after zero. On an early September night at Fenway Park, I was matching zeros with Mike Mussina, who I respected as a smart and durable pitcher. But I was only matching Mussina with zeros in the runs column. There were other zero totals that Mussina accumulated that I hadn't matched. He hadn't allowed a hit, a walk, or a base runner through eight innings and was three outs away from a perfect game.

I was the last pitcher to throw a perfect game two years earlier, and now I was competing against a pitcher who was trying to throw his own perfect game. Having been in that nerve-wracking position, I understood what Mussina was thinking and feeling as he worked through every pitch. When a pitcher knows he can't make one mistake, one tiny mistake, every pitch is more physically and mentally demanding. No matter how many times I told myself to just throw my pitches in the late innings, I thought about my perfect game on every pitch. My pursuit of a perfect game was different because we had a 5–0 lead after two innings, so I wasn't thinking about winning and losing. Mussina was pitching a perfect game in a game that might go into extra innings and I was part of the reason why. With a scoreless ninth, I could have potentially blocked Mussina from getting a perfect game. If Mussina was perfect through nine and the score was still 0–0, that wouldn't have been an official perfect game. He would have had to remain perfect in extra innings.

Anyway, I failed to make that happen as the Yankees scored an unearned run against me to take a 1–0 lead. Mussina retired the first two batters in the ninth and then had to face Everett. On an 0-2 fastball, Everett punched a single to left field to ruin the perfecto. Mussina put his hands on his hips, shook his head, and grimaced. He won the game, 1–0, but he lost the chance at history. The next time I saw Mussina, I tried to compliment him about his near-perfect game, but he wasn't interested in having that discussion. I like Mussina and we got along pretty well, but he wasn't the type who was going to reflect on the game, as great as it was.

I stopped thinking and caring about baseball when our world changed on September 11, 2001. Like millions and millions of Americans, I was devastated by the terrorist attacks on the World Trade Center and the Pentagon. I had played in New York for twelve years and still had an apartment in New York, so I considered that my home. After those attacks, I was in Tampa with the Red Sox. I was depressed and so angry and I wanted to be in New York. To help people, to console people, to do whatever I could to try and help the city, my city, heal. After Boston's season ended, I sat in my apartment and watched the Yankees lose to the Arizona Diamondbacks in the World Series, and that was depressing. Those players were my friends and my old teammates; even if I had just competed against them all season, I was sad when they lost. All that sadness helped me decide it was time for me to say good-bye to baseball. The Red Sox offered me a contract for 2002 and the Expos were interested, too, but I didn't want to pitch anymore.

I never dreamed I would be so miserable as a retired player, but I was. It was almost an identity crisis that I experienced because I didn't have baseball to lean on anymore. I remember telling friends and family members that I was going to pursue some business ventures, perhaps do some speaking engagements and look for a real job. When I sat down at my desk to craft a résumé, my pen never budged and the sheet of paper remained blank because I had no practical job experience. That was such a scary moment that I dropped the pen. I'm guessing every retired athlete has that kind of wakeup call at some point. It just showed how wrapped up I still was in baseball and how I wasn't over it.

When my old buddy Al Leiter called me in 2003 and asked if I was interested in pitching with him on the Mets, it sounded like a great idea. I was a pitcher who just couldn't let go, so Al's invite meant that I could return to the life that I loved. I was forty, I hadn't pitched in more than a year, I had a painful hip condition, and I tried to come out of retirement and pitch.

Why? Because I was desperate to pitch again, desperate to rekindle that feeling of being on the mound and getting batters to swing and miss or pop out or ground out. I wanted that fix, but my comeback didn't last long.

I always thought it would be my arm that ended my career, but it was my hip that stopped me. I had a pretty long stride in my drop-and-drive pitching style, and I just didn't have enough power to drive forward with the lower half of my body. I would push forward, but then I would pull up on the landing because my hip felt like it had an ax stuck in it when I tried to land. I had a cortisone shot in the hip and that gave me some relief. Two weeks later, the pain returned. I asked myself, "How many more of these shots am I going to have to get?" That was when I started to get miserable again. I pitched only five games with the Mets before I retired again. It was over, truly over, this time.

Golf was my savior. I played every day for about three or four years and went from being terrible to being able to play a decent round. But I can genuinely say it took me about ten years to put the end of my baseball career in perspective. After I retired, whenever the clock would hit 7:05 p.m., which is usually the time the first pitch is thrown, I would feel as if something was amiss in my life. The same held true every February because I was so accustomed to reporting for spring training. I would feel as if I should be throwing a baseball somewhere and getting ready for the season. There's such a structured life for baseball players, and that can be a detriment. All our luggage is carried by someone else. All our reservations are made by someone else. We are given cash to pay for our meals. We are told what time to show up, and the bus or the airplane takes us to the next destination. It's so regimented, but it's all being done for you and it all works out for you. That's not the real world.

Becoming a broadcaster for the YES Network has been a life-saver for me because it has kept me close to the game and allowed me to feel like I'm still connected to a team. I do need to know when pitchers and catchers are reporting for spring training because that impacts my work schedule. I do need to know when the Yankees play the Red Sox because I will be announcing those games. What I have learned about myself is that I need to be around baseball. It doesn't mean I have to put on a uniform and run out on the field, but I want to be able to reach out and touch the game. I can do that as an announcer.

My style as an announcer is to find a way to say what I used to say in the dugout as a player, but with more of a filter. I look for patterns and tendencies and I try to read at bats. I have attended the same kind of scouting meetings these teams have held before a series, so within the first few at bats of a series, I can tell how a team is planning to pitch a batter. If the Red Sox attacked Gary Sanchez with sliders on the outside corner in three straight at bats, it's obvious they believe he's been anxious lately and will probably chase those pitches out of the zone. In that situation, I can discuss Boston's strategy and how Sanchez can counter what the Red Sox are doing to him. If I was still sitting in the dugout, I would be saying the same thing to my teammates.

Since I'm such a player's advocate and since I know how difficult it is to play this game, I had to determine a comfortable way to critique a pitcher's performance. I resolved this by acting as if I was critiquing one of my own starts. With that approach, the words flow smoothly as I say, "They should have stayed away from the fastball in that spot because the batter was obviously ready for it" or "He hung a slider in the worst place a pitcher can hang a slider."

When I provide those critiques, I'm actually thinking about the many times I did those same things. I lived in the same cleats as those failed pitchers, so I want to bring that emotion and insight to the air.

I'm very aware of what I say during games, and it's pivotal that I remain true to myself as a broadcaster. I have a job to do now. The YES Network is my team. I put a headset on, I watch the game, and I speak candidly about what's happening on the field. And that means the good, the bad, and the ugly. If I didn't do that, I would lose credibility as a broadcaster. When I have to analyze managerial decisions and player performances, I'm drawing on more than thirty years of experience around professional baseball. There are times where I will criticize the manager or a player because it's appropriate. My mantra is this: To be a good broadcaster, you have to tell the truth.

"Coney knows the game, he studies the game, and he's passionate about the game," said John J. Filippelli, the president of production and programming for YES. "When he's in the booth, you can feel that he's living through every pitch and every play as if he was still pitching."

When I first started working for YES, I was reluctant to speak with the players before the game because I didn't want to be intrusive. It's kind of strange because reporters will tell you I was as accommodating as any player they ever covered, but as an announcer, I didn't want to interfere with a player's preparation. As the years have passed and I've grown more comfortable in my position, I do like to hang around the batting cage because, again, that keeps me close to the game. I can't pitch anymore, but man, can I talk about pitching.

And sometimes I don't talk. I scold. During a game between the Yankees and the Mets in May 2013, I was surprised when Matt Harvey threw a changeup to Lyle Overbay and he laced it for a run-scoring single. Harvey had struck out Overbay on a changeup in his previous at bat, so I blasted him and catcher John Buck for choosing that pitch again. With Harvey firing 98-mile-per-hour fastballs and 91-mile-per-hour sliders, I didn't think he needed to mess around with a changeup. I was so immersed in that sequence that I probably went overboard in critiquing them. If Harvey or Buck heard my assessment, they probably would have been ticked. As luck would have it, both Harvey and I are Jay-Z fans. I bumped into Harvey at Mr. Carter's concert at Yankee Stadium a few months later.

"You know, I crushed you pretty good for throwing that changeup," I said to Harvey.

Harvey told me we were cool. He agreed that the change was a bad pitch and said he could tell Overbay was expecting it. I was relieved that he handled it as well as he did. He even asked me a few questions about the way I pitched in certain situations. In the end, I made those comments about Harvey because I have so much passion for the art of pitching.

I've talked with CC Sabathia about different ways to grip a slider and how power pitchers can become finesse pitchers, which are the types of conversations I still love having. All pitching, all the time. In A. J. Burnett's last season with the Yankees, he approached me and wanted to talk about his mechanics. He seemed confused by what the Yankees were suggesting he try to do with his windup, and he asked me if I had ever adjusted my mechanics during the season. I smiled and told Burnett I was the king of re-creating myself and that I made changes all the time. I didn't want to have a deep discussion about his mechanics because I'm not a coach and I never want to step on anyone's toes, but I told Burnett he should try to simplify things. If I focused on one simple thought related to my delivery like, for instance, the placement of my hands, it made me more comfortable.

In more than a decade of broadcasting, I've never had a player complain to me about something I said, which is a streak I'm proud of and which I hope speaks to my honesty. I occasionally walk through the Yankee clubhouse to chat with some players, but I don't do it too often because it's a much different atmosphere from when I played. Before games, I would routinely hold court with reporters because I enjoyed it, and I also thought it helped my teammates who disliked dealing with the media. These days, there are times where I only see a few players by their lockers, so it's not worth hanging around in there.

But the clubhouse isn't my home anymore. The booth is. When 7:05 rolls around, I still get the same itch I got twenty years ago. I'm eager for the game to start. I want to see if the umpire is giving any extra room off the corners, I want to study the interaction between the pitcher and the catcher, and I want to see how the pitchers are attacking the hitters. I'm in the booth with one of the best seats in the house. It's not the same as throwing a baseball. Nothing is. But this is a pretty sweet alternative. This is enough to fulfill my baseball fix.

EXTRA INNINGS

WINNING THE BATTLE WITH BONDS

I THREW SIZZLING FASTBALLS THAT WERE up and in to Barry Bonds, the most prolific home run hitter of all time, and I lived to talk about it. Fortunately for me, I only faced Bonds during the first six seasons of my career when I sported a fastball that hovered in the mid-90s and I could throw it past some of the best hitters in baseball.

Bonds slugged 762 career homers, but he only managed one against me in forty-five plate appearances and, interestingly enough, that came in his first at bat. My explanation for this revolves around fortunate timing as I faced Bonds when my fastballs resembled aspirin tablets and when he was still growing as a hitter. Eventually, steroid suspicions or not, Bonds became the most fearsome hitter in the major leagues. Ten of Bonds's best season home-run totals occurred after 1992, the last season that I pitched against him.

When I was with the Mets and Bonds was the left fielder for the Pittsburgh Pirates, I thought he had a little hole in his swing so I was able to beat him with inside fastballs that I elevated. Usually, I threw fastballs above the belt and right at the hands on the inside corner and they handcuffed him. Year after menacing year, Bonds got much better at covering up that hole, but, when I faced him, it was an area I exploited. And, if I got ahead in the

347

count, I would also use my splitters down and away to see if he would chase them.

Still, although Bonds was 7 for 40 (.175 average) against me with five strikeouts, five walks, and that one homer, that doesn't mean I was thrilled to face him. I feared Bonds, just like the other 448 pitchers who allowed at least one homer against him. In fact, I showed Bonds the ultimate respect by walking him with the bases loaded during a game in 1991. The Mets were already losing to the Pirates, 1–0, in the third inning so I couldn't afford to allow another run to cross the plate, but I also didn't want Bonds to put a ball into the gap or hit one over the fence. I threw five pitches, my kind of pitcher's pitches just off the corners, and he only fouled off one so I was more comfortable with walking him than letting him swing at an appealing pitch. Those were the only two runs I allowed in eight innings as we lost, 4–3, in fifteen innings.

I was in my last full season with the Red Sox as Bonds smashed a record-setting seventy-three homers in 2001, but I have often wondered how I would have attacked Bonds in that season. Since Bonds had such a great eye and once walked 232 times in a season, it would have been problematic for the 2001 version of me to go up and in with fastballs again because he probably wouldn't have swung at those pitches. But I definitely would have tried to expand the zone to see if I could have tempted him with the same type of pitches that had worked in the past. Still, my fastball had lost several miles per hour in velocity, so it would have been very, very tough for me to continue to retire the older, wiser, and better Bonds.

Every so often, someone will notice my statistics against Bonds and will ask me how I managed to dominate him. I tell them that I didn't really dominate Bonds and that our matchups need to be put into context. It was early in our careers and I used my above-average fastball to exploit a small area of the plate. There are numerous hitters who were far inferior to Bonds and they pummeled me. Again, it's all about timing and perspective. Long before Bonds became the greatest home run hitter of all time, I challenged him with fastballs and lived to talk about it. But I would never boast about it.

NOTHING BUT FASTBALLS FOR CAL

I TRIED TO GIVE CAL RIPKEN JR. hints about what I was doing without ever saying a word. I was the starter in the final game of Ripken's glorious career in 2001 and I wanted him to know that it was going to be a matchup filled with fastballs. No sliders, no splitters, and no trickery. For everything that Ripken had meant to baseball in playing day after day for the Baltimore Orioles, I decided to try and help him have another special moment.

After my first couple of pitches, Ripken stared at me. He later said, "It was almost like I could read his mind and he was saying, 'OK, it's going to be nothing but fastballs today.'" So the talented Ripken was a mind reader, too, because that was what my expression was saying. By giving Ripken a knowing grin and some optimistic eyes, I hoped he would figure out that I had no desire to change arm angles or nibble at the corners with breaking pitches.

Here's my best fastball, Cal, I basically said with my pitches. *Let's see how far you can hit it.*

That wasn't what Joe Kerrigan, my manager with the Red Sox, wanted me to do. Before the game, Kerrigan told me I should challenge Ripken the way I normally would, but that was white noise because I had already decided that I was going to throw all fastballs. And, if Ripken happened to knock one of them out at

Camden Yards, I would have watched him soak up his fifty-eighth ovation of the game and maybe even tipped my cap to him.

There was so much love and affection for Ripken in Baltimore that night. Bill Clinton, the forty-second president of the United States, was one of the 48,807 people who were fortunate enough to be in attendance. Those fans saw the starting lineup of the 1981 Orioles, Ripken's first team, trot onto the field before the first inning. They saw Cal's number 8 etched into the outfield grass. They saw a one-hundred-foot picture of Ripken displayed on the warehouse wall behind right field and they chanted "Thank You, Cal" with reverence. As a supporting actor in Ripken's finale, I admit that I got caught up in the tributes to the man who broke Lou Gehrig's seemingly unbreakable record of 2,130 consecutive games played by playing in 2,632 straight games. In my Forrest Gump–like relationship with Ripken, I also faced him in the final game of that illustrious streak, a game in which he went 0 for 3.

I thought my plan for Ripken was a perfect honor to a great baseball ambassador, but a problem occurred because my fastballs kept sinking and cutting, and that made them nastier pitches. I was trying to throw straight fastballs to Cal, but my pitches kept darting and moving, and that wasn't supposed to be part of the plan. Now I wasn't trying to put a baseball on a tee for him, but I was trying to give him something decent to hit.

The fans were standing and shouting during Ripken's first at bat, which they pretty much did for him all night long. That at bat was actually Ripken's best chance for a hit as he drilled my 1-0 fastball to left field, but he didn't elevate the ball enough, and the liner died at the warning track. By Cal's second at bat, I could sense he was aware of my plan to feed him fastballs.

"I was sitting on the bench and I'm thinking, 'Is he going to do this all game?'" Ripken later said. "The next time I went up there, I took another look out at him, and I got another fastball. And, after that, I was just looking for a fastball on every pitch. He still had a good fastball. It's not like it was easy to hit."

When Ripken swung at a 2-0 fastball in his second at bat, the pitch sank and he got under it and popped out to shortstop. In the millisecond after he swung, I twisted my head to watch the flight of the ball and said "Damn" in frustration. Most of the players in the Orioles' dugout saw me do that, so now they all knew my plan.

With an accomplished hitter like Cal, it wasn't as if I could lob the ball in there at 80 miles per hour because that would have messed him up even more. So I kept trying to throw him my best stuff and said: *Here it is, hit it.* I wanted to throw the fastballs right down the middle, but they had life on them and I couldn't control that.

The flashbulbs were popping and everyone seemed to be standing and praying when Ripken strode to the plate for his third at bat in the eighth inning. We were winning, 4–1, and I was pitching well, so the fans anticipated that this might be Cal's final at bat. I even saw some fans wiping away tears. They roared so much that Cal didn't even get in the batter's box until he removed his helmet and tipped it to them. Once again, I wanted Ripken to feast on fastballs. With a 2-1 count, my fastball cut toward the outside corner and Ripken belted it to center. I whipped my body around and turned to look at Trot Nixon camping under the fly ball. It was the first and only time in my career that I had wished a batter had hit the ball about fifty feet farther.

"I didn't control myself as much as I should have," Ripken recalled. "It was more of my anxiousness because I knew what was coming. I kind of started my swing early because I was trying not to be late."

A few years later, Ripken and I spoke at Yankee Stadium, and he thanked me for what I had done in his final game. We discussed the mentality of the pitcher-hitter matchup, how I didn't need to say anything to him that night and he still detected what I was trying to do. I had some competitive battles with Cal and held him to 12 hits in 55 at bats (.218 average) by trying to be unpredictable and by using my slider a lot.

"That slider had a bigger break than you'd expect and he generated such spin on that pitch," Ripken said. "The only way I could describe it is to say it was a Wiffle ball–like slider or a Frisbee-like slider."

On Ripken's last night, there was so much deserved emphasis placed on him, including by me, that I didn't think too much about the fact that it could be my final game, too. And for about a year, that was my last game. I didn't pitch in 2002, and I returned briefly with the Mets in 2003. But my career was a footnote to Ripken's memorable finale in Baltimore. I tried to help send Cal out with a bang. I really did, but my fastballs didn't cooperate.

MANNY BEING MANNY

My MISSION WAS TO DECEIVE hitters. Tease them, frustrate them, and make them look foolish. I always thought I could outwit hitters by preparing, studying, and being smarter than them. But when I reflect on some of the batters who outsmarted me, the first player I think about is Manny Ramirez. Yes, Manny Ramirez.

We all know Ramirez was one of the best right-handed batters of his generation, an imposing hitter with excellent pitch recognition, vicious bat speed, and tremendous power. But there was a goofy and sometimes petulant side to Ramirez, so he didn't get enough credit for being a hitting savant, which he was. Ramirez could look and act silly, but he was serious, so serious, about hitting.

"I think Manny was as good a hitter as I've ever seen," Derek Jeter once said.

I signed a minor league contract with the Red Sox for the 2001 season, which received slightly less attention than Ramirez's eight-year, $160 million free agent deal with Boston. He was a devastating hitter, a hitter so formidable that his flaws, like shoddy defense and a detached attitude, were accepted.

After trying to retire Ramirez across several seasons, I had the opportunity to witness his preparation for games with the Red Sox, and it was impressive. While Ramirez could be a moody sort, he was always smiling when he had a bat in his hands. And I don't remember too many days in which Ramirez wasn't lugging around a bat. I bet Ramirez is swinging a bat right now, hoping he can add to his career total of 555 homers.

"I just love the game," Ramirez once said. "I just like to compete, that's it."

As Ramirez angered teammates, managers, and owners, the popular phrase to explain away his foolish actions was "That's Manny being Manny." But, as a pitcher who was trying to stop Ramirez, "Manny being Manny" was also a way to lament his offensive prowess. To me, it meant that Manny was so disciplined that he would stand in the batter's box and wait for one pitch, the pitch he thought he could crush. With that approach, Ramirez used his patience to try to set up pitchers, which was what I wanted to do to him.

In the final month of the 1999 season, Manny outsmarted me in a game between the Yankees and the Indians, his first team. On that September day, my brain was focused on the notion that Ramirez had previously swung wildly at one of my sliders and missed it by about two feet. It was surprising to see such an advanced hitter miss a pitch by that much, which should have been a clue to me that I was being baited. I don't recall the precise pitch when Ramirez flailed at that slider. It might not have even been in that game, but, in that moment, my vision was of Ramirez being clueless against my sharp-breaking slider.

With a 1-1 count in the fifth inning, I decided to sneak in a slider to try and get a second strike. I didn't snap my wrist enough and hung the pitch, and Manny was definitely waiting for it, his eyes gleaming as he destroyed it. The ball soared into the sky and kept soaring until it landed in the last row of seats in left field, almost clipping the scoreboard at Jacobs Field. Manny's moon shot traveled 471 feet and was one of the longest homers ever blasted against me.

I'm not ashamed to say Manny fooled me. Like I said, he was an intelligent hitter with a plan, and he set a trap for me and prevailed. After the homer ended my day, Ramirez had a gratified look on his face, an expression that said, *Yeah, I got another one*. Ramirez was 12 for 39 (.308 average) with 11 strikeouts against me, but that was his only homer. Obviously, it was a memorable one.

As Manny's teammate, I saw him bait pitchers all the time, and I think it was misread by some people as Manny being indifferent. If Ramirez took a fastball down the middle for a called third strike, it could be misconstrued as him being disinterested. But that wasn't true. Those called third strikes sometimes happened because Manny had baited the pitcher and was now sitting on a breaking pitch. The pitcher might have won the battle with a fastball, but Manny might have slammed a breaking pitch in the next at bat. Manny always had a well-conceived plan and he was loyal to it.

Based solely on Ramirez's superb statistics (a slash line of .312/.411/.585, 2,574 hits, and 9 top-ten MVP finishes), he should have coasted into the Hall of Fame on the first ballot. But Ramirez failed two drug tests late in his career and has never received more than 24 percent of the vote in three years on the ballot, drastically short of the 75 percent needed to receive a plaque in Cooperstown.

I don't have a vote for the Hall, so it's not my decision to say if Ramirez should be in Cooperstown. With that being said, if someone asked me to name a clever batter who had outwitted me, Ramirez's is the first name that would tumble out of my mouth. I guess it was just Manny being Manny.

INTIMIDATED BY GWYNN

Hɪs ʜᴀɴᴅs ᴡᴇʀᴇ ɪɴᴄʀᴇᴅɪʙʟʏ ǫᴜɪᴄᴋ, quicker than any batter's hands I had ever seen. No matter what type of pitch I threw, he would wait and let the baseball travel farther so that he could uncover whether it was a fastball, a slider, or a splitter. And then he would unleash his smooth swing and collect another hit. He intimidated me.

The batter I am describing is Tony Gwynn, an eight-time batting champion and the man with those lightning-quick hands. Because Gwynn had such trust in his hands and his eyes, he was supremely confident that he would make contact with the baseball and he would usually try to smack it to the opposite field. He was such a magician in the way he wielded the bat that the legendary Ted Williams called him "Houdini."

Gwynn's intimidation of me started in a strange place, on a day when I helped the Mets squash his Padres, 9–1. I gave up one run on three hits in seven innings in that game in September 1987, but, afterward, I spent a lot of time thinking about Gwynn. He had two hits against me and I marveled about his quickness to my teammates. Welcome to our world, kid, they basically said.

Since Gwynn had the ability to wait so long on pitches, he forced me to second-guess how I pitched to him. After that first game,

I never had a dependable plan for opposing Gwynn, which was a rarity for me. I always had a plan to attack hitters. I usually had multiple plans for attacking hitters. But with Gwynn, I just tried to mix my pitches up and see if I could catch him off guard with different sequences.

How did my mix-it-up approach work? Not very well. In the early 1990s, I decided to steer away from my fastball and throw more sliders and splitters to see how Gwynn would react. In doing that, I helped transform a singles hitter into a power hitter. On May 13, 1991, Gwynn sauntered to the plate in the first inning at Shea Stadium and clubbed my first pitch into the right field seats for a two-run homer. It was Gwynn's first homer in a span of 397 plate appearances, dating back to July 15, 1990. Great strategy on my part, huh?

I kept trying anything to confuse Gwynn, but I was probably confusing myself. With Gwynn batting and a runner on first on May 13, 1992, I threw over to the base three times. I had a below-average pickoff move so I was trying to keep the runner close to the base, but I think I was also delaying the inevitable against Gwynn. After the count drifted to 3-2, I tried to trick Gwynn with a slider. He wasn't fooled, belting it into the right field seats.

"It was supposed to be down and in," I told reporters. "I suppose it wasn't enough of either."

Gwynn was such a skilled hitter and such a great contact hitter that pitchers lamented how he didn't have any weaknesses that could be exploited. I'm surprised that Gwynn was only 11 for 37 (.297 average) with two homers off me because I would have guessed that his statistics were much better. He was a .338 hitter with 3,141 career hits and hit .300 or better for 19 straight seasons. My statistics against him say that I performed decently, but my stress level was always high and I'm also guessing he hit a lot of bullets right at my fielders. From the first time I spied Gwynn's

quick hands and disciplined approach, I never felt relaxed pitching to him. No matter what I threw, I was bracing for him to slap it for a hit. I wasn't alone.

"When you watched Gwynn play every day, you became immune to how great he was," said John Flaherty, a former teammate with the Padres. "Just put him down for two hits every day."

The last time I ever pitched to Gwynn came in the sixth inning of Game 3 in the 1998 Would Series between the Yankees and the Padres. In a scoreless game, Gwynn rapped a two-run single off me. Of course he did. As aggravated as I was at that time, I can now say it was a predictable result. I could never figure him out.

PRIME TIME

WITHOUT EVEN PEEKING AT STATISTICS, I knew which batters excelled against me and, unfortunately, that was why I knew Deion Sanders so intimately. I knew his slightly open stance, I knew the way he held his hands up high, and I knew his slashing swing. I knew way too much about Neon Deion.

Sanders's success against me was one of the main reasons he was featured in Atlanta's lineup when the Braves played my Blue Jays in the 1992 World Series. Not only did Sanders finish with glossy career stats off me (9 for 15, .600 average), I was very aware of how comfortable he was against me, which, whether he realized it or not, gave him a mental edge, too.

Sanders was a phenomenal athlete, talented enough to play professional football and baseball, but he was an average hitter who relied a lot on his speed. He once led the National League in triples with 14 and once stole 56 bases, but he was a .263 hitter who I should have been able to retire if I executed my pitches expertly. The Braves had other players who were superior hitters, like David Justice and Terry Pendleton, but Sanders could smack a fastball, and he punished my fastballs.

Since I knew Sanders preferred fastballs, I would throw

splitters, sliders, and curves early in the count to try and fool him, but he was disciplined and wouldn't swing. Invariably, I would fall behind in the count and I would be forced to throw fastballs; he was always patiently waiting for them, and he always made solid contact. If Sanders and I opposed each other today, my guess is I'd be hesitant to throw a fastball, I'd fall behind in the count, and he would eventually connect off a fastball.

Pitchers can be their own worst enemies by being too passive and that's what happened with me and Deion. Mentally, I created more problems against Sanders by fretting and adjusting too much. Instead of focusing on what I did well, I stressed out about every hit Sanders had against me, picturing line drives shooting into the outfield every time I faced him. I shied away from fastballs, but I should have thrown him more fastballs, just fastballs that were located better. Because I was paranoid about Sanders's success, I became defensive, I didn't attack enough, and the quality of my pitches suffered.

Far from a mound and years after my last pitch in the majors, fellow airline travelers were filing past my first-class seat. Like everyone else, I just wanted the plane to depart.

But, suddenly, I saw a bald, athletic, and impeccably dressed man boarding the plane. I smirked. It was Sanders and, seconds later, he was easing into the seat beside me. After a minute or two, I said, "You were pretty tough on me when you hit."

He glanced at me, but he didn't even study my face. Then there was silence. I realized Sanders didn't recognize me. It was more amusing than it was annoying.

"Hi, Deion," I said, as I extended my hand, "I'm David Cone."

Sanders was momentarily surprised and did a double take before saying, "Oh, OK. Hey, how are you doing? You're the reason I got to play in the World Series."

Yes, I was. All I could do was laugh at the exchange. In another back-and-forth between us, one that didn't involve a bat and a ball, Sanders was still dominating me. Although Sanders didn't recognize me, my guess is that he would have recognized my fastball.

Epilogue

CONE'S CLINIC

ON A BUSY SPRING TRAINING morning with the Yankees in 1996, I waited patiently to have a conversation with Catfish Hunter, a pitching legend. Hunter was part of the pregame festivities at George Steinbrenner's new ballpark in Tampa and I was starting the game, but I was distracted as I roamed around the clubhouse. I needed to quiz Hunter about a story I had been told a decade earlier. Finally, I cornered Hunter and he confirmed that it was true.

Here's what the Hall of Fame pitcher and 224-game winner shared with me: If Hunter gave up a homer to a batter on a certain pitch, he would frequently throw the same pitch to the batter in the next at bat. And if the batter hit a second homer, Hunter would repeat his approach in the third at bat. Same pitch and same location.

"Let me see you try and hit three straight homers," Hunter would say.

Was Hunter a masochist? Not at all. He was aggressive and fearless. The lesson from Hunter's story is that he believed in his pitches and he would never shy away from challenging batters, even if a batter had connected for a few hits. I loved this approach because it's a way for pitchers to show confidence in themselves, to keep throwing strikes and to keep attacking.

When I advise young pitchers, whether it's the twelve-year-old Little Leaguers or the sixteen-year-old high school varsity pitchers, I've referenced this kind of aggressive and fearless approach because there is a lot of wisdom wrapped up in what Hunter did. For those young pitchers who want to be smart and prepared on the mound, I compiled my eleven lessons for them. Let's take a visit to Cone's Clinic.

FIND THE STRIKE ZONE

Every pitcher must throw strikes, consistently pumping pitches into the zone to prove that he can be effective. While this is a no-brainer, it still needs to be reinforced. If a pitcher is hesitant to throw strikes or is tossing pitches off the backstop, there's no reason to leave him in the most important position on the field. He can persist and try to become reliable at putting the ball over the plate. But if the inconsistency continues, there are eight other positions he can try.

BE AGGRESSIVE

Once a pitcher finds the strike zone and is pelting it with strikes, he can't get scared out of the zone just because he has allowed some blistering hits. This was the premise of Hunter's strategy and this is why he challenged a home run hitter with the same pitch. Pitchers need to attack batters and that requires them to be able to throw pitches to both sides of the plate and remain in the zone. Be aggressive and fearless, like Hunter.

PREPARE TO MAKE ADJUSTMENTS

The art of pitching is contingent on making adjustments because changes will happen during every game. Your pitches won't be as sharp. The batters will become more aggressive. The umpire will miss a few calls. It will start to drizzle and the mound will get soggy. Every time something jarring happens, the pitcher must take a deep breath and be prepared with a Plan B. Having a Plan C and D doesn't hurt, either.

UNDERSTAND "LESS IS MORE"

When I was nine years old, my father told me I didn't need to throw at full speed all the time, which seemed ridiculous to a kid who wanted to throw the ball as hard as he could. During workouts, he instructed me to throw at 100 percent of my strength and then decrease my power to 75 percent and eventually to 50 percent. I had a strong arm, but I didn't throw enough strikes so my dad was helping to minimize my erratic pitching by focusing on control over velocity. It was a tough adjustment for a nine-year-old. But, as pitchers advance to higher levels, throwing softer and trying to trick batters with less velocity can be just as useful as trying to blow them away with fastballs.

TRUST YOUR INSTINCTS

I was a creative pitcher, constantly searching for different ways to collect outs. If that meant throwing sidearm, I did it. If that meant changing my arm angles, I did it. If that meant including a hesitation in my delivery, I did it. I tried these things because they felt natural to me. That's why a pitcher must trust his instincts and do whatever feels comfortable to him on the mound. I clashed with some pitching coaches because they had specific rules that they thought every pitcher should follow, an approach that I strongly disagree with because there are many different styles a pitcher can use to be successful. The pitcher is the one who is throwing the baseball so he needs to do it in a way that feels satisfying to him.

SPINNING THE BASEBALL

I have studied pitching for more than four decades and I believe it's OK to tinker with throwing curveballs by the time you're twelve years old, an opinion that will cause many coaches, athletic trainers, and physicians to frown. I know there's a risk, but I think it's smart for a young pitcher to learn how to spin the baseball. Now I want to be clear: I'm not saying a kid should throw thirty or forty curves in every game. I would limit young pitchers to throwing curves in practice and make sure a knowledgeable and experienced coach or parent is monitoring them. If you tell a twelve-year-old he can't throw curves for a few years, he's going to try and imitate Dellin Betances when coaches aren't around anyway. Instead of having pitchers sneak in those curves, let them do it with proper supervision.

My dad taught me how to throw curves, but he studied me closely and I was only permitted to throw about ten in a game. In some games, I wasn't allowed to throw any. I had to prove to my father that I wouldn't overthrow them and that I wouldn't snap them off too hard, which can cause an injury. That happened to me. As a thirteen-year-old, I hurt my arm by overthrowing curves and my father wouldn't let me pitch for the rest of the season. Despite that setback, I still think it's worthwhile to let youngsters experiment with curves because there's value in gaining a feel for spinning the baseball.

ADMIT WHEN THERE'S SOME PAIN

Since I just discussed throwing curveballs, it's only natural that I should give some advice on injuries. Injuries can be as inevitable as walking batters and giving up homers. During my professional career, I rotated my arm in bed as soon as I woke up because I wanted to see how much pain I would have to endure that day. A twelve-year-old doesn't have to do that, but a twelve-year-old must be careful because his tendons, ligaments, and growth plates haven't fully formed yet. That's why I stress that a pitcher needs to be taught and supervised when he spins the baseball. And if a pitcher feels some soreness in his arm, he needs to report it to his parents or his coach. Don't be a hero. There is no shame in saying, "This hurts." That's actually the smart thing to say.

USE THE POWER IN YOUR LEGS

I've never been a big dude. I weighed about 140 pounds as a fifteen-year-old and about 185 as a major leaguer. Because of my smallish size, my father taught me a drop-and-drive style of pitching in which my legs helped generate a lot of my power. I used my right leg to push hard off the pitching rubber and then I drove forward and used my lower body to help extend toward the plate with a long stride.

When I was developing as a pitcher, most coaches focused on

my upper body and how important it was to keep my non-throwing shoulder close to my body to avoid "flying open" and scattering my pitches. That is crucial. But I always felt it was even more critical to keep my left hip raised and pointed toward third base for as long as possible because I could gather my body together in my delivery and then glide forward. To me, the lower body is more important than the upper body because a pitcher's power comes from the ground up.

POSSESS MENTAL AND PHYSICAL TOUGHNESS

Everyone who has ever thrown a baseball will experience some horrendous games, but a pitcher must be mentally tough enough to forget about the dreary performances and move on to the next game. That's not easy. I didn't become comfortable doing that until I was in my twenties. Failure is inevitable for pitchers, but the way we deal with failure will help determine how successful we will be. Obviously, Derek Jeter wasn't a pitcher, but he turned the page on difficult games and looked ahead with more ease than anyone I've ever seen. I think the pitcher needs to be the toughest and most prepared player on the field. If he is tough, he will show his resilience on a disappointing day. If he is prepared, he will be ready to react on a dismal day.

THROW THE RIGHT PITCH

A smart pitcher knows the best pitch he can throw isn't necessarily a fastball, a curve, a slider, or a changeup. It's the pitch he can throw with conviction. Because, if a pitcher believes in what he's about to throw, he'll throw it with more confidence.

Hall of Fame pitcher Tom Glavine has said, "You are a vastly different pitcher when you know you can make a pitch versus hoping you can make a pitch." I think that quotation should be plastered on the walls of every dugout. To Glavine, pitchers must have the mind-set that throwing strikes isn't a significant hurdle because they have done it before, even if only in practice. When pitchers have that trust, that confidence, and that belief, that doesn't mean they're automatically going to execute a great pitch. But it does mean they've put themselves in a better position to make that pitch.

TAKE CHARGE AND ENJOY THE JOURNEY

I had an insatiable passion for pitching because I loved the challenge and I loved being the center of attention. I think most pitchers are drawn to the mound for the same reasons and because they want to control the action. Well, once you get there, make sure you stay in control. The pitcher has more power than anyone because he can dictate the pace of the game. Nothing happens until a pitcher is ready to throw the baseball. When there are runners dancing off the bases and the intensity has risen and the pitcher feels like he's the silver ball bouncing around inside a pinball machine, he can always slow things down by taking his time. Remember, you're in control.

Pitching is exhilarating and deflating, delightful and depressing, and stimulating and stressful. But, as you sweat through inning after inning, you have to make sure it's enjoyable, too. Yes, there will always be tension because it's a pressure-filled position, but the adrenaline rush I felt after striking out batters was a feeling only pitchers can explain. I made a comeback at the age of forty with an injured hip because I desperately missed pitching. If a team wanted me, I'd make another comeback in my fifties right now. Well, probably not. But when you're holding the baseball on the mound and you're the person everyone is watching and you're getting the chance to throw your best pitch against their best hitter, be sure to enjoy the journey. To me, there's none like it.

ACKNOWLEDGMENTS

I really can't thank Jack Curry enough for his dedication to this project. I'm sure there were times when he was frustrated about this undertaking, but he never gave in and never gave up. With his relentless attitude, he would have been a great pitcher. Jack's character is the reason why I quickly agreed to do this book with him. He's the consummate professional and he's always had a keen eye for the nuances of pitching and the personalities of the men who do it for a living.

I must acknowledge my parents for their love and support. Ed and Joan Cone were more than supportive parents. They were the reason I fell in love with baseball. Mom was a great athlete and taught me the importance of having a positive attitude, even in the toughest of times. She worked full-time while raising four kids. She was a rock and I miss her dearly. Dad worked the graveyard shift, but still found time to coach me throughout my childhood. We spent countless hours working in our backyard and he even introduced me to Wiffle ball, which is what inspired me to call our yard Coneway Park and Conedlestick Park. I had big dreams and my parents were the inspiration for those dreams.

I was blessed to have three caring siblings. Christal, Danny, and Chris taught me many life lessons and always looked out for their little brother. As I built a pitching career, I was fortunate to have Joe Presko as a coach when I was a teenager and thankful to have the great Mel Stottlemyre as my coach with the Mets and the Yankees. I'm forever grateful that Carl Blando, the Royals' scout who signed me, believed in a skinny Kansas City kid.

Andrew Levy is my business partner, but much more than that, he's been a trusted and reliable friend. In many aspects of my life, Andrew is my go-to guy and I appreciate how loyal and honest he is.

John Filippelli is my boss at the YES Network, but he's also a close friend. I love talking about baseball with Flip and I'm thankful for his support. Like a great baseball team, YES has a terrific roster and I'm grateful to work with so many talented people.

During this process, David Black, a literary agent extraordinaire, was a constant source of passion and positivity. Sean Desmond, a superb editor, reviewed what Jack and I had written and made recommendations that made the prose even better.

From the time I picked up a baseball as a boy until now, there have been countless people who have had lasting impacts on my life. I would need to write another book to acknowledge all of them, but you know you are. Thanks to all.

David Cone

When I first approached David Cone about writing a book that dug inside the mind of a major league pitcher, he was standing in the Yankee Stadium press box. After I explained why his creative mind made him the ideal pitcher for this book, David said, "I like the idea. Let's do it."

So we did it and I'm happy and proud that we did it. I'm grateful that David agreed to collaborate on this project and I'm thrilled that he shared his knowledge with me and with you. Thanks to Coney's insight in this book, and across the last twenty-five years that I've known him, I now have a doctorate in pitching. And, if you've reached this point in the book, David's wisdom has made you a lot smarter about pitching, too. He's a pitching savant.

Every book needs an architect, a person who can build the thoughts and theories into something concrete. Sean Desmond, an enthusiastic editor, was that talented architect for us. With style and skill, he gave us the guidance and the freedom to complete this book.

Every author deserves a literary agent as talented and devoted as David Black. Smart, tough, and optimistic, David is a problem solver. He doesn't see problems. He sees solutions. I'm thankful to have him as an agent, but the first word I use to describe him is "friend."

While I worked on the book, John J. Filippelli, my boss at the YES Network, was endlessly encouraging. I appreciate his passion for the project. My YES colleagues Michael Kay, Bob Lorenz, Jared Boshnack, and John Flaherty are loyal friends who all lent advice or lent an ear when I shared Cone's latest pitching revelations. Jeff Quagliata and James Smyth, the Rivera and Jeter of researchers, provided vital assistance.

Ian O'Connor, Joel Sherman, Mike Vaccaro, and Don Burke are great friends and great journalists who offered valuable insight on many chapters. Andrew Levy is another great friend and, as an original Conehead who has been David's friend for three decades, was a valuable resource.

In addition to asking Cone a thousand questions, I also interviewed more than twenty-five other current and former major league pitchers about David and about his pitching philosophies. I thank them for their time and their observations.

I am fortunate to have so many relatives and friends who asked for updates about this book and who gave me unwavering support. I wrote some of this book while visiting St. Kitts, so I'm thankful to my island friends for their goodwill.

Acknowledgments

My parents, Jack and Bea, would have loved this book and would have paraded around Jersey City telling their friends to buy it. Instead, Rob, my brother, will handle that role. I thank Rob for introducing me to baseball, a love affair that turned into my career.

In *Full Count,* David describes the pitcher-catcher relationship as being "like a dance" in which each side needs to be in sync. I'm grateful that Pamela, the love of my life, danced through this process with me. She was an editor, a cheerleader, and a confidant. By the time the book was finished, she knew almost as much about pitching as me.

And, when the book was done and David had helped me succeed in showing what it's like inside the frenetic mind of a pitcher, the first thing I did was listen to a song by Damian Marley and Nas. It's called "Count Your Blessings."

Jack Curry

INDEX

Index

ABOUT THE AUTHORS

David Cone is the current color commentator for the New York Yankees on the YES Network. He made his MLB debut in 1986 and continued playing until 2003. Cone pitched the sixteenth perfect game in baseball history in 1999. He was a five-time All-Star and led the major leagues in strikeouts each season from 1990–92. A two-time twenty-game-winner, he set the MLB record for most years between twenty-win seasons with ten. He was a member of five World Series championship teams—1992 with the Toronto Blue Jays, and 1996, 1998, 1999, and 2000 with the New York Yankees. He currently lives in New York City.

Jack Curry is an award-winning sports journalist who is an analyst on the Yankees' pregame and postgame shows on the YES Network, where he's worked since 2010. He has won four Emmy Awards as part of YES's Yankee coverage and is also a columnist for YESnetwork.com. Before joining YES, he covered baseball for twenty seasons at the *New York Times,* first as a Yankee beat writer and then as a national baseball correspondent. Curry is the co-author with Derek Jeter of the *New York Times* bestseller *The Life You Imagine.* He currently lives in New Jersey.